UNIVERSAL
ORLANDO
2011

The Ultimate Guide to the Ultimate
Theme Park Adventure

Seth Kubersky with **Kelly Monaghan**

Universal Orlando
The Ultimate Guide To The
Ultimate Theme Park Adventure

Published by
The Intrepid Traveler
P.O. Box 531
Branford, CT 06405
http://www.intrepidtraveler.com

Copyright © 2011 by Kelly Monaghan
Tenth Edition
Printed in the United States
Book design by Jana Rade
Cover photo © 2010 Chip Litherland Photography
Maps designed by MapGorilla.com
ISSN: 1543-6233
ISBN: 978-1-887140-90-4

Publisher's Cataloguing in Publication Data.
    Monaghan, Kelly; Kubersky, Seth
    Universal Orlando: the ultimate guide to the ultimate theme park adventure. Branford, CT: Intrepid Traveler, copyright 2011.
    Revised and updated edition of Universal Studios Escape (2000).
    Includes five maps.
    PARTIAL CONTENTS: Universal Studios Florida. -Islands of Adventure. Seuss Landing. Lost Continent. Jurassic Park. Wizarding World of Harry Potter. -CityWalk. -Resort Hotels.
    1. Universal Orlando--Description and travel--Guidebooks. 2. Theme parks--Orlando region, Florida--Guidebooks. 3. Hotels--Orlando region, Florida--Guidebooks. I. Title. II. Intrepid Traveler.
    917.5924

Trademarks, Etc.

Other Books by Kelly Monaghan

Seaworld, Discovery Cove & Aquatica:
Orlando's Salute to the Seas

The Other Orlando:
What To Do When You've
Done Disney & Universal

Home-Based Travel Agent:
How To Succeed In Your Own
Travel Marketing Business

The Travel Agent's Complete Desk Reference

Air Courier Bargains:
How To Travel World-Wide For Next To Nothing

Fly Cheap!

Air Travel's Bargain Basement

About the Authors

Kelly Monaghan has been covering the "other Orlando" for over sixteen years. In addition to this book, he is the author of *Seaworld, Discovery Cove, & Aquatica: Orlando's Salute to the Seas*. Over the years he has written other travel-oriented books about how to travel on the cheap and how to be a home-based travel agent. He offers a home study course for those who wish to expand their travel horizons with — and profit from — their own travel marketing business at **www.HomeTravelAgency.com**

Seth Kubersky is an author, artist, and entertainment professional who has been based in Orlando for fourteen years. After graduating from the College of William and Mary in Virginia, Seth began his career at Universal Studios Florida, where he was a technician for the *Ghostbusters*, *Terminator*, and *Barney* shows, and an entertainment supervisor for Mardi Gras parades, Halloween haunted houses, and other special events. He has been interviewed as a 'theme park expert' on Rudy Maxa's satellite and broadcast radio shows. As an independent theater producer, he has worked on stages across Central Florida, from dinner shows and Fringe Festivals to the Shakespeare Center and Centroplex. His arts & entertainment opinion column "Live Active Cultures" appears in each issue of the *Orlando Weekly* alternative newspaper.

Photo Credits

All photos by the authors, except as noted.

Table of Contents

List of Maps

CHAPTER ONE:

PLANNING YOUR ESCAPE

Have you heard about the magical kingdom that's emerged in the middle of Florida? There, the halls of an enchanted castle reverberate not with the squeals of little girls playing princess, but the screams of grown men and women having the ride of their lives. In this fantasy land, you can enjoy a mystical medieval meal with an actual adult beverage. And you can find all this family fun inside a resort that doesn't require spending a single valuable vacation second sitting on a shuttle bus or monorail. For Orlando visitors willing to wander beyond the usual World, an extraordinary alternate Universe is waiting.

You're forgiven if Mickey immediately came to mind as you read the last paragraph. After all, the Mouse has been the Big Cheese of Florida tourism ever since 1971, when Walt Disney World opened on 43 sprawling square miles of scrubland southwest of the Orlando, in Lake Buena Vista. Two decades later, Disney's domination of Orlando's attraction industry was still essentially unchallenged. By then, this new and improved version of California's Disneyland had been expanded to include hotels, water parks, nightclubs, and multiple theme parks. But when Universal Studios, in distant California, announced plans for an East Coast edition of their famous Hollywood tour, Mickey was spooked enough to rush the Disney-MGM Studios (today known as Disney's Hollywood Studios) into construction.

Universal's entry in the Florida theme park sweepstakes was dubbed Universal Studios Florida. When it opened in 1990, it quickly became Orlando's number-two attraction. But as just one theme park to Disney's many it seemed doomed to perpetual also-ran status. It didn't help that some of its signature attractions were initially plagued by breakdowns, saddling the park with a reputation for unreliability that haunted it for years.

That all changed in 1999 when Universal Studios Florida reinvented itself as Universal Orlando Resort, adding a second theme park, a nighttime entertainment complex, and several hotels. For the first time, Walt Disney World had competition worthy of the name and Orlando had its second multi-park, multi-hotel, multi-activity, all-in-one, never-need-to-leave-the-property vacation destination. Then, in June 2010, almost exactly 20 years after opening their original park, Universal Orlando raised the stakes again by opening "The Wizarding World of Harry Potter," a highly anticipated expansion that resets the bar for theming and thrills.

Universal Orlando is no mere Mouse copycat. It represents a new departure in theme park and resort destinations that is very shrewdly positioned in the marketplace to build its own following and capitalize on any decline of the Disney brand. It is sure to capture the imagination of both theme park veterans and a new generation of vacationers hungry for entertainment experiences designed with the twenty-first century in mind.

Just What Is 'Universal Orlando'?

Universal Orlando bears a superficial resemblance to Disney World in that it is a multi-park, multi-resort vacation destination. But whereas Disney sprawls over a vast area, Universal Orlando is comfortably compact, allowing its guests to spend less time getting around and more time enjoying themselves. And while Disney World harkens back to an earlier time, Universal is very much of the moment, with an eye to the future.

There are two theme parks here. The original movie-studio-themed **Universal Studios Florida** (USF) is still going strong. It continues to add new thrills using the very latest in technology. Almost literally next door is **Islands of Adventure** (IOA), an attraction that takes the whole notion of "theme park" to the next level, with awesome rides and exceptional dining.

CityWalk is an entertainment and restaurant complex that lies between the theme parks. This is very much an adult experience, although several restaurants will also appeal to the younger set. CityWalk recognizes the ethnic diversity of America in a way that is new to theme park entertainment. It also sets a new standard for luxury, with an ultra-gourmet restaurant. And CityWalk rocks. It boasts the world's largest Hard Rock Cafe and Hard Rock Live, a performance space that hosts some of pop music's biggest names.

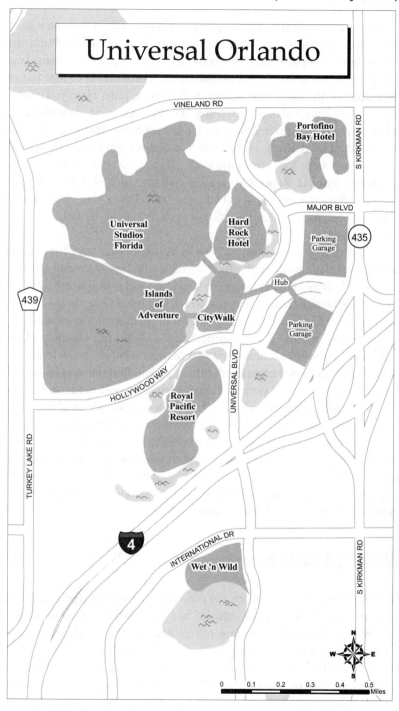

The clearest signal that Universal intends to go mano-a-mano with the Mouse is the proliferation of themed, on-property resort hotels. **Portofino Bay Hotel** has set its sights on becoming Orlando's premiere resort hotel. This ultra-luxury property is a photographic reproduction of that favorite destination of the international jet set, Portofino, Italy. Here you can unwind in the splendor of high-tech suites and dine in a world-class restaurant before catching a complimentary motor launch to the theme parks. More casual is the **Hard Rock Hotel**, which radiates a hip California sensibility and is just steps away from the front gate to Universal Studios Florida. The **Royal Pacific Resort** evokes the romance of far-off Bali, just minutes away from the theme parks by foot or boat. Two additional properties have long been rumored but they do not yet have names, let alone projected completion dates.

Just a stone's throw away is **Wet 'n Wild**, a water park that Universal now owns. It has not been officially rolled into the "Universal Orlando" brand, but it is included in some ticket options and is well worth a visit. In addition to the hundreds of acres on which Universal Orlando sits, Universal owns more land nearby, fueling rumors of yet more future expansion.

Universal Orlando is a family destination. But, unlike some parks we could name, Universal seems to recognize that "families" come in all sorts of different packages. Parents with little ones will find this an almost ideal place for their kids. And yet families with teenagers will not have to worry about complaints that the rides are "lame." Best of all, adults who have yet to have kids, or who have grown kids, or who have left the kids at home, or who never plan to have kids at all can come to Universal Orlando without feeling that they're in a kiddie park. And those snobbish sophisticates who think theme parks are beneath them may find themselves won over by the dazzling architecture, the luxurious accommodations, the gourmet food, and the wide array of nighttime entertainment.

When to Come

There are three major questions you must ask yourself when planning a visit to Universal Orlando: How crowded will it be? What will the weather be like? When will my schedule allow me go? For most people, the third question will determine when they go, regardless of the answers to the other two. The dictates of business or the carved-in-stone school calendar will tend to dictate when you come to Orlando. For those who can be flexible, however, carefully picking the time of your visit will offer a number of benefits. And parents should bear in mind that school officials will often allow kids out of classes for a week if you ask nicely.

During slow periods, the crowds at Orlando's major theme parks are noticeably thinner than they are at the height of the summer or during the madness of Christmas week. On top of that, hotel rates are substantially lower and airfare deals abound. Likewise, Orlando in winter can seem positively balmy to those from the North, although it's unlikely you will find the temperature conducive to swimming (except in heated pools). Spring and fall temperatures are close to ideal.

Let's take a look at these two variables: the tourist traffic and the weather. Then you can make a determination as to which dates will offer your ideal Orlando vacation.

Orlando's Tourist Traffic

Most major tourist destinations seem to have two seasons — high and low. For most of Florida, the high season stretches from late fall to early spring, the cooler months up North. Low season is the blisteringly hot summer, when Floridians who can afford it head North. Orlando, thanks to its multitude of family-oriented attractions, has five or six distinct "seasons," alternating between high and low, reflecting the vacation patterns of its prime customers — kids and their parents.

The heaviest tourist "season" is Christmas vacation, roughly from Christmas Eve through January first. Next comes Easter week and Thanksgiving weekend. The entire summer, from Memorial Day in late May to Labor Day in early September, is on a par with Easter and Thanksgiving. There are two other "spikes" in attendance: President's Week in February and College Spring Break. Various colleges have different dates for their Spring Break, which may or may not coincide with Easter; the result is that the period from mid-March through mid-April shows a larger than usual volume of tourist traffic.

The slowest period is the lull between Thanksgiving and Christmas. Next slowest (excluding the holidays mentioned earlier) are the months of September, October, November, January, and February. Tourism starts to build again in March, spiking sharply upward for Easter/Spring Break, then dropping off somewhat until Memorial Day.

It would be nice to know how theme park attendance rises and falls from month to month. That information is a closely guarded trade secret, but fairly reliable annual estimates are available. Here are annual attendance figures for Orlando area parks for 2009 as estimated by the trade groups TEA and AECOM Economics:

Rank*	Park	Attendance
1	The Magic Kingdom	17,233,000
3	EPCOT	10,990,000
4	Disney's Hollywood Studios	9,700,000
5	Disney's Animal Kingdom	9,590,000
7	SeaWorld Orlando	5,800,000
8	Universal Studios Florida	5,530,000
9	Islands of Adventure	4,627,000
12	Busch Gardens Tampa	4,100,000

*Numbers represent the parks' **national** rankings. Disneyland, California, was number two, Disney's California Adventure was number six, Universal Studios California was number ten.*

In other words, on any given day, the largest crowds will tend to be at the Disney parks. If you've been a Disney regular, Universal Orlando will seem quite manageable by comparison.

The best advice is to avoid the absolutely busiest times of the year if possible. The slow months of fall and spring are ideal. Even January can be enjoyable if you're not the sunbathing type. If you come during the summer, as many families must, plan to deal with crowds when you arrive and console yourself with the thought that Disney is likely even busier.

■ The Best Day of the Week to Visit

A fair bit of advice has been written about the best days of the week to visit the various Orlando area theme parks, and we've written our fair share of it. In the fullness of time, however, such guidance has shown itself to be of limited use, for a number of reasons. First, if you're anywhere near normal, theme park crowds are going to seem overwhelming most of the time anyway. Second, there's a problem with averages. You could well arrive on the "slowest" day of the week only to find that there's been an atypical blip in attendance.

That being said, one popular view has it that Saturday and Sunday are good days to visit Universal Orlando on the theory that most folks start their vacations on the weekend and that most of those who come to Orlando go to Disney first. Following this theory, Monday through Wednesday become the "busy" days. Recently, however, the trend has seemed to be quite the opposite, with fewer people in the parks on weekdays and bigger crowds on the weekends. Go figure.

Finally, there is no reason to cram a visit into a day or two (although many people insist on doing just that). If you decide to make Universal Orlando your primary Orlando destination, you can get a fourteen-day Orlando FlexTicket (see *The Price of Admission*, below) that offers unlimited admission to both Universal Orlando parks, as well as some others nearby. The per-day cost of these tickets is quite reasonable and they remove the insane pressure that comes with a park-a-day touring schedule.

■ The Best Time of Day to Visit

If it's hard to guess which day of the week is best, it is possible to give sound advice on what time of day to come to the parks, regardless of the day of the week or the time of year.

For optimum touring conditions, plan on arriving at the park early, very early. The gates open anywhere from 15 minutes to an hour prior to the official opening time. The parking lot opens even earlier. This is especially true during busy periods; if you are visiting during one of the lulls you can probably afford to sleep in a bit.

Arriving crowds peak at about 11:00 a.m. and then level off. Many families and the faint of heart start leaving at about 4:00 p.m. Thus, your best shot at the more popular rides is before 11 and after 4. During the heat of the day you can catch the shows in the large theaters that offer posted starting times and shorter lines. You may also find that in the hour before closing many rides have no lines at all.

Of course, CityWalk is another matter. Things don't start hopping there until 8:00 or 9:00 p.m. and the place stays open until 2:00 a.m. Factor that in to your planning. You might find that a day that starts at seven and ends at two the next morning isn't much of a vacation.

Orlando's Weather

Orlando's average annual temperature is a lovely 72.4 degrees. But as already noted, averages are deceptive. Here are the generally cited "average" figures for temperature and rainfall throughout the year:

	High (°F)	Low (°F)	Rain (in.)
January	71	49	2.3
February	73	50	3.0
March	78	55	3.2
April	83	59	1.8
May	88	66	3.6

	High (°F)	Low (°F)	Rain (in.)
June	91	72	7.3
July	92	73	7.3
August	92	73	6.8
September	90	73	6.0
October	85	66	2.4
November	79	58	2.3
December	73	51	2.2

(Source: Orlando/Orange County Convention & Visitors Bureau)

Use these figures as general guidelines rather than guarantees. While the average monthly rainfall in January might be 2.3 inches over the course of many years, in 1994 there were 4.9 inches of rain that month and in 1996 almost 4 inches fell in the first two days alone. In June of 2005, Orlando International Airport recorded 16.74 inches of rain, over twice the historic average. The same holds for temperatures, especially in the winter months. January of 1996, 2001, and 2010 saw lows dip into the twenties.

Orlando's weather is most predictable in the summer when "hot, humid, in the low nineties, with a chance of afternoon thunderstorms" becomes something of a mantra for the TV weather report. Winter weather tends to be more unpredictable with "killer" freezes a possibility. As to those summer thunderstorms, they tend to be localized and mercifully brief (although occasionally quite intense) and needn't disrupt your touring schedule too much. For safety resons, outdoor rides like roller coasters will temporarily close during lightning storms. Also, June through September is hurricane season, with late August and early September the most likely time for severe weather.

Gathering Information

Universal Orlando maintains a number of phone lines that provide recorded information about prices, opening hours, and special events. These numbers can also be used to get in touch with Universal Vacations if you are interested in booking a package. Toll-free numbers that work in the United States and Canada are (800) 711-0080 and (888) 322-5537. Here you can get general park information, buy tickets, and make hotel reservations. For the hearing impaired, there is a TDD line at (800) 447-0672. If you are calling from other countries outside the U.S. or are already in Orlando, the number to call is (407) 363-8000, which is the main switchboard.

■ The Internet

There are a number of resources on the Internet you may want to check out before your trip. The main Universal Orlando site can be found at www.universalorlando.com, and has perhaps the most "official" information. It has sections on both parks, CityWalk, and the resort hotels, as well as information about upcoming special events. If you are interested in booking a package vacation that includes a hotel room and other add-ons, the web site for Universal Vacations is www.univacations.com.

An excellent source of pre-trip intelligence can be found at www.disboards.com. The "dis" in disboards stands for "Disney Information Station," but the site has a discussion board devoted exclusively to Universal Orlando. On the home page, scroll down and click on the link for "Universal Studios/Islands of Adventure Forums." Another site, www.ioacentral.com, devoted primarily to Islands of Adventure, also has a very active discussion forum, as does www.orlandounited.com.

Getting There

Universal Orlando is located near the intersection of the Florida Turnpike and Interstate 4 (abbreviated I-4 and pronounced "Eye Four"). It is bounded by Kirkman Road on the east, Vineland Road on the north, Turkey Lake Road on the west, and I-4 on the south. Universal Boulevard runs through the park property from the International Drive tourist district to Vineland Road.

There are four entrances to the park complex. The main entrance is via the Universal Boulevard overpass from International Drive. There are also entrances from Kirkman, Vineland, and Turkey Lake. The Kirkman Road entrance sits on a main thoroughfare and is quite busy. The other entrances seem almost anonymous by comparison. Perhaps because of that, they tend to be the lesser used and, therefore, the quickest ways into the park. All entrances feed cars down broad, palm-lined boulevards to a toll-plaza-like entrance between the two huge, multilevel parking garages sandwiched between Universal Boulevard and Kirkman Road.

Practically speaking, the entrance you wind up using will probably depend on the direction from which you approach.

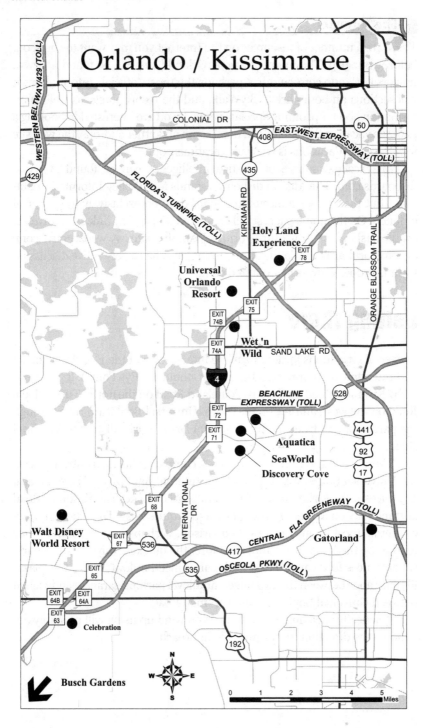

Orlando / Kissimmee

From International Drive

If you are staying in one of the many hotels in the International Drive area, your obvious approach is up Universal Boulevard, crossing I-4 to the main entrance. This approach provides a nice view of the Royal Pacific Resort and Islands of Adventure as you cross the Interstate.

From the south on I-4

Note: This is the route you will be taking if you are coming from the airport via Route 528 ($1.75 toll), which joins I-4 south of Universal.

Coming from the south (that is, traveling "east" on I-4), the most direct route into the park is to take Exit 75A, International Drive, and turn left at the top of the ramp. This puts you on the Universal Boulevard approach. There are two other alternatives, however. On especially busy days, when the overpass at Exit 75A can be backed up, you might save a little time by getting off at Exit 74, Sand Lake Road. Turn left off the ramp, under the Interstate, and then right almost immediately onto Turkey Lake Road. You can't miss it; just follow the "Universal Orlando" signs. Just opposite Dr. Phillips High School, you will see the Universal sign on your right. Your third choice is to drive past Exit 75A and take the left hand Exit 75B, which feeds you onto Kirkman Road; the entrance to the park will be on your left at the first light.

From the north on I-4

Visitors approaching from the north (that is, traveling "west" on I-4) have a choice of using Exit 75B or, a little further along, Exit 74B. Of the two, Exit 74B offers the most direct route to parking. It takes you to Hollywood Way, where you turn right and head straight ahead to the parking garages. It is also the better choice if you are staying at Royal Pacific Resort. If you are heading to the Hard Rock Hotel, Portofino Bay Resort, or any of the hotels along Major Boulevard, use Exit 75B.

From Florida's Turnpike

Whether you are coming from the north or south, take Exit 259 and follow the signs to Tampa via I-4, then get off I-4 at either 75B or 74B.

Parking at Universal Orlando

Whichever entrance you use, you will arrive at the tollbooth entrance to the two huge parking structures; one is five levels high, the other six, and they hold a total of 20,000 cars. At the booth, an attendant will collect your daily parking fee of $14 ($20 for RVs, buses, and trailers). Annual Pass holders can show their pass for **free** admission to the parking lots. Parking is **$3** between 6:00 and 10:00 p.m. (except during special events), and is free after 10:00 p.m. Don't bother asking the booth attendants for maps to the park or parks you'll be visiting that day; they don't have them. You'll be able to pick up these guides later as you enter the parks.

Once you have paid the parking fee, you will be directed to your parking space. The parking structures are ingeniously designed so that as one level fills up cars are routed directly to the next level, without having to corkscrew upwards as you do in most multistory parking lots. If you arrive early, you will be directed in such a way that the two parking structures are filled in the most efficient way possible. However, the structures are often understaffed later in the day, leaving drivers to fend for themselves, so drive cautiously if arriving after noon.

One of the great things about Universal Orlando's parking is that most of it is covered, thus protecting you and your car from the broiling Florida sun and those sudden afternoon downpours. During the busy summer season, however, the open roof is filled fairly early in the day to spare the lot attendants the worst of the sun and heat. Great for the employees, not so great for you. You can ask the attendant to direct you to sheltered parking on one of the lower levels. It may take some polite persistence but it can be done.

The various sections in the two structures are named after movies or characters (Jaws, Jurassic Park, Cat in the Hat, and so forth); rows are indicated by numbers, with the first digit indicating the level. Thus "Jaws 305" would be on the third level. As always in these situations, it's a good idea to make a written note of your parking lot location. Better yet, take a picture of your row number with your cell phone or digital camera!

Universal Orlando claims that the farthest parking space is just a nine-minute walk from CityWalk. That may be stretching (or shrinking) the point, but moving walkways (when operating) speed your journey.

Handicapped Parking. Handicapped parking spaces are provided close to the main entrance on Level 3. Follow the signs for handicapped parking and you will be directed accordingly.

Preferred Parking. If you'd like to shave a few minutes off your walk, you can pay $18 ($4 for annual passholders) for a parking space that's almost as close to the main entrance as the handicapped spaces.

Valet Parking. Get in the Hollywood spirit by having an attendant park your car for you as you pull up right at CityWalk. The fee is $12 if you stay for less than two hours and $22 for over two hours. Overnight parking is not permitted. Preferred Annual Pass holders pay a flat rate of $12 no matter how long they stay. Just follow the signs. If you are coming just for lunch Monday through Friday, between 11:00 a.m. and 2:00 p.m., you can have your parking stub validated at most full-service CityWalk restaurants. A stay of under two hours is **free** and two to four hours is $12, but a stay of over four hours will cost you the full $22, even with validation. If you leave your car in valet overnight you'll face a $25 fee in the morning.

Passenger Drop-Off. If you're in a generous mood, you can drop your family off near CityWalk before you go off to park the car. Look for the signs directing you to the drop-off area, which is just across Universal Boulevard from the Valet Parking area.

Parking for Resort Guests. If you are staying at one of the on-property resort hotels, use any of the entrances and follow the signs to your hotel. All of the hotels have separate gates, with separate, paid parking facilities for guests. Non-guests can also use these lots but at rates higher than those charged to guests and considerably higher than the fee levied at the main theme park parking garages. In other words, the hotel parking lots do not provide an economical alternative to parking in the main parking structures, nor do they offer much in the way of additional convenience.

Alternatives To Driving

If you are staying at an off-site hotel, look into the **Super Star Shuttle** bus service that ferries guests at area hotels to Universal Orlando, SeaWorld, and Wet 'n Wild. There are about eight separate routes and hotels as far afield as downtown Orlando and the Route 192 corridor in Kissimmee participate in this program. The service is typically **free** to guests, but some hotels may charge a small fee. In theory, you must be a guest of a participating hotel to use this service, but this is seldom if ever enforced. Hotels near a pickup point cheerfully send their guests next door to catch the shuttle.

Unfortunately, information on routes, schedules, and which hotels are currently participating is hard to come by. The best bet is to ask the hotel you are planning to book whether they participate in the program. Once at Universal Orlando, you can stop by the bus station between the parking garages and CityWalk to see which routes service which hotels. The service runs from the hotels to Universal Orlando all day, with fewer departures in the afternoon. Return trips don't start until about 4:00 p.m. You should be able to pick up a printed schedule for your route from your hotel or the driver.

If you are staying along the International Drive corridor, you can hop on the **I-Ride Trolley** to reach the corner of Kirkman Road and Major Boulevard (stop number five on the Main Line). From there, follow the walking directions given below. The trolley is $1.25 for those 13 and older and 25 cents for those 65 and older. Kids 12 and under ride **free**. Exact change is required. All-day and multi-day passes, which are a good deal, are available at many hotels and retail shops along I-Drive, but not on the trolleys. For more information, call toll-free (866) 243-7483 or view a route map on the Internet at www.iridetrolley.com.

You can also reach the parks via public transportation; Orlando's **Lynx buses** cost $2 ($1 for seniors 65 and older), exact change required. A weekly bus pass costs $16. Route 21 links downtown Orlando with the I-Drive corridor, passes through the Major Boulevard hotel area (see *Chapter Six: Staying Near the Parks*), and stops near the Hub in Universal Orlando. Getting from the Walt Disney World area to Universal is tricky, but possible. Take Lynx Route 50 from Disney's Ticket & Transportation Center to SeaWorld and switch to the I-Ride Trolley. For more information, call (407) 841-5969 or visit www.golynx.com on the Internet. On the web site you will be able to download maps of the routes that interest you.

It is actually possible to **walk to the parks** and a few people do it. If you are staying at one of the hotels located along Major Boulevard on the Kirkman Road side of the property (see *Chapter Six*), you can reach CityWalk in 15 to 30 minutes, moving at a purposeful pace. From Major Boulevard, follow the signs for valet parking and you will find an escalator that takes you to CityWalk. If you are staying on the other side of I-4, at a hotel near Universal Boulevard and I-Drive, you are looking at a much, much longer walk. Coming from this direction, use the escalator leading up from the bus station.

If you are staying at an on-site resort hotel (See *Chapter Five: The Resort Hotels*), you can use the **free water taxis** to CityWalk or the **shuttle buses** that drop you near Universal Studios Florida.

You can neatly solve all your transportation problems by taking a **taxi, van, or limo** from the airport and staying at an onsite hotel for the duration of your stay. Quicksilver Limos (888-468-6939) is a small local firm that provides town car and stretch limo services. They will stop en route to let you stock up on groceries and such for your room and they offer an innovative "three-way" option. They will take you from the airport to Universal, then a few days later from Universal to Walt Disney World, and finally back to the airport, all for $155. For a family of four, it's a bargain for the convenience and comfort. The web site, www.quicksilver-tours.com, has a full price list.

Otherwise, Mears Transportation offers walk-up shuttle van service from the airport for $29 round trip per person, $23 for children 4 to 11. No reservation is necessary. Taxi fare from the airport runs $30 to $40.

Staying at one of Universal's resort hotels without the temptation of a car is a great way to maximize your vacation enjoyment. If you are staying on in Orlando, you can always rent a car in your hotel at the end of your stay.

Arriving at Universal Orlando

From your parking space, you will walk to the nearest of a series of escalators and moving sidewalks that will funnel you to "**the Hub**," a large circular space on the third level with access from both parking structures and from the bus station. In the Hub, you can rent a wheelchair ($12), but not strollers or electric convenience vehicles. For those, you'll have to wait until you reach the theme parks. The Hub also has restrooms and a few vending kiosks if you just can't wait to get that Universal T-shirt or hotdog.

Tip: You can rent a wheelchair here and then "upgrade" to an ECV once you reach the park.

From the Hub, past an efficient security check, it's a straight shot along more moving sidewalks to CityWalk, Universal's dining, shopping, and entertainment venue. In CityWalk, you can continue straight ahead to Islands of Adventure or hang a sharp right and head for Universal Studios Florida.

Whichever park you choose to visit, you will cross a bridge over the artificial canal system that links the resort hotels to the parks and arrive at an attractive entrance plaza where you will find a row of ticket windows and, nearby, a Guest Services window, of which more later.

Once inside the park gate, be sure to pick up a "2-Park Map" from the racks just past the entrance. The large fold-out brochures contain maps of both parks and a listing of rides, restaurants, and helpful information such as the show times of many attractions. On the front will be listed the parks' official opening and closing times and the dates for which the information is valid, which could be for just the day on which you receive it or for several days or weeks.

If you forget to pick up a map at the entrance, don't despair. You will find maps near the cashier's desk in shops scattered throughout the parks.

Opening and Closing Times

Universal Orlando is open 365 days a year. In the slow seasons, the parks may open at nine and close at six. During the high season, the parks may open earlier than the official time and close at eleven. The gates may open a few minutes prior to the "official" time and certain hotel packages may include "early entry" access to select attractions an hour prior to the posted opening time. But if you can't enter early you can stay late. Typically, the last visitors aren't shooed out until an hour or more after closing time.

As noted previously, opening and closing times can also be affected by special events. If the park will be closing early, there should be a large sign posted near the entrance gates informing you of this sad fact. You can also double-check today or tomorrow's official hours by calling (407) 363-8000.

Tip: Take your time leaving the parks at night unless you're absolutely exhausted (a strong possibility). Strolling slowly through these magical streets under a moonlit sky, hand in hand with that special someone, is an unforgettable experience when you are among just a handful of people in the park.

The Price of Admission

Universal Orlando has a variety of ticket options, with a variety of bells and whistles, that seem to change with astonishing regularity. So take this section with a grain of salt. If past experience is anything to go by, the information below will change before the next edition comes out. The number, variety, and configurations of passes offered may very well change and, of course, prices are subject to change without notice.

▎ Buying Tickets

Your best bet is to buy tickets on the Universal Orlando web site before you come to Orlando, more for the time savings than the modest discounts offered. Universal is making a major push to encourage people to pre-order online and is offering some attractive online-only ticket options to encourage you to do just that. All online options allow you print out your admission ticket at home, ready to take to the gate, or pick up at the parks using the electronic kiosks just outside the entrance. Swipe the same credit card you used to make the purchase, enter the confirmation code you received at the time of purchase, and you will receive a ticket you can take to the gate. It's simple and fast.

Note: Although online prices on multi-day tickets are discounted $10 from the price charged at the gate, an online "processing fee" of $2.15 eats into the discount; one-day tickets are actually more expensive online. This fee may be waived for certain ticket types. Below, you will be given the "bottom line" for all ticket purchases.

If you prefer to have your tickets sent to you, FedEx shipping (domestic and international) is available for $14 to $19. If you use a travel agent, allow several weeks to receive your tickets. You can also visit your local AAA office if you are a member, or try the services of Ticketmania, described later.

If you must wait to purchase tickets until you are in Orlando and can't use the Internet, you can purchase tickets at the park when you arrive for your visit. If you have only one or two days to spend at Universal Orlando, save precious time by buying tickets at the park a day or so before your visit, perhaps during a visit to CityWalk. A good time to purchase tickets at the park is in the late afternoon. Tickets can be purchased at the Universal Studios store in the Orlando International Airport, where many tourists begin their Orlando adventure. You might also look around for an Internet cafe or borrow a computer to get those online-only offers and discounts.

Note: The electronic kiosks outside the front gates of the parks are there specifically for the pickup of tickets already purchased online, and cannot be used to purchase tickets.

Tickets can also be purchased at the resort hotels (*Chapter Five: Resort Hotels*) at the concierge desk. There is no extra charge for this service. However, once you check in you will no doubt want to start using your front of the line privileges in the parks immediately (see below), so once again you are losing precious time. Better to have your tickets in hand before you arrive.

▋ Ticket Options

In 2010, Universal radically revamped their ticket prices, eliminating the popular "unlimited ticket" option and replacing it with a tiered pricing structure dubbed "Universal's Select." Similar to Disney's "Magic Your Way" system, the new pricing encourages purchasing longer passes by increasing the base ticket cost but reducing the premium for adding additional days and parks. All multi-day tickets must be fully utilized within **14 days** after the first use, and include 14 nights of free admission to CityWalk's clubs. Whatever your choice, children under three are admitted **free**.

For the most recent information you should check www.universalorlando. com and click on the "Tickets" link, although as noted below, the web site does not always list every type of ticket available. Another excellent source of intelligence about the latest prices and special admissions offers is the DISboards web site mentioned earlier. If you have any questions as to what may or may not be available at the time of your visit, post a question there and you should get a speedy answer. If you'd prefer to get your information straight from the horse's mouth, you can try emailing Universal at customer.support@tickets.universalstudios.com or call (407) 224-7840.

All that being said, prices (including 6.5% sales tax and $2.15 online fees where appropriate) were as follows when this book went to press (the online prices are listed in parentheses):

Base Ticket: 1 Park Access
(Universal Studios Florida **or** Islands of Adventure)

	Adults	Children (3-9)
1 Day	$ 84.14 ($ 86.29)	$ 73.49 ($ 75.64)
2 Days	$127.79 ($119.29)	$113.94 ($105.45)
3 Days	$143.76 ($135.27)	$127.79 ($119.29)
4 Days	$154.41 ($145.92)	$136.31 ($127.81)
7 Days	$181.04 ($172.54)	$159.74 ($151.24)

Park-To-Park Ticket: Two-Park Access
(Universal Studios Florida **and** Islands of Adventure)

	Adults	Children (3-9)
1 Day	$116.09 ($118.24)	$105.44 ($107.59)
2 Days	$154.41 ($145.92)	$140.57 ($132.07)
3 Days	$159.74 ($151.24)	$143.76 ($135.27)
4 Days	$165.06 ($156.57)	$146.96 ($138.46)
7 Days	$191.69 ($183.19)	$170.39 ($161.89)

(Another form of multi-day pass, the Orlando FlexTicket, which offers admission to other theme parks in addition to the Universal parks, is discussed a little later.)

At press time, a special offer allows you to add unlimited Wet 'n Wild visits to any 3-day or longer ticket for an additional $25. Again, be aware that Universal changes its ticket options frequently.

▌ CityWalk Party Passes

CityWalk's entertainment venues levy a "cover charge" in the evenings. If you wish, you can purchase a CityWalk Party Pass for $12.77, including tax. It offers admission to all entertainment venues for the evening, so you don't have to pay a separate cover at each club or restaurant. Be aware that all tickets (except 1 Day passes) include admission to CityWalk's clubs, which is an excellent incentive to buy the multi-day pass. So be sure to check your pass before plunking down money for a Party Pass you don't need. For more on the CityWalk Party Pass, see *Chapter Four: CityWalk*.

■ Annual Passes

Universal Orlando offers three Annual Pass options.

Two-Park Annual Power Pass:
    All ages: $149.09 (FL residents only)
Two-Park Preferred Annual Pass:
    All ages: $244.94 ($234.29 for FL residents)
Two-Park Premier Annual Pass:
    All ages: $308.84

What's the difference? The **Annual Power Pass** (currently available only for Florida residents) comes with about 25 blackout dates (Christmas, Spring Break, and the week around July 4th), does not include parking, and offers no additional discounts. The **Preferred Annual Pass** is valid 365 days a year, includes free parking, and entitles the holder to a host of attractive discounts on food, merchandise, and stays at the resort hotels. Since parking is $14 a day, you need only visit six days during the year before the additional cost of a Preferred Annual Pass pays for itself — and that doesn't take into account any in-park discounts! And to sweeten the deal, Universal's "FlexPay" lets you pay for any Annual Pass in 11 interest-free payments, with a $79 down payment. There is no online discount, so save yourself $2.15 by buying in person.

The **Premium Annual Pass** adds a few nifty perks not offered by the Preferred Annual Pass. These include free self-parking in the Preferred Parking area or free valet parking, free Universal Express Plus access to rides and attractions after four o'clock, admission to all CityWalk clubs for the passholder and a guest (passholder only on weekend nights), one non-peak Halloween Horror Nights ticket, eight bottles of water, and other benefits.

In addition to the freedom to come and go as you please, Preferred and Premier Annual Passes confer a number of other benefits, including 10%-20% discounts on tickets to Blue Man Group, AMC Cineplex, CityWalk, and the parks. Preferred passholders also receive a 10% discount on souvenir purchases and food (not alcohol and not at walk-up stands) in the parks, while Premier passholders receive 20% off merchandise and 15% off food. The Preferred Pass will get you a 10% discount on food in many of City-Walk's restaurants; Premier provides a 5%-10% bump.

The special rates at the resort hotels, which can shave as much as 30% off the daily rate, are an especially attractive perk for annual passholders. Annual passholder rates are usually available during the slower times of year, so don't expect any deals at Christmas, Spring Break, or during the height of the summer rush. There are additional discounts and privileges that change from time to time; they are outlined in the brochure you receive with your Annual Pass. Any changes will be announced in the annual passholders' newsletter, which is published quarterly.

For the very latest information on Universal's Annual Passes visit www.universalorlando.com/annualpass or call (800) 564-5764.

Florida Resident Specials

Universal frequently makes special annual pass offers designed to encourage those who live closest to the parks to visit more often. Usually these are available only to Florida residents but there have been some offers that have included residents of Georgia as well.

A typical Florida Resident Special involves a reduced price for admission to both parks during slower periods of the year. For example, at press time a $105 3-day /2-park pass valid for 6 months was offered (a $45 savings). To get these deals you must be able to show proof of Florida residence such as a Florida drivers license or some other document linking you to a Florida address. You may also need a coupon from a soda or fast-food sponsor. The best way to find out what Florida Resident Specials are currently available is to visit www.universalorlando.com and click on the "Florida Residents" link under the "Tickets" drop-down menu.

The Star Treatment

If an Annual Pass doesn't offer enough ego gratification, consider a **Non-Exclusive VIP Tour**. For $150, plus tax, you can join a group of up to 11 other VIPs for a five-hour escorted behind-the-scenes tour of the park of your choice. Not only will you see things that ordinary visitors don't, you will be whisked to the head of the line for "at least eight" attractions and be guaranteed the best seats. These tours start at 10:00 a.m. and noon.

If you'd like to corral up to 11 close friends, you can all take a private eight-hour **Exclusive VIP Tour** ($2,000). That gives you nearly 60 percent more time at a slightly higher per-person cost. What's more, this tour starts when you want it to and can be customized to your group's special interests. The group must be preformed; that is, you can't join another group. Nor does your group have to total 12. You can bring five friends or ten, or go all by yourself. The cost remains the same.

If you'd like to do a VIP Tour of both parks, that can be arranged, too. There is a **One-Day, Two-Park Non-Exclusive VIP Tour** ($185), a **One-Day, Two-Park Exclusive VIP Tour** ($2,500), and even a **Two-Day, Two-Park Exclusive VIP Tour** ($3,750). Again, the Exclusive tours are for a group of up to 12.

But there's a catch: VIP tours **do not** include regular admission to the park. You can get more information about both kinds of VIP tours, as well as additional options, by calling (407) 363-8295 from 9:00 a.m. to 6:00 p.m., Monday through Friday (to 5:00 p.m. on weekends). You can also request a VIP tour reservation by email at viptours@universalorlando.com. Reservations must be made at least 72 hours in advance (two weeks prior during summer and holiday periods) and a credit card hold is required. If you must cancel your reservation, do so at least 72 hours prior to the tour; otherwise, your credit card will be charged.

If you can afford it, this is a terrific way to see the parks. The guides are personable and extremely knowledgeable. Becoming a guide is a lengthy and highly competitive process and only a few who apply make the cut.

▌ The Orlando FlexTicket

Several of the non-Disney theme parks, namely Universal Orlando, Sea-World, Wet 'n Wild, Aquatica, and Busch Gardens Tampa, have banded to-gether to offer multi-day, multi-park passes at an extremely attractive price. This option is called the Orlando FlexTicket and it works like this:

Five-Park, Fourteen-Day Orlando FlexTicket:
(Universal Studios Florida, Islands of Adventure, SeaWorld,
Wet 'n Wild, Aquatica)

Adults:	$276.85
Children (3 to 9):	$255.55

Six-Park, Fourteen-Day Orlando FlexTicket Plus:
(adds Busch Gardens, in Tampa)

Adults:	$319.45
Children (3 to 9):	$298.15

These passes are valid for 14 consecutive days, beginning the day you first use them. They offer unlimited visits to the parks they cover. As for parking, you pay at the first park you visit on any given day. Then show your parking ticket and Orlando FlexTicket at the other parks on the same day for complimentary parking. The five-park option includes free bus transportation from SeaWorld to Busch Gardens Tampa. FlexTickets purchased at Universal Orlando also provide 14 days' admission to "select" CityWalk nightclubs.

Remember, these tickets expire. That is, if you use an Orlando FlexTicket for only five days, you can't return a month later and use the remaining nine days. These passes offer excellent value for the dollar; the five-park pass works out to less than $20 a day! On top of that, they offer the come and go as you please convenience of Annual Passes, albeit for a much shorter time.

Passes may be purchased on Universal's web site, at any of the participating parks' ticket booths, or through your travel agent before coming. You cannot print these tickets at home, so online purchases will incur $14 to $19 in shipping charges. There are a number of attractive vacation packages now being offered that include the Orlando FlexTicket plus hotel accommodations in the International Drive area and other benefits. For more information, call Universal Vacations at (800) 711-0080, or contact your nearest travel agent.

Which Price Is Right?

First, it is a good strategy to purchase your tickets online at the Universal Orlando web site. This gets you a $8.50 discount on multi-day tickets, though one-day tickets are $2.15 more expensive online. But mostly what the online option does is save you time.

If your schedule only allows one day at Universal Orlando, with little likelihood of ever returning, the choice is both simple and complicated. Simple because you'll only need a one-day pass, complicated because you must choose between two wonderful parks or try to do both parks in one day. If you will be visiting at a busy time of year, our advice is to choose one park. If the one-day, two-park option is available when you visit, it will pretty much give you a "Universal's Greatest Hits" sort of experience with many attractions missed for lack of time. However, if you are visiting during a slow period, are staying at an on-site hotel (which gives you preferred access to rides), or know you will be skipping kiddie attractions and "aggressive" rides like the roller coasters, then you can probably comfortably do two parks in a single day. Conversely, if you will only be doing the aggressive thrill rides, then the two-park option might also work for you, especially if you are staying on site.

But don't try to cram both parks into a single day. There is just too much to see, do, and savor. In fact, Universal's multi-day option is so reasonably priced that you really owe it to yourself to slow down and smell the roses. But if you only have one day available, please try to avoid the temptation to do both parks.

So let's say you have one day. Which park should you choose? If you've already visited Universal Studios Florida, then you will probably opt for Islands of Adventure. Even if this is your first visit to Orlando, you may still choose Islands of Adventure. After all, with Harry Potter's much-publicized arrival, it's the one all your friends back home will want to hear about. On the other hand, if you hate roller coasters and soaking water rides and love live shows (or if it's raining), you might find Universal Studios Florida more to your liking. Read the chapters that follow and make your own decision.

If you have two days, then the most sensible option is to purchase a 2-Day Base Ticket and visit each park on different days. If you want to spend three or four days in the parks, additional discounts kick in that make the Park-to-Park Access option most attractive.

After four days, however, the cost of parking (5 days times $14 is $70!) makes it more economical to purchase a Preferred Annual Pass for one member of your party, and 7-Day Park-to-Park tickets for the rest. And if you are considering a stay at one of the resort hotels, remember that an annual pass will entitle you to special rates, if you come at the right time of year. For example, annual passholder rates at the Hard Rock Hotel can sometimes be $60 less than the best rate available. A three-day stay and the annual pass pays for itself!

Think twice before grabbing a Power Pass, however. This option makes sense only if you have figured a way around paying for parking. The dollar difference between a regular annual pass and the Power Pass is roughly six days of paid parking. Factor in the blackout dates and the money you lose by not getting a discount on meals and shopping and the Power Pass looks even less attractive. At about $60 more than Preferred, the Premium Annual Pass is recommended for locals who like late afternoon express access, the added luxury of preferred or valet parking, and Halloween Horror Nights. If you don't plan on taking advantage of those perks, it might be hard to make the additional investment pay off.

The Orlando FlexTicket is also an excellent buy for people whose main interest is Universal and who have two weeks to spend in Orlando. You can spend one day each at the other parks and the remaining ten or eleven days coming and going as you please at the two Universal parks. The per-day cost is roughly $19 to $23, which is a lot of entertainment bang for the buck.

If you have any doubts about whether you will enjoy the theme park experience, you can hedge your bets. You can upgrade any pass to a more expensive pass while you are still in the park. The price you pay will be exactly what you would have paid if you'd purchased the more expensive pass when you first arrived.

Discounts

Getting a discount to Universal Orlando is a good bit harder than it used to be, but it is still possible to save a few bucks. Here's how.

AAA. Members of the American Automobile Association receive a modest discount for all members of their party, up to six people, at the gate on the two-day Universal Orlando pass only. The policies on AAA discounts change frequently, so double-check by calling one of the toll-free numbers given earlier. AAA members can also buy their tickets through a local AAA club office, in which case the discount will no doubt be better and will vary from club to club. Once inside the parks, your AAA card is good for a 10% discount at the shops and restaurants.

Fan Club. Members of the Universal Fan Club get an array of discounts. Membership is free but the catch is you must enroll through your employer, which must participate in the program. The Fan Club program is available to companies with more than 100 employees (more than 50 for Florida firms). For information on how to get your company enrolled, ask your Human Resources manager to call (866) 886-5027, extension 1. For more information, log on to www.universalfanclub.com.

Medical Discounts. Disabled guests receive a 15% discount. If you have a medical condition that prevents you from enjoying Universal's more intense or active rides — even if you do not consider yourself "disabled" — go to the "Guest Services" window near the ticket booths to inquire about a disability discount. This is a good strategy for grandparents who know they'll be sitting out the *Hulk, Dragon Challenge*, and some of the other more aggressive rides. You will not be asked to prove you have a disability or other medical condition.

Ticket Brokers. Another major source of discounts is ticket brokers. There are dozens of them scattered around the tourist areas, many of them located in hotel lobbies. Ticket brokers concentrate on the major attractions and the dinner shows that are an Orlando staple. Discounts for the major theme parks aren't as good as they used to be. At most you will be able to shave a few bucks off the price of the popular Universal Orlando passes. At worst, you will pay full price in exchange for the convenience of not waiting in a long ticket line at the parks.

One place worth checking out is the Official Visitors Center at 8723 International Drive, operated by the Orlando/Orange County Convention and Visitors Bureau. It is about a mile south of Universal Orlando. There you will find plenty of discount tickets and the free Orlando Magicard, which offers a broad array of discounts at hotels, restaurants, and attractions.

On the Internet. Ticket brokers are cropping up on the Internet. One of them, Ticketmania, offers Universal Orlando passes for a few dollars off the gate price, depending on the pass. They currently offer free pickup at their Kissimmee store, $6.95 home delivery, or delivery to an Orlando-area hotel for $13. The Ticketmania web site is www.ticketmania.com.

Timeshare Come-ons. Some ticket brokers advertise Universal tickets for an eye-popping $20 or even for free. The catch is, you must agree to sit through a presentation on timeshare properties. There's "no obligation," of course, but you can expect to be subjected to a concentrated hard sell. Another thing to consider before going for these super-cheap tickets is that the tickets Universal sells to the timeshare tour folks are heavily restricted; for example, they do not allow park-to-park access.

Travel Agents. Bona-fide travel agents (there is a strict screening process) receive complimentary one-day admission to the parks. For more information on how to apply, visit www.universaltravelagents.com.

Vacation Packages. If you purchase a vacation package from your travel agent, one that includes airfare, hotel, and a rental car, as well as passes to Universal Orlando, you are probably getting a very good buy on the tickets. If you are making Universal Orlando the primary focus of your trip, these package deals offer excellent value and make a lot of sense.

Universal Express

Long lines are the biggest complaint people have about theme parks. Wouldn't it be great if you could just get on every ride without having to cool your heels in line for an hour or more? Well, at Universal Orlando there are three closely related programs that let you do just that.

■ Universal Express Plus

This program allows you to buy your way to the front of the line (see *Notes and Comments*, below) by purchasing a small card with a magnetic stripe that gives you one-time Express access to every ride or attraction with an Express queue. You can buy a pass for one park or both and the cards will only work on a single day starting one hour after park opening. Unlike Disney's "FastPass" system, Universal Express Plus can be utilized whenever you choose; you don't have to pick up a ticket and then return later at an assigned time.

To find out how much you will pay for this privilege, go to the tickets page on the Universal Orlando web site and look for the "Express Plus Passes" link. Recently, passes have been selling in advance online for $20 for a one-park pass during slower periods, all the way up to $70 for a two-park version at peak periods like Christmas. Prices go up a notch on weekends. Prices may also be higher when purchased in the parks, where they are only available for same day use. There are very few days, it seems, on which the pass is not available; since those are usually slower days, that might not be a problem.

Quantities are limited (the exact number issued is a closely guarded secret) and once they're gone for the day, they're gone. At each ride, your card will be "swiped" by an attendant using a hand-held device. If there is no hand-held device, the attendant will scribble a notation on the card. Either way, the result is the same: one ride per attraction.

■ Universal Express Plus for Resort Guests

Guests at the on-site resort hotels (see *Chapter Five*) get the best deal of all. At no extra charge, they can use their room keys (which look like credit cards and are personalized with the guest's name) to gain immediate access to the Universal Express Plus queues. Simply show your key to the attendant at the express queue and you are in. Better yet, you can use this perk all day and ride each ride as many times as you wish.

At check in, you will be given a key for every member of your party, so everyone staying in the same room can take advantage of this perk at his or her own discretion. Even if your family tours the parks as a group, the official policy is to check every card, so make sure every member of your party has theirs. However, occasionally families are waved through after a single card is produced. Your key card will be examined carefully by an attendant. This is to make sure that your room key is still valid.

Your room key gives you Express access on the day you check in and all day the day you check out. So you can check in very early and, even though your room isn't ready, get a room key to use at the parks. When you check out, hang on to your room key and use it at the parks for the rest of the day.

■ VIP Unlimited Express Pass

This new option combines a two-park ticket with unlimited Express usage. One day costs $191.69 ($181.04 children 3 to 9) during "non-peak" times, and $209.79 ($199.14 children) during "peak." Additional days are also available, up to $406.82 for a 7-Day Park-to-Park VIP Peak ticket. If you're visiting during a busy season and you want to re-ride your favorites multiple times, this may be a good option, but a stay in a Universal hotel could be more cost-effective.

■ Notes and Comments on Universal Express

You may sometimes hear Universal Express Plus referred to as "Front of the Line" or FOTL. Some people mistakenly take this to mean that they will quite literally be placed on the ride ahead of everybody else who is waiting. Not so. In effect, you are placed on a separate, shorter queue. You **will** experience a short wait, at least at peak times. The official word is that it will be no more than 15 minutes although at peak times it can be longer. Usually it is much less. Of course, rules and policies may change, so check with Guest Services or your resort hotel concierge for exceptions and restrictions at the time of your visit.

Not all rides accept Universal Express Plus. Certain popular rides, including *Hollywood Rip Ride Rockit* and *Harry Potter and the Forbidden Journey* may be excluded, as are low-capacity attractions like *Pteranodon Flyers*. The rides and attractions that do accept it will be indicated by the Universal Express Plus logo on the map you pick up when you enter the theme parks.

Tip: There is actually a downside to Universal Express Plus on some rides like *Revenge of the Mummy, Men In Black,* and *Dragon Challenge*. Because you miss the queue line, you miss the setup for the ride's story line. Consequently, you don't experience the ride to its fullest. So our advice is to use the Universal Express Plus system only when absolutely necessary or after you have ridden a ride a few times.

Universal Express Plus is not the only way to jump to the front of the line. A few rides in each park offer "**single rider lines**" that can cut your waiting time dramatically. These are indicated in the *Good Things To Know About...* sections of *Chapters Two* and *Three*.

If you are seriously considering popping for these passes, pause for a moment to consider this: If there are three people in your party and Universal Express Plus costs $40, that's a $120 daily investment. That could be more than the difference between a night's stay at an on-site resort and what you're already paying to stay elsewhere. Remember that a one-night stay at an on-site resort gives you two days of **free** front of the line access!

Meal Deal

Universal offers an "all-U-can eat" option for those who can content themselves with a limited menu of fast food eateries. Here are the prices, including tax, as we went to press.

One-Park Meal Deal:

Adults:	$21.29
Children (3 to 9):	$10.64

Two-Park Meal Deal:

Adults:	$25.54
Children (3 to 9):	$12.77

There are a number of catches, however. First, drinks are not included, although you can purchase a "Sipper Cup" for $7.44 entitling you to 79-cent soft drink refills. No full-service restaurants are included and the list of participating restaurants changes seasonally, so you may not be happy with the selection. Kids must order from a special Meal Deal kids menu. You are limited to one entree and one pretty boring dessert each pass through the line. You can't game the system by ordering a whole pizza. And so it goes. Sometimes, you can add an entree at participating CityWalk restaurants for $6, a slightly better deal.

Aside from the fact that the Meal Deal encourages us to overeat and offers only fast food options, the savings aren't even all that great. On the other hand, if you like fast food fare and can eat three or four meals . . . well, you know who you are.

The Meal Deal can be purchased online, at the ticket windows, or at any participating restaurant. At the first restaurant you go to, show your ticket and get a wrist band that identifies you as a Meal Deal diner. The offer is only good for the day of purchase.

Good Things To Know About . . .

Here are some general notes that apply to both of the theme parks at Universal Orlando. Notes that are specific to the individual parks are included in the appropriate chapter.

▇ Access for the Disabled

Universal Orlando makes a special effort for its disabled guests. (In fact, you are likely to see disabled people among the staff at the parks.) Special viewing areas are set aside at most shows; there are even kennels for guide dogs that cannot accompany their masters on some rides.

Wheelchairs can be rented in the Hub (see above under *Parking*), as well as inside the parks, for $12 per day. Electric convenience vehicles (ECV) can be rented just inside the entrances to both parks; the rate is $50 per day. For either, you must provide a $50 cash deposit or credit card imprint, and a signed rental contract. A one-week advance reservation is recommended for ECVs, which tend to sell out quickly. Call (407) 224-4233 to make reservations at either park.

Tip: You can rent a wheelchair at the Hub (near the parking garages) and then "upgrade" to an ECV once you reach the park. When you return the ECV, you will have a wheelchair waiting for the trip back to the Hub.

Auditions

If you think being a performer at Universal Orlando would be a lot of fun, you are not alone. To whet your appetite, check out the Universal Audition Hotline at (407) 224-7622 or visit universalauditions.com, where they announce upcoming tryouts and give details on exactly what they're looking for. Who knows? This could be your big break.

Babies

Little ones under three are admitted **free** and strollers are available for rent if you don't have your own. There are also diaper changing stations in all the major restrooms (men's and women's). But that's as far as it goes. Make sure you have an adequate supply of diapers, formula, and baby food before you head for the park. Strollers and "kiddie cars" can be rented just inside the entrances of both parks. Single strollers are $15 per day and doubles are $20; single kiddie cars are $18, doubles are $23.

Baby "Swaps"

All rides can accommodate parents whose little ones are too small to ride. One parent rides, while the other waits in a holding area with the child. Then the parents switch off and the second parent rides without a second wait in line. It's a great system.

Breakdowns

Rides break down. They are highly complex mechanical wonders and are subjected to a great deal of stress. Some mechanical failure is inevitable. If you are on a ride when it breaks down, you may receive a pass that will give you priority access to the ride once it's working again.

■ Car Trouble

If you return to your car and find the battery dead, Universal will give you a free jump start. Raise the hood to alert the attendants. If the problem is more serious, they will help you get help.

■ Drinking

Universal Orlando provides beer at outdoor stands and in all sit-down restaurants and at many fast-food outlets as well. Wine is also available. Hard liquor is served at many restaurants and at walk-up windows in CityWalk. The legal drinking age in Florida is 21 and photo IDs will be requested of anyone appearing 30 or younger. Try to feel flattered rather than annoyed. Although you can drink as you stroll about, taking alcoholic beverages through the turnstiles as you leave the parks is not allowed.

■ Emergencies

As a general rule, the moment something goes amiss, speak with the nearest Universal employee (and one won't be far away). They will contact security or medical assistance.

First Aid. Each park has two first aid stations. See the chapters on the individual parks for information on locations.

Lost Children. It happens all the time, and there's a good chance an alert employee will have spotted your wandering child before you notice he or she is gone. Rather than frantically search on your own, contact an employee. Found kids are escorted to Guest Services and entertained until their parents can be located.

Lost Property. Go to Lost & Found on the Front Lot at Universal Studios Florida or in the Port of Entry at Islands of Adventure and report any loss as soon as you notice it. The Guest Services window in CityWalk also has a lost and found section. Be prepared to provide as accurate a description as possible. Universal has an excellent track record for recovering the seemingly unrecoverable.

■ Guest Services

The friendly folks at Guest Services can answer just about any question you have. If you have a problem or complaint while in the parks, seek out the Guest Services office at the front of the park (in the Front Lot at USF and in Port of Entry at IOA). If you have a question you can call (407) 224-4233 and press the number 9 to speak with a Guest Services representative. You might want to program this number into your cell phone.

Happy Hour

Boozers rejoice! Most, if not all, of Universal Orlando's bars have generous happy hours. Times vary with the season. Some places may have happy hour from 3:00 to 5:00 p.m., while others will run from 4:00 to 7:00 p.m., allowing for extended discount drinking. What's available at what price also varies but half-price domestic drafts and margaritas are fairly standard happy hour offerings.

Leaving the Parks

You can leave either park at any time and be readmitted free the same day. Just have your hand stamped on the way out and look for the "same day reentry" line when you come back. You will also have to show your ticket again, since some tickets only allow admittance to one park. Those with annual passes can skip this formality.

Most people use this system when they visit the restaurants in CityWalk or go back to the hotel for a quick afternoon nap, but it's a good idea for Mom and Dad to have their hands stamped when leaving the park for the day, just in case you need to check back with Lost & Found.

Lockers

Electronically controlled lockers are available at both parks and allow unlimited in-and-out all-day access. They cost $8 or $10 a day, depending on size, and accept both bills and credit cards. The more "aggressive" rides restrict what you can carry with you, so lockers are provided and their use is mandatory. They are usually free for a short period of time, which varies with the length of the lines. After that, a hefty fee is charged for each half hour or so of use, to a daily maximum of $14. Should you overstay your welcome you can usually find a sympathetic ride attendant to open them for you; otherwise, you will have to pay to retrieve your stuff. Water-related rides also provide lockers, but charge a flat rate of $2 per hour.

Pets

If you have pets, inform the attendant when you pay for your parking and you will be directed to the Universal Studios kennels. Pet boarding is $15 a day (50% off first pet for Premier annual passholders) for each animal. The accommodations are comfortable, if not precisely luxurious. You supply the food, they supply the bowl and water. However, Universal's staff will not feed or care for your pet; they won't even touch it. If your pet needs to be walked or fed at specific times, you must return to the kennel and take care of it yourself. Kennels close two hours after park closing;

after that, you'll have to appeal to Security to spring your pet. Pets are not only welcomed but pampered at the resort hotels. See *Chapter Five: The Resort Hotels*.

▊ Phone Numbers

Although most are mentioned elsewhere, here is a handy list of important phone numbers:

General Info:	(407) 363-8000
TDD Line:	(407) 224-4414
Guest Services:	(407) 224-6350 - Main number
	(407) 224-4233 - USF and IOA
Lost & Found:	(407) 224-4244 - USF
	(407) 224-4245 - IOA
Universal Vacations:	(407) 224-7000 or (800) 711-0080
Audition Hotline:	(407) 224-7622
Jobs:	(407) 363-8080
Event Hotline:	(407) 224-5500
Merchandise:	(407) 224-5800
Hard Rock Hotel:	(407) 503-7625
Portofino Bay:	(407) 503-1000
Royal Pacific:	(407) 503-3000

▊ Priority Seating

Some restaurants in the parks and most in CityWalk offer "priority seating," which is subtly different from a reservation. It means that the restaurant will give you the first table that will accommodate your party that becomes available at or after the time you requested.

▊ Shopping at Home

Forgot to buy a magic wand for your favorite wizard? Here's a magic spell you can use. Visit www.universalorlando.com/Merchandise or call 877-318-2732 to purchase from a selection of souvenirs, including a limited array of Harry Potter merchandise.

▊ Smoking

Florida state law prohibits smoking in all restaurants. Smoking is not permitted in lines to the rides and attractions either. In fact, Universal has tried to take things a step further by limiting outdoor smoking to specified areas, marked on the maps with purple signs bearing a lit cigarette symbol. This system has met with only partial success and complaints about smoking in `nated areas are frequently heard. Bear in mind that many foreign- Universal Orlando and most of them come from countries where .ca's fetish with secondhand smoke seems quaint, if not downright .rd.

◢ Visiting the Resort Hotels

The resort hotels offer plenty of atmosphere along with good restaurants and bars. You don't have to be a hotel guest to enjoy them. Feel free to stroll over from CityWalk or the theme parks for a meal or drinks or just to look around. Or take the complimentary water taxis from the dock in CityWalk; some people don't realize that they are open to all and not exclusively for hotel guests.

A Note on Costs

Let's face it, visiting a theme park resort destination is not precisely a budget vacation, and Universal Orlando is no exception. A three-day visit by a typical family of four will cost over $600 in admissions alone. Of course, compared to other forms of entertainment, Universal Orlando offers excellent value for the dollar, as most people will agree.

Nonetheless, most of us must keep an eye on how much money we are spending, so throughout the book you will be given a quick idea of how much things like restaurants and hotels cost using dollar signs.

For restaurants, estimates are for an average meal, without alcoholic beverages. In the case of full-service restaurants, estimates are based on a "full" meal consisting of an appetizer or salad, an entree, and dessert. At the end of the book, you will find a list of hotels that are off Universal's property but convenient to the parks. Hotel estimates are based on one night's stay in a double room. The cost rankings are as follows:

	Restaurants	Hotels
$	Under $15	Under $100
$$	$15 - $25	$100 - $150
$$$	$25 - $40	$150 - $200
$$$$	Over $40	Over $200

As for fast-food prices, you don't have to worry about comparison shopping within the parks; a burger will cost the same no matter which cart or window you buy from. (The exception is some independent franchises in

CityWalk). Rather than repeat prices in the following chapters, here is a sampling of standard costs for quick-service consumables:

Double Cheeseburger w/ fries: $8.99

Hot Dog w/ chips: $7.29

Deli Sandwich: $7.89

Pasta: $6.89/ with meatballs: $7.89

Chicken Strips, Salad, or Sandwich: $7.99

Fried Chicken or Fish Basket: $7.99

Cheese Pizza: $3.79 slice/ $18.79 pie

Soda: $2.49 22oz/ $2.99 32oz

Hot Tea/ Coffee/ Hot Chocolate: $1.99

Milkshake: $2.99 reg/ $3.59 large

Popcorn: $2.99 reg/ $4.49 bucket

Frozen Slush: $3.75 virgin $7.75 alcoholic

Soft Serve: $2.99 cup/ $3.99 waffle cone

Draft Beer: $6 20oz / $8 pilsner

Pastries and Cakes: $2.50 - $4.89

Cheeseburger: $7.69

Turkey Leg: $8.99

Meatball Sub: $6.19

Chinese Entree: $8.29

Chef or Tuna Salad: $7.49

Funnel Cake: $4.99

Personal Pizza Pie: $6.79

Bottled Water: $2.75

Bottled Juice: $1.99

Pretzel or Churro: $2.99

Novelty Ice Cream: $3.25

Fruit Cup: $2.99

Ice Cream Float: $3.99

Wine: $6 glass

Accuracy and Other Impossible Dreams

While this book strives to be as accurate, comprehensive, and up-to-date as possible, these are all unattainable goals. Any theme park worth its salt is constantly changing and upgrading its attractions. Restaurants change their menus; shops revamp their choice of merchandise with the seasons and even the theme of the shop itself. On top of that, some attractions are seasonal; that is, they operate only when the crowds come.

What are most likely to change, alas, are prices. Like any business, Universal reserves the right to change its prices at any time without notice, so it's possible that prices will be revised after the deadline for this book. If you do run into price increases, they will typically be modest.

The Intrepid Traveler, the publisher of this book, maintains an entire web site with updated information about Universal Orlando and other non-Disney attractions in the Orlando area. Log on to the blog for the latest on prices and new rides and attractions:

■ **http://www.TheOtherOrlando.com/tooblog**

CHAPTER TWO:

UNIVERSAL STUDIOS FLORIDA

"Ride The Movies!" The brilliant ad slogan coined by Steven Spielberg says it all. In creating its first Florida theme park, Universal Studios built on the lessons learned over three decades at their original Hollywood movie-themed attraction, and injected a giant jolt of high-tech thrills. Over the last twenty years, much of the park's film-making "edutainment" has given way to some of the world's greatest thrill rides. But the cinematic spirit still thrives here among meticulously detailed, working movie sets that can make the simple act of sitting down to eat a hot dog seem like an adventure.

When Universal Studios Florida opened in 1990, it instantly became the number two draw in Orlando, right after Mickey's realm down the Interstate. With just over 100 acres and a price tag of a mere $650 million, Universal couldn't match Disney in size and scope. But that didn't mean Universal was willing to accept perennial also-ran status. There are a number of elements that set Universal Studios Florida apart from Disney and, say some, make it superior to Disney.

For starters, while Disney's Hollywood Studios remained comparatively static during the 2000s, Universal Studios Florida went through an amazing evolution. Of the opening day attractions, only the *E.T. Adventure* remains essentially unchanged. Former headliners *Kongfrontation*, *Earth-*

quake, *Jaws*, *Alfred Hitchcock*, *Hanna Barbera*, and *Back to the Future* have all been replaced or radically revamped from their original incarnations, and numerous new adventures have been added. So if your last visit here was in the late 90s, it's a whole new park to you.

The word that visitors and locals most frequently use to differentiate Universal from Disney is "adult." Whereas Disney World is perceived by many as a kiddie park that adults will enjoy, they see Universal as a park conceived with grown-ups in mind. There are a number of reasons for this:

Adult Themes. Many Universal attractions are based on films and shows that appeal primarily to adults — *Jaws*, *Disaster!*, *Terminator*, *Revenge of the Mummy*, and *Twister* are a far cry from *Honey, I Shrunk the Kids*.

Intensity. Whereas Disney (at least in its early days) would tend to tone down rides in the development stage lest they frighten young children, Universal Studios seems to delight in seeing just how intense they can be. *Revenge of the Mummy* is a prime example.

Beer and Wine. Beer and wine are readily available at Universal. And not just in the restaurants. Don't be surprised to see a beer vendor plying the lines on hot summer days. Some of the sit-down restaurants serve pretty decent wines by the bottle or glass and at a few places you can get a mixed drink. One of these, Finnegan's in the New York section, is a full-fledged Irish pub and a very good one at that.

There are two other elements that, while not necessarily contributing to the "adult" nature of the park, tend to set Universal apart:

Film Production. Universal Studios Florida is a working studio. While there's not as much production as there once was, virtually every corner of the park was designed in such a way that it could serve the needs of Universal's own film makers as well as those of other producers who use the facility to shoot films, TV shows, and television commercials. The New York set can be "dressed" to stand in for virtually any urban setting in the world, so they say, and was even flooded for Creed's "My Sacrifice" music video. While most filming takes place inside the Studio's soundstages, don't be surprised if you see a film crew at work in the streets during your visit. You are welcome to watch if you are discreet.

Pyrotechnics. If Universal Studios Florida has a stylistic signature, something that tells you that this is a Universal attraction and not someone else's, it has to be their lavish use of fire, fireworks, and loud explosions. You can almost feel your eyebrows singe on *Disaster!*, *Twister*, *Revenge of the Mummy*, and *Jaws*.

Eating in Universal Studios Florida

Universal is unlikely to win kudos from die-hard gourmets. Still, it seems to do a pretty good job of holding prices down while serving food most people will enjoy. And if you want a step up from the standard carnival fare, Finnegan's and Lombard's Seafood Grille, the two full-service restaurants in the park, have at least a dish or two that's better than average. Try the Catch of the Day at Lombard's or one of the Irish specialties at Finnegan's, for example, and you will feel well fed indeed.

For most families, however, the fare will be of the standard fast-food variety — most of it pretty good and not too outrageously priced. The prices of modest choices in the full-service restaurants are roughly equivalent to the prices at the fast food joints. So for about the same amount or just a few dollars more, you can enjoy the luxury of table service, constant refills of your iced tea, and best of all, air conditioning. It's an option worth considering.

In addition to the standard eateries, which are described in detail later, there are innumerable street-side kiosks, offering a wide variety of drinks and snacks, that appear and disappear as the crowds and weather dictate.

Shopping in Universal Studios Florida

It's easy to spend more on gifts and souvenirs than on admission. The standard, all-American souvenirs (T-shirts and the like) are priced slightly higher than their off-park equivalents, though some of them are very nicely designed. More upscale clothing, with the Universal logo displayed very discreetly, is sometimes available. When it is, it tends to be expensive but well made.

Rather than lug purchases with you, take advantage of Universal's package pickup service. Most shops will be happy to send your purchases to the It's A Wrap shop, near the front entrance, where you can pick them up on the way out. Or you can simply save all your shopping for the end of your visit and stop into the Universal Studios Store while the rest of the crowd is rushing to the gate at closing time. This shop has a good, although not complete, selection of merchandise from virtually every other shop in the park. You can also shop by phone by calling (407) 224-5800.

Another option is to visit the Universal outlet store in the nearby Festival Bay Mall on International Drive. They offer a selection of discontinued and discounted Universal merchandise, and rumor has it they sometimes carry items that are still currently on sale in the parks. All of Universal Studios Florida's shops will be touched on later.

Good Things To Know About...

Here are some notes that apply specifically to Universal Studios Florida. General notes that apply to both parks will be found in *Chapter One*.

▮ First Aid

There is a first aid station on Canal Street, across from *Beetlejuice's Grave-yard Revue* and just beside Louie's Italian Restaurant. You'll also find help at Family & Health Services on the Front Lot.

▮ Getting Wet

The *Curious George* play area in Woody Woodpecker's KidZone is straight out of a water park, and kids who visit there will not be able to resist the temptation to get absolutely drenched. On cooler days when a wet child could catch a chill, bring a towel and a change of clothes.

▮ Height Restrictions and Other Warnings

Due to a variety of considerations, such as sudden movements and the con-figuration of lap restraints, a few rides will be off-limits to shorter (typically younger) guests. The following rides have minimum height requirements:

Woody Woodpecker's Nuthouse Coaster	36 in. (91.4 cm.)
Jimmy Neutron	40 in. (101.6 cm.)
(Stationary seating is provided for shorter kids.)	
Men In Black	42 in. (106.7 cm.)
Revenge of the Mummy	48 in. (121.9 cm.)
Hollywood Rip Ride Rockit	51 in. (130 cm.)

In addition, any child under 48 inches must be accompanied by an adult on all these rides (except the *Mummy* and *Rockit*, which they can't ride at all) and must be able to sit upright without help.

▮ PG-13 Ratings

Universal urges "parental discretion" for kids under 13 on the following rides and attractions:

Beetlejuice's Graveyard Revue
Terminator 2: 3-D
Twister
Universal Horror Make-Up Show

In addition, *Jaws* may be too intense for very small children. Most par-ents seem to ignore the warnings. In this day and age (sadly, perhaps), it's hard to imagine a child being shocked by anything.

Reservations

Both Lombard's Seafood Grille and Finnegan's accept dining reservations. They are highly recommended at any time and especially if you are visiting during the busy season, although a reservation is not an absolute guarantee of avoiding a short wait. You can make your reservations first thing in the morning when you arrive or by phone up to 24 hours in advance. The number to call is (407) 224-3613.

Single Rider Lines

To help shrink long lines, "Single Rider" lines can cut you to the front of the queue provided you are willing to be separated from your party. *Hollywood Rip Ride Rockit, Men In Black,* and *Revenge of the Mummy* have a single rider line open most of the time, and *E.T. Adventure* sometimes opens a single rider line when things get busy. Single rider entrances may shutter if there is too much demand (or not enough), so you can't always count on this option.

Special Diets

Lombard's Seafood Grille and Finnegan's can provide kosher meals with 48 hours advance notice. Call Food Services at (407) 363-8340 to make arrangements. The 2-Park Map's list of dining spots calls out restaurants offering "healthy side choices," which usually means vegetarians can be accommodated.

Universal eliminated trans-fat oil from its menus in 2007. Still, if you're on a low-fat regimen, sticking with salads and fruit plates is probably the best strategy. Lombard's has a nice selection of seafood and salads.

Special Events

The year is sprinkled with special events tied to the holiday calendar. The events listed here, with the notable exception of Halloween Horror Nights, are usually included in regular admission, but separate admission is sometimes charged for evening events.

Among the holiday-themed events Universal Studios puts on are:

Mardi Gras. New Orleans' pre-Lenten bacchanalia comes to Florida in the form of a nighttime parade, complete with garish and gaudy floats, plenty of baubles and beads that are flung into the outstretched hands of the crowd, and concerts by classic and current musical artists.

Fourth of July. Universal Studios used to celebrate America's birthday with a fireworks display you could feel in the core of your being as well as see and hear from CityWalk. In recent years, they've scaled back to simply presenting their *Universal 360 Cinesphere Spectacular* (described later in this chapter). Most often, these shows continue nightly through the entire month of July, although this is not guaranteed.

Christmas. Ho, ho, ho! It's a Hollywood version of a heartwarming family holiday, complete with a scaled-down version of New York's famous Macy's Holiday Parade, giant balloons included.

New Year's Eve. Expect a wild street party, often with a live pop concert being taped for later television broadcast. There is an awesome fireworks display at midnight and the park stays open until 1:00 a.m.

Halloween Horror Nights. Universal's wildly popular after-hours frightfest is held on selected nights in late September through Halloween weekend. After the daytime guests depart, the park is turned into an elaborately themed bacchanalia of the bizarre, featuring famous Hollywood monsters alongside original horrors from the fiendish minds of Universal's fearmasters. The heart of the event is the half-dozen-plus haunted mazes in which visitors scream and shuffle past movie-quality tableaus of terror. Rock musicals, gory magic acts, and bawdy comedy shows (like the long-running "Bill & Ted" pop-culture satire) are staged, and most of the major rides are open. The park's thoroughfares are filled with fog and lurching "scareactors," but relax: they observe a strict "no-touching" policy.

Plans for 2011 are not yet announced, so check www.halloweenhorrornights.com for official info, or horrornightnightmares.com and behindthethrills.com for juicy rumors. A separate admission of roughly $75 is required, with various discounts available. The event is intense in every sense: loud, claustrophobic, suggestive, scatological, and alcohol-saturated. It is not for children, nor for many adults. If you intend to attend, do so on a "non-peak" night (Sunday to Thursday) or brace yourself for overwhelming crowds. Purchase tickets in advance, and arrive well before the event start time. Lines for the mazes build within an hour of opening, so see as many as you can early; then see shows until the final hour of the night. Express Passes are sold (for $40 to $80) though on peak nights you may face long waits even with them. An "RIP" guided tour, though pricey, is your only prayer for seeing everything on busy nights.

Play like a kid ... live like a 'King.'

Top: Seuss Trolley Ride in Islands of Adventure
Bottom: Hard Rock Hotel lobby

Above: Welcome to Universal Studios Florida

Right: Mel's Diner, just like you remember it. (Hollywood)

Below right: I'm ready for my close-up, Mr. DeMille. (KidZone)

Below left: What's real? What's fake? (Hollywood)

Above: Getting discovered at Schwab's. (Hollywood)

Left: Girl meets Jaws. (San Francisco-Amity)

Below left: Krusty wants YOU! (World Expo)

Below right: The Mummy's minion beckons. (New York)

Above: A mouse-sized world (different mouse). [KidZone]

Right: Just for the kids. (KidZone)

Below right: Woody and friend. (Hollywood)

Below left: The fun of horror make-up. (Hollywood)

Above: Lombard's Landing. [SF/Amity]

Left: Rip Ride Rockit will take you to new heights. (Production Central)

Below left: Kwik-E-Mart minus Apu. (World Expo)

Below right: Men in Black. (World Expo)

Above: Somewhere on the Lower East Side, circa 1930. (New York)

Right: Noble Steed enchants a young admirer. (Production Central)

Below: Touring a theme park is darned hard work. (Universal Studios)

Above: The Caro-Seuss-el. (Seuss Landing)

Left: A beacon for adventurers. (Port of Entry)

Below left: The Mystic Fountain speaks. (Lost Continent)

Below right: An exotic streetscape. (Port of Entry)

Above: Welcome to Islands of Adventure. (Port of Entry)

Right: Yes, it's a restaurant — Mythos. (Lost Continent)

Below right: Gourmet eats at Mythos. (Lost Continent)

Below left: Here be griffins. (Lost Continent)

The Shooting Script: Your Day at Universal Studios Florida

It is perfectly possible to spend a full day at Universal Studios Florida and see everything. This is especially true if you are staying in one of the on-site hotels, which will give you preferred access to virtually all the rides and attractions. It is also true if you have heeded the advice in *Chapter One* and arrived during one of the less hectic times of year. A slower touring pace is preferable, which multi-day ticket options, including the Orlando Flex-Ticket, make possible.

If circumstances or perversity have led you to ignore this sage advice, you will have to plan carefully and perhaps purchase a Universal Express Plus pass (see *Chapter One: Planning Your Escape*) to ensure seeing as much of the park as possible in a one-day time span. At the very least, you will be able to see enough to feel satisfied. Not everyone, after all, will be equally interested in all of the attractions, and missing a few won't break anyone's heart. Even at less busy times, you might want to consider following some of the strategies set forth in this section. Lines for more popular rides can grow long enough to make the wait seem tedious even in slack periods.

A little later, you'll get a blow-by-blow description of every attraction, eatery, and shop in the park. This section provides an overview, some general guidance, and a step-by-step plan for seeing the park during busier periods.

Doing Your Homework

You can arrive at Universal Studios knowing nothing about any of the films or TV shows on which its attractions are based (although it's hard to imagine that being possible), and have a perfectly good time. Indeed, you don't need to understand a word of English to be entertained here, as the happy hordes of foreign tourists prove.

Nonetheless, there is one attraction that will benefit from a bit of research prior to your visit. *E.T. Adventure* will make a lot more sense to those who have seen the film. This is especially true for younger kids who might find E.T.'s odd appearance a bit off-putting if they haven't seen the film. Fortunately, this is the kind of homework that's easy and fun to do. Netflix will have all the research material you need. While you're at it, you might want to add *Shrek* and *Jimmy Neutron* to your queue, if only to whet the kids' appetites for their visit.

What To Expect

Universal Studios Florida uses the "back lot" as its organizing metaphor. The back lot is where a studio keeps permanent and semi-permanent outdoor sets that can be "dressed" to stand in for multiple locations. USF consists of six such sets — Hollywood, Woody Woodpecker's KidZone, World Expo, San Francisco/Amity, New York, and Production Central — in addition to the Front Lot. You will find a helpful map of the layout of the sets in the **2-Park Map** brochure, which you can pick up at the entrance gates or in many of the shops throughout the park. Each set will be discussed in detail in the sections that follow.

It will also help to have a basic idea of the different types of rides, shows, and attractions Universal Studios Florida has to offer. Each type of attraction has its own peculiarities and dictates a different viewing pattern.

Rides. As the term indicates, these attractions involve getting into a vehicle and going somewhere. Some, like *E.T. Adventure*, are the descendants of the so-called "dark rides" of old-fashioned amusement parks; you ride through a darkened tunnel environment lined with things to look at. *Men In Black* adds exciting elements of interactivity to the old formula, while *Revenge of the Mummy* takes this concept to the cutting edge and beyond!

Rides are the first major attractions to open in the morning and should be your first priority. Rides have a limited seating capacity, at least compared to the theater shows. They don't last long either; most at Universal are no longer than five minutes. They tend to be the most popular attractions because of the thrills they promise (and deliver). The result: Lines form early and grow longer as the day wears on and more people pack the park.

Theater Shows. Whereas the rides offer thrills, theater shows offer entertainment and, occasionally, education as well. Theater shows can be live (like the *Horror Make-Up* show), on film (like *Shrek*), or a combination of both (like *Terminator*). They occur indoors, out of the heat and sun, in comfortable theaters. They last about 25 minutes on average. Most film shows start running soon after opening time and run continuously. Live shows start about midday and have their show times listed in the 2-Park Map.

Because they seat 250 to 700 people at a time, a long line outside a theater show may be deceptive. Many times you can get in line as the next group is entering and still make the show. This is not always true during the busier times, however. Ask an attendant if getting in line now will guarantee a seat at the next show.

Amphitheater Shows. These shows differ from theater shows in that they take place in larger semi-open auditoriums that do not offer the luxury of air conditioning. They start about midday, with show times listed in the 2-Park Map brochure.

Outdoor Shows. These are small-scale shows involving a few entertainers. They occur on the streets at set times announced in the 2-Park Map.

Displays and Interactive Areas. These two different types of attractions are similar in that you can simply walk into them at will and stay as long as you wish. That's not to say you won't find a line, but, with the exception of *Fievel's Playland*, lines are rare at these attractions.

All the Rest. There's a great deal of enjoyment to be derived from simply walking around in Universal Studios Florida. The imaginative and beautifully executed sets make wonderful photo backdrops and, when things get too hectic, you can even find a grassy knoll on which to stretch out, rest, and survey the passing scene.

Academy Awards

If you have a limited time at Universal Studios Florida, you probably won't be able to see everything. However, it would be a shame if you missed the very best the park has to offer. Here, then, is a list of Academy Awards:

The Simpsons. Simulator thrills and Simpsons satire! What a combo.

Terminator 2: 3-D Battle Across Time. With this show, the award for "best 3-D show in Orlando" moved from Disney to Universal.

Shrek 4-D. Another boffo 3-D entertainment that solidifies Universal's preeminence in the genre.

Curious George Goes To Town. Just for kids and just wonderful.

Revenge of the Mummy. Eternal torment has never been such fun.

Universal Horror Make-Up Show. Fun and games with dead bodies and strange critters.

Runners-Up

These aren't on the list of the best of the best but they make many other people's lists and they are very, very good.

Hollywood Rip Ride Rockit. A one-of-a-kind coaster for thrill ride junkies and music fans alike.

Men In Black: Alien Attack. A ride-through video game pits you against the universe.

E.T. Adventure. A bicycle ride to E.T.'s home planet is like *it's a small world* on acid.

Jaws. A wet and wild updating of those old haunted house rides on the boardwalk. Ride it at night.

The One-Day Stay

If you are staying at an on-site hotel and thus have preferred access or have purchased a Universal Express Plus pass (see *Chapter One*), then you can largely ignore the following advice and proceed as you wish.

1. Get up early. You want to arrive at the park before the official opening time. Allow at least half an hour to park your car and get to the main entrance. If you arrive extra early, don't worry, there will already be people there waiting and Universal Studios will do its best to keep you all amused, usually by having costumed characters come out to mix and mingle and pose for photos.

2. Since you were smart enough to buy your tickets the day before, you don't have to wait in line again, at least not for tickets. Position yourself for the opening of the gates and go over your plan one more time.

3. As soon as the gates open, move briskly to *Hollywood Rip Ride Rockit*, using the single rider line if available.

4. After riding *Rockit*, head quickly past "Mel's Drive-In" around the lagoon to *The Simpsons Ride*.

5. Continue next door to *Men In Black*. Use the regular queue if this is your first time on *MIB*; otherwise use the single rider line.

6. Next stop is *Jaws*. After *Jaws*, do *Disaster!*

Option: If *E.T. Adventure* is high on your list, go there first and then head for *Jaws*; if not, save *E.T.* for late in the day when many of the kiddies and their exhausted parents will have left.

7. Ride *Revenge of the Mummy* using the single rider line.

8. See *Shrek 4D*, then ride *Jimmy Neutron* if the line is short. If the line looks too long, head on to *Twister*, then *T2*. Now the time has come to start checking out the theater and amphitheater shows. The *Universal Horror Make-Up Show* is a short walk from the *T2* exit and well worth seeing.

9. At this point, you will have been on the most popular rides and seen a show or maybe even two. The crowds are beginning to get noticeably larger and the sun is high in the sky. Take a break, maybe eat lunch. If the park is particularly crowded and you feel you are "running late" you may want to limit your lunch to quick snacks you can carry with you as you move from

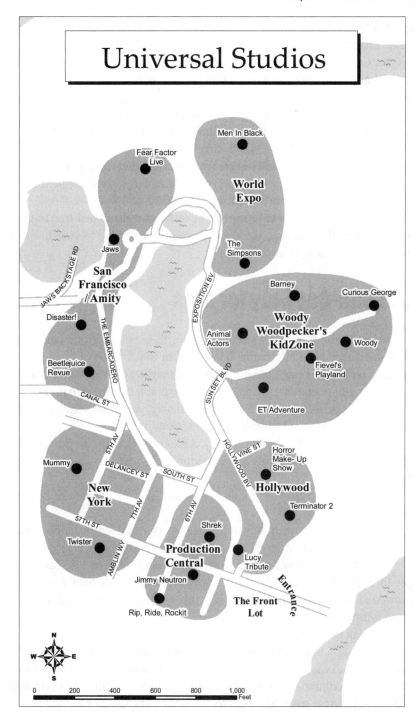

Universal Studios

Men In Black

Fear Factor Live

World Expo

Jaws

The Simpsons

San Francisco / Amity

Barney

Curious George

Disaster!

Woody Woodpecker's KidZone

Animal Actors

Woody

Beetlejuice Revue

Fievel's Playland

ET Adventure

Mummy

Horror Make-Up Show

New York

Hollywood

Terminator 2

Twister

Shrek

Production Central

Hollywood

Lucy Tribute

Jimmy Neutron

The Front Lot

Rip, Ride, Rockit

Entrance

JAW'S BACKSTAGE RD

THE EMBARCADERO

EXPOSITION BV

SUNSET BLVD

CANAL ST

5TH AV

DELANCEY ST

SOUTH ST

HOLLYWOOD BV

VINE ST

7TH AV

6TH AV

57TH ST

AMBLIN WY

N
W   E
S

0   200   400   600   800   1,000
Feet

line to line. There are plenty of outdoor kiosks dispensing this kind of portable "finger food."

10. Continue your rounds of the shows you want to see and check in periodically at any rides you missed (or would like to try again). You may be pleasantly surprised.

11. As the crowd thins toward closing time, circle back to the rides you missed. A great time to find shorter lines to even the most popular rides is about an hour before the official closing time.

12. The park doesn't lock the gates at the scheduled closing time. So this is a good time to buy your souvenirs; you'll have saved some prime touring time and won't have to lug them around for so long.

Many of the smaller eateries will be open as well, so feel free to grab a well-earned dessert. And you'll still have plenty of time to visit *Lucy: A Tribute* before heading to your car.

The One-Day Stay for Kids

For selfless parents who are willing to place their child's agenda ahead of their own, here is an alternative one-day plan that will serve the needs of younger children — age eleven and below, maybe seven or eight and below. Often it happens that young children are better equipped to handle the more intense rides than their elders. Presumably, you know your own child and will be able to adapt the following outline as needed.

1. Get to the park bright and early. As soon as you are in, ride *Jimmy Neutron* (if your kids are over 40 inches tall). Afterwards, visit *E.T. Adventure*.

2. If you have very young kids, it'll be too early for *Barney* so head to see *Shrek 4-D*.

3. Depending on your kids' tolerance, check out *Men In Black*, *Jaws*, and *Disaster!*, in that order. (Take note of height restrictions.)

4. Next, check show times for *Barney* and *Animal Actors on Location!* See them in the appropriate order. Try to steer your little ones away from *Barney's Backyard*, *Fievel's Playland*, and *Curious George*, explaining that you'll return later.

5. Break for lunch.

6. After lunch, let the kids burn off steam at *Fievel's Playland*, *Barney's Backyard*, and *Curious George* while you get some much-needed rest and plot out the remainder of the day. Remember, too, that the heat of the day is the best time for your little ones to get soaked at *Curious George*.

■ THE FRONT LOT ■

In movie studio parlance, the front lot is where all the soundstages, as well as the administrative and creative offices, are located — as opposed to the back lot, which contains the outdoor sets. Here at Universal Studios Florida, the Front Lot is a small antechamber of sorts to the theme park proper, which can be looked on as one huge back lot. On the Front Lot you can take care of minor pieces of business on your way into the park — like renting a stroller — and here you can also return when things go wrong — to register a complaint at Guest Services, or seek nursing aid for an injured child, or check Lost & Found for that priceless pearl earring that flew off in *Revenge of the Mummy*. You will find the following services on the Front Lot:

■ To your left as you enter the park are . . .

Lockers. There are two small bays of electronically controlled lockers. The rental fee is $8 for the day with in and out access, and the machines accept both bills and credit cards. If these are full, you can find more lockers (including some larger and more expensive ones that are handy if you have a lot of stuff) on the other side of the plaza.

Mail. You'll find a small U.S. Postal Service drop box to the right of the lockers. Stamps are available at On Location (see below).

Phone Cards. Also near the lockers is a phone-card vending machine.

Stroller & Wheelchair Rentals. Wheelchairs are $12 a day and strollers $15. Double strollers are $20. Slightly more elaborate strollers, called "kiddie cars," feature a kid's steering wheel and cup holders and rent for $18 and $23 respectively (when available).

A motorized "electric convenience vehicle" (ECV) is yours for $50 for the day. ECVs and wheelchairs require a $50 deposit and a signed rental agreement; ECVs can be reserved a week in advance and this is highly recommended. You must be over 18 to rent an ECV. Both ECVs and wheelchairs can be transferred from park to park.

■ To your right as you enter the park are . . .

Guest Services. This office performs a wide variety of functions. You can pick up information and brochures about special services and special events. If you have a complaint about anything in the park, make your feelings known here. They also field compliments. So if some Universal employee has made a positive difference to your experience in the park, make a note of their name and take a moment to share your experience here. It really does make a difference for those outstanding employees.

Guest Services will also exchange some (but not all) foreign currency, to a maximum of $500, for a flat fee of $5. If you exchange the limit, that works out to a one percent fee, a better deal than you'll get elsewhere.

If you've come to Universal Studios Florida for the day and like what you see, Guest Services can upgrade your one-day pass to any of Universal Orlando's multi-day pass options. The price you paid for your one-day pass will be deducted from the price of the multi-day pass. In other words, you will pay exactly what you would have paid had you purchased the multi-day ticket in the first place.

There are some simple rules: Upgrades must be purchased before you leave the park. Everyone in your party who wants one must show up with their one-day pass stub in hand. Free or complimentary passes are not eligible for upgrades.

Upgrades are non-transferable and Universal enforces this feature by requiring your signature on the pass and requesting photo ID when you return, which can be the next day or five years hence. The pass stays valid until you use it. If you really liked your visit, you can also sign up for an Annual Pass here.

ATM. Next to the Studio Audience Center is an outdoor ATM, where you can get a cash advance on your Visa, MasterCard, or Discover credit card at any time. The machine is also hooked into the Cirrus, Plus, NYCE, AFFN, and Maestro systems for those who would like to withdraw money from their bank account back home. There is a $2.50 fee for those not using a GE Money card.

Studio Audience Center. There is far less television production at Universal than there used to be, but *TNA Wrestling* and *Family Feud* are regularly produced here. If anything is being taped on the nearby sound-stages during your visit to Universal Studios, this is the best place to get information and tickets. A show can have an audience of 50 to 300 and tape one to six episodes on a single day.

Each show will have a minimum age requirement, which can vary greatly. Tickets are free and distributed on a first-come, first-served basis. Show up early, but try not to be disappointed if you come up empty. You can call (407) 224-4233 (press option 5) to see what might be available during your visit. They say they usually know about tapings only two weeks or so in advance.

Family & Health Services. Nursing aid is also available here, under the Studio Audience Center marquee, should you need it. There is also a "family bathroom" if, for example, you need to assist a disabled spouse. A special room is set aside for nursing mothers. If you just need to change a diaper, you will find diaper-changing facilities in restrooms located throughout the park.

Lost & Found. The Studio Audience Center window does double duty as Lost & Found. Items that if lost elsewhere would probably be gone forever have a surprising way of turning up at theme parks. The good feelings the park experience generates must make people ever so slightly less larcenous. Universal personnel always check the rides for forgotten belongings. Items are kept for 30 days. You can call (407) 224-4244.

Lockers. Here are more of those electronic lockers, with still more lockers just around the corner in a narrow, easy to overlook passageway that leads to Hollywood Boulevard and the *T2* theater. Daily rental is $8 or $10, depending on size, and allows unlimited in and out access.

Shopping on the Front Lot

In the Front Lot, Universal has shrewdly located a number of shops that cater to the needs of both the arriving and departing guest.

If you left the camera at the hotel or find yourself short of film, your first stop should be **On Location**. They can also help with sunscreen, sunglasses, and tote bags. In addition you will find a constantly rotating inventory of T-shirts, baseball caps, and the like.

If you have your photo taken by a roving photographer in the park, there's no obligation to buy a print, but if you just can't resist, this is where you view and claim your pictures. All pictures are digital and are held for three days. They only print them out if you order. Prices range from $20 for a single 8 x 10 to $30 for more elaborate packages.

Studio Sweets, a small shop on your left as you enter the park, sells scoop-your-own bulk candy at caviar prices. There is also a wide assortment of tinned cookies, chocolate- and caramel-dipped apples, and fudge.

By far the largest store in the park, the **Universal Studios Store** is located just next to (in fact, it surrounds) Studio Sweets. Here you will find a representative sampling of the wares to be found in the various smaller shops scattered about the park. If you want to save all your souvenir shopping until the end of your visit, you should be able to get something appropriate here. Just be aware that the selection is not exhaustive and that the special item you admired elsewhere might not be for sale here.

There are plenty of T-shirts for men, women, and children. Even with the inevitable Universal Studios logos, much of the clothing displayed here is very stylish and in impeccable taste. Prices are moderate, with the occasional pricey item on offer. They haven't forgotten toys for the kids and, of course, the Universal Studios Store has a generous selection of other souvenir merchandise, everything from refrigerator magnets to mugs, emblazoned with various film and TV series names, faces, and logos.

It's A Wrap (studio lingo for "we've finished shooting the movie") is a nifty name for this vest-pocket souvenir stand that thoughtfully straddles the exit to the park. That means, if you're on your way to the car and suddenly remember that you forgot a present for Auntie Em, you can run back and get something without reentering the park. The selection is limited, running heavily to T-shirts and gewgaws like key chains and the like, although there is a small selection of sale items offering some nice bargains.

HOLLYWOOD

Hollywood is probably the smallest "set" at Universal Studios Florida. It is about two city blocks long, stretching from *Lucy: A Tribute* near the park entrance to The Garden of Allah motel near the lagoon. Along the way is an imaginative and loving recreation of the Hollywood of our collective subconscious. The Hollywood set was primarily a shopping and dining venue until the opening of *Terminator 2: 3-D Battle Across Time* made it a major stop on everybody's tour of Universal's Greatest Hits.

Terminator 2: 3-D Battle Across Time

Rating: * * * * +
Type: A "3-D Virtual Adventure"
Time: About 20 minutes
Our Take: The most exciting 3-D theater attraction in Orlando

When the Governator swore "I'll be back," he wasn't kidding! Most attractions based on movies are created and developed by specialists at the parks. With *T2:3D*, "King of the World" James Cameron (director of box-office behemoths *Titanic* and *Avatar*) and his *Terminator* star Arnold Schwarzenegger set out to prove they could do it better themselves. And, boy, did they ever! Reports are that $60 million was spent to create this show. You'll get their money's worth.

You step off Hollywood Boulevard into the newly rebuilt headquarters of Cyberdyne, the not-so-nice corporate giant of the *Terminator* flicks, which is out to refurbish its image and show off its latest technology. The pre-show warm-up, which takes place in a large anteroom to the theater itself, features a delicious parody of the "Vision of the Future" corporate videos and television commercials that were all the rage in the early Aughts. The pre-show also gets the plot rolling: Sarah Connor and her son John have invaded Cyberdyne and commandeered the video screen to warn us against the new SkyNet project (which sounds remarkably like the Bush-era National Missile Defense system). According to these "terrorists" (as the Cyberdyne people describe them), SkyNet will enslave us all. The Cyberdyne flack who is our host glosses over this "unfortunate interruption" and ushers us into the large auditorium. There we settle into deceptively normal looking theater seats, don our "protective glasses," and the show begins.

And what a show it is. Without giving too much away, suffice it to say that it involves a spectacular three-screen 3-D movie starring Ah-nold himself, along with Linda Hamilton and Eddie Furlong (the kid from *Terminator 2*). In one of the more inspired touches, the on-screen actors move from screen to stage and back again, Arnold aboard a roaring motorcycle.

While the Terminator franchise has moved on, with two more films and a TV show released since *T2:3D* premiered, this attraction preserves the series at its peak popularity. Though the film's celluloid projectors are showing their age, the special effects remain spectacular, and the slam-bang, smoke-filled finale still has people screaming and shrieking in their seats.

Note that the huge interior queue can hold over 1,100 people, while the theater holds 700 people; with shows starting every 30 to 45 minutes, the line moves fairly quickly.

The Universal Horror Make-Up Show

Rating:	* * * * *
Type:	Theater show
Time:	25 minutes
Our Take:	Hilarious! Universal's best-kept secret

How to take something gory, gruesome, and downright disgusting and turn it into wholesome, funny family fare? Universal has solved the problem with this enjoyable (not to mention educational) foray into the ghastly art of make-up and special effects for the horror genre. The key is a horror make-up "expert" with a bizarre and goofy sense of humor who is interviewed in a studio make-up lab by an on-stage host and straight-man. During a laugh-filled 25 minutes, our expert leads us through a grisly show-and-tell of basic horror movie tricks and gimmicks. It's a roaring success that many call "Universal Studios' best-kept secret."

Tip: The subject matter is undeniably gross and the performers are given fairly wide latitude to ad-lib. Some people may find either the subject matter or the humor (or both) beyond the bounds of good taste. The easily offended, then, should give this show a miss. Universal rates it PG-13.

Using the inevitable volunteer from the audience (to very amusing effect), we learn how harmlessly dull knifes can be made to leave bloody trails on bare human flesh and, thanks to video projected onto two screens, we get a brief history of extreme makeup from Lon Chaney to modern masters Tom Savini and Rick Baker. Also on hand are mechanical werewolf heads like those used for the still stunning transformation scene in *An American*

Werewolf in London. The show ends with a preview of a new, remotely controlled monster and yet another dirty trick played on a "volunteer."

This show actually instructs while it entertains. Everyone will have a keener understanding of basic horror effects, and young children will be sternly warned about the importance of safety at all times. ("Don't do this at home . . . Do it at a friend's house!")

The waiting area for this show is the lobby of the Pantages Theater, where you can peruse memorabilia displays from Universal's horror-movie history while waiting for the show to begin.

This is the best show at Universal and it just seems to get better and better every year. The performers, all skilled improvisers, play off the audience, making every show slightly different and rewarding repeat visits.

The best seats in the house. If all you want to do is enjoy the show, the oft-repeated Universal refrain is absolutely true — every seat's a good seat. Exhibitionists hoping to be selected as a volunteer should be aware that the performers have a predilection for young women seated in the middle, close to the stage.

Lucy: A Tribute

Rating:	* * +
Type:	Museum-style display, with video
Time:	Continuous viewing
Our Take:	Best for adults with a sense of history

Lucy: A Tribute is a walk-in display honoring the immortal Lucille Desiree Ball. It's hard to miss, since you bump into it almost as soon as you enter the park. There's hardly ever a crowd, so feel free to breeze on by and take it in later. If you run out of time . . . well, truth to tell, you haven't missed much. Still, fans of the great redhead (and who isn't?) will find at least something of interest here, even if it's just a reminder to pull down those Lucy videos at home and take a four hundredth look.

The "tribute" is simply a large open room ringed with glassed-in display cases, like shop windows, crammed with Lucy memorabilia — photos, letters, scripts, costumes, and Lucy's six Emmys. One of the more interesting windows contains a model of the studio in which the ground-breaking *I Love Lucy* show was shot. It was the first show shot with the three-camera method still used today. A fascinating footnote: The sets in those days of black-and-white TV were actually painted in shades of gray (furniture, too) to provide optimum contrast on the home screen.

Continuously running videos feature Bob Hope and Gale Gordon reminiscing about Lucy, while brief clips remind us of just how much we really did love Lucy. You'll hear the people next to you saying, "Oh, I remember that one," or "I lo-o-o-ved that one." There's some interesting material here about Lucy's career before she became a television icon and an interactive *I Love Lucy* trivia quiz.

Selected Short Subjects

■ Hollywood Celebrities

Hollywood Boulevard is a great place for star spotting. **Stars of yesteryear,** like Marilyn Monroe and Lucy and Desi, as well as famous **cartoon characters**, have been known to put in appearances. Lately, the Simpsons have been showing up in a large RV to mix and mingle with the crowds along the Boulevard. You can have your photo taken with them or even get an autograph.

■ Musical Entertainment

From time to time, usually during the park's busier periods, you will find a fifties-style group holding forth on a small stage outside Mel's Diner. The groups vary in size and composition, but the doo-wop nostalgia blast is virtually guaranteed to please.

■ Universal Studios Radio Broadcast Center

On your left as you proceed down Hollywood Boulevard is a fairly inconspicuous radio studio. From here popular disk jockeys from around the world have broadcast live to the folks back home, and local stations frequently use it for "remotes." Peek in and check out the clever ceiling treatment inside.

■ Trick Photography Photo Spot

Near the lagoon, you will find a spot where you can take your own souvenir photo using the "hanging miniature" technique pioneered in the early days of filmmaking. Position your camera on the stand and follow the fool-proof instructions. There are even footprints telling you where to place your subjects. Then you can photograph your family in front of the (real) Pantages Theater, with the (painted) Hollywood hills and the rest of the Los Angeles skyline stretching into the distance. Even if you don't have a camera, take a peek to see how it works. It's nifty.

Eating in Hollywood

■ Beverly Hills Boulangerie

What: Sandwiches, sweets, and coffee

Where: At the corner of Hollywood Boulevard
and Plaza of the Stars

Price Range: $

This faux-bistro blends the current craze for coffee bars with a tasty array of breakfast and dessert baked goods. It's an unbeatable combination. If you're visiting during one of the less crowded times of year (so you don't have to dash right off to *Shrek*), you might want to pause here for a fortifying if calorie-laden breakfast. Sit outside on sunny days to entertain yourself with the passing people-watcher's parade.

There are gigantic blueberry, banana-nut, and bran muffins and roly-poly chocolate croissants. If you subscribe to the when-on-vacation-start-with-dessert philosophy, why not start the day off right with an eclair, or a slice of raspberry cheesecake? Choices range from basic pastries and muffins to lavish cakes for around $5 and fancy cappuccinos.

Later in the day, you can stop in for a smoked turkey, roast beef, or ham and Swiss sandwich on your choice of baguette or croissant. Or soothe your conscience with a Health Sandwich of Swiss cheese, sprouts, cucumbers, and avocados. Sandwiches are in the $8 range and come with a tasty side of potato salad and fresh fruit. You can also get salads here if you purchase them with soup ($5) or a sandwich ($9).

■ Mel's Drive-In

What: Fast-food burger joint

Where: At the end of Hollywood Boulevard,
across from the lagoon

Price Range: $

Remember the nostalgia-drenched drive-in restaurant from *American Graffiti*? Well here it is in some of its splendor. No curvy car hops, alas, but you will see a few vintage cars parked outside.

Inside, you will find a fairly typical fast-food emporium with fifties decor. Place and pay for your burger or hot dog and fries order at the cashier, then step forward to pick it up, wrapped in paper. If the food and non-service won't bring back memories of those great cheeseburgers and real-milk shakes you had way back when, at least there are jukeboxes to flip through at the tables. An outdoor seating area looks out to the park's central lagoon.

63

The menu is limited, but the chili is hearty. Soft drinks, shakes, and root beer floats are the beverage choices here. Mel's is a good spot for a quick bite with kids who like no surprises with their meals.

■ Schwab's Pharmacy

What: Ice-cream parlor
Where: In the middle of Hollywood Boulevard
Price Range: $

Schwab's is famous in Hollywood lore as the place where a sharp-eyed talent scout discovered a sweater-clad, teenaged Lana Turner sipping soda at the counter. At Universal Studios, Schwab's lends its name to a small, black-and-white tiled, vaguely forties-ish ice-cream parlor featuring Ben & Jerry's cones, milk shakes, sundaes, and ice cream floats, as well as double scoop sundaes and banana splits. Although there are a few tables, Schwab's is primarily aimed at those looking for a quick take out snack.

In keeping with its namesake's primary business, Schwab's also has a small supply of over-the-counter headache and heartburn remedies, but keeps them under the counter, so ask. For those intent on spending the whole day riding *Hollywood Rip Ride Rockit*, Schwab's very thoughtfully provides Pepto-Bismol.

■ Cafe La Bamba

What: Cafeteria-style barbecue restaurant
Where: Across from Mel's and the lagoon in the
        Hollywood Hotel
Price Range: $ - $$

Cafe La Bamba serves up ample portions of rotisserie chicken and barbecued ribs at moderate prices. On top of that, the ambiance is a cut above your average fast-food restaurant. Evoking a Spanish mission courtyard with adobe walls and tiled floors, it offers some charming corners just a few steps away from the cafeteria lines, plus a delightful outdoor seating area that looks across to Mel's and the lagoon.

At the **Cantina Bar**, you can get a frozen alcoholic drink, beer, or specialty drinks like "Potion of the Aztecs."

Note: This restaurant only operates during peak season.

Shopping in Hollywood

Hollywood Boulevard funnels visitors from the studio entrance to the central lagoon and serves as a primary route for visitors on their way out. Much of it has been given over to a variety of shopping experiences. The Boulevard itself is an imaginative recreation of major Hollywood facades, some of which still exist and others of which have vanished into the realm of cherished memories. It makes for a pleasant stroll and a fitting introduction to the movie-themed fun that awaits you in the rest of the park.

Silver Screen Collectibles opens onto the Plaza of the Stars, just across the street from the Universal Studios Store. At the other end, it merges with *Lucy: A Tribute*. Expect to find T-shirts and other merchandise featuring cartoon characters. Betty Boop merchandise is prominently featured. The real star of the shop, however, is the special Lucy section, strategically located at the entrance/exit to *Lucy: A Tribute*. Here you will find the Lucy Collection, a series of DVDs. In addition, you'll find a generous selection of books, which the true Lucy fan will find to be invaluable references, and a series of T-shirts in homage to the great redhead.

You can't miss **Cyber Image** if you see *Terminator 2: 3-D Battle Across Time* (and you should); you walk right through it when you leave the theater. Here's your chance to dress just like Arnold in pricey black leather, muscles not included. For the less well heeled there are T2 and superhero T-shirts. DVDs of *The Terminator* and other sci-fi films are usually available.

Studio Styles is the small jewelry store sandwiched between Schwabs Pharmacy and the now-defunct Darkroom photo developers (remember film?). It offers costume and semi-precious earrings, necklaces, and pins. "Olympia" beads and charms ($5-$20) are featured, as are souvenir coins and watches. Check out the reproduction rings based on baubles worn by Marilyn Monroe and Claudette Colbert ($150-$200).

Next to Mel's Diner, under the sign that says "Williams of Hollywood," you'll find **Theatre Magic Shop**, a fascinating boutique that gives away (well, *sells*) the secrets of the magician's trade. The target audience is the absolute beginner and most of the magic kits sold here come with an instructional DVD to help bring you up to speed quickly. The big seller is "The Levitator," a trick that lets you magically spin cards in mid-air. There are frequent magic demonstrations timed to attract the crowds pouring out of the nearby *T2* and *Horror Make-Up* shows.

WOODY WOODPECKER'S KIDZONE

Although its intense thrill rides have brought Universal Studios Florida a reputation as an "adult" theme park, it hasn't forgotten the kiddies. Woody Woodpecker's KidZone, located along a winding avenue off the central lagoon, is a perfect case in point. If you have children under ten, you could very easily spend an entire day here, with only an occasional foray to sample other kid-friendly attractions in the park. There's a nice balance here, too, from stage shows to play areas to kiddie-scale "thrill" rides. They will be described in roughly the order you encounter them as you wend your way deeper into Woody's KidZone.

Tip: At the end of the Hollywood set, past Cafe La Bamba, look for the Gardens of Allah Villas on your right. Cut through here for a shortcut to Woody's KidZone and the *E.T. Adventure.*

Animal Actors On Location!

Rating: * * * +
Type: Amphitheater show
Time: About 20 minutes
Our Take: Fun for just about everybody

This awww-inspiring spectacle shows off the handiwork of Universal's animal trainers and their furry and feathery charges. It's all done with the droll good humor and audience participation that characterize all of Universal's shows. Volunteers are pulled from the audience to serve as foils for several amusing routines.

The show alternates between live action on stage and video footage on a large overhead screen showing clips of animal actors in a surprising variety of films, from comedies to horror flicks. In one especially fascinating segment, we learn how birds can be filmed in flight using a large fan and some trick camera work.

Just which animals you see will depend to some extent on which "stars" are available when you visit. But you can probably count on a display by a well-trained if slightly mercenary bird and a bit that uses a child volunteer from the audience. If you're lucky, an orangutan will provide comic relief.

In between the fun and games, the show sneaks in a few points about the serious business of producing "behaviors" that can be put to use in films. Most interestingly, when an animal balks at performing a trick, the trainer doesn't merely gloss over the rough spot and get on with the show. Instead, he works patiently with the animal until the behavior is performed correctly. We learn that what for us is light entertainment is serious business for the folks (both two- and four-legged) on the stage.

The best seats in the house. There really are no bad seats for this one. However, if you'd like a shot at serving as a landing strip for that mercenary bird, try sitting in the middle of the middle section.

E.T. Adventure

Rating:	✻ ✻ ✻ ✻
Type:	Gondola ride
Time:	5 minutes
Our Take:	Kids love this one (some adults do, too)

Based on the blockbuster movie that crossed sci-fi with cuddly toys, the *E.T. Adventure* takes us where the movie didn't — back to E.T.'s home planet. In a filmed introduction to the ride, Steven Spielberg, who directed the film, sets up the premise: E.T.'s home, the Green Planet, is in some unspecified trouble, although it looks like an advanced case of ozone hole, which is turning the place a none-too-healthy-looking orange. You have to return with E.T. to help save the old folks at home. How to get there? Aboard the flying bicycles from the film's final sequence, of course. The fact that Spielberg doesn't bother to explain how we'll survive the rigors of interstellar travel aboard mountain bikes tells us that this ride is aimed at the very young. After this brief setup, the doors ahead open and we line up to tell a staffer our first names and get the "passports" we will need for the journey.

Passports firmly in hand, we walk through a cave-like tunnel into the misty, nighttime redwood forests of the Northwest. This set is a minor masterpiece of scenic design and some people think it's the best part of the adventure. As we wend our way along a winding "nature trail" among the towering trees, we make out the animated figure of Botanicus, a wise elder from E.T.'s planet, urging us to hurry back. Here, too, we glimpse the jury-rigged contraption E.T. used to communicate in the film.

At the staging area, we hand in our passports and collect our "bikes" (look for E.T. to pop his head out of the basket on the front), which are actually 12-passenger, open-sided gondolas hanging from a ceiling track. They have bicycle-like seats, each with its own set of handlebars.

The best seats in the house. On the whole, the left side of the gondola provides better views than the right, especially of the city. Best of all is the far left seat in the first row.

This ride might be likened to a bike with training wheels. It has many of the aspects of more thrilling rides — sudden acceleration, swoops, and turns — but toned down so as not to be truly frightening. In the first phase of the ride, we are zipping through the redwoods, dodging the unenlightened grown-ups who want to capture E.T. for study and analysis. This section can be a little scary for small kids and a little loud for older adults. Soon, however, we are soaring high above the city in the ride's most enchanting interlude. We rise higher until we are in the stars themselves and are then shot down a hyperspace tunnel before we decelerate abruptly and find ourselves in the steamy world of E.T.'s home planet.

It's an odd cave-like environment but soon, apparently buoyed by our arrival, the place perks up and we are flying through a psychedelic world of huge multicolored flowers in wondrous shapes, past talking mushrooms and plants (or are they creatures?) with dozens of eyes. All around are little E.T.s, peeping from under plants, climbing over them, and playing them like percussion instruments. It's all rather like Disney's *it's a small world* on acid.

All too soon, E.T. is sending us back to our home, but not before a final farewell when those passports pay off cleverly. Listen carefully!

Some are captivated by this ride, but it has a few flaws. Spielberg authorized a whole new cast of characters for this ride (culled from the obscure paperback sequel *E.T. and the Book of the Green Planet*) but, other than Botanicus, they are hard to identify, much less get to know. Also, the humans in the woods look a bit like department store mannequins. Still, the ride will appeal to younger children and their timid elders, who can get a taste of a "thrill" ride without putting the contents of their stomachs at risk.

This is also one of the few rides at Universal where seeing the film on which it is based will definitely add to the appreciation of the experience. Without this background, much of the ride may seem merely odd. This will be especially true for younger children who will be better able to empathize with E.T. and his plight if they've seen the movie.

E.T. is one of Universal's most popular rides for people of all ages, with the result that the lines can become dauntingly long. On busy days, there can be another wait of 15 to 20 minutes once inside before you reach the ride itself.

Tip: When the *Animal Actors* show lets out (about 25 minutes after the posted show time), the crowds stream over to get on line for *E.T.* Time your visit accordingly.

Note: There are two Universal Express entrances in this ride, one outside and a second shortly after you enter the forest inside the building.

Fievel's Playland

Rating:	* * *
Type:	Hands-on activity
Time:	As long as you want
Our Take:	For young and very active kids

Based on Steven Spielberg's charming animated film, *An American Tail*, about a shtetl mouse making his way in the New World, *Fievel's Playland* is a convoluted maze of climb-up, run-through, slide-down activities that will keep kids amused while their exhausted parents take a well-deserved break.

Don't forget to bring your camera for great photo ops of the kids amid the larger-than-life cowboy hats, victrolas, water barrels, playing cards, and cattle skeletons that make up this maze of exploration.

The highlight is a Mouse Climb — a rope tunnel that spirals upwards. At the top, kids can climb into two-man (well, two-kid) rubber rafts to slide down through yet another tunnel to arrive at ground level with enormous grins and wet bottoms. Don't worry, there's also a set of stairs to the top of this water slide.

Photo op: A shot of your kid hitting the bottom of the slide makes a great souvenir and a ground-level video monitor of the top of the slide lets you know when your little darling is about to descend.

This is a place you can safely let the kids explore on their own. The ground is padded. However, kids less than 40 inches high will have to drag a grown-up (or maybe a bigger sibling) along to ride the water slide. There's seldom a wait to get in to *Fievel's Playland* but long lines do form for the water slide. If time is a factor and if you will be visiting one of the water-themed parks on another day, you can tell the kids that there are bigger, better water slides awaiting them tomorrow.

Note: Even though this attraction is aimed squarely at the kiddie set, don't be surprised if your young teens get in the spirit and momentarily forget that romping through a kid's playground is not the "cool" thing to do.

A Day in the Park with Barney

Rating: * * *
Type: Theater show with singing
Time: About 20 minutes
Our Take: For toddlers and their long-suffering parents

According to the publicity, Universal's *Barney* attraction is the only place in the United States where you can see Barney "live." For some people, that may be one place too many. But for his legions of adoring wee fans and the parents who love them, this show will prove an irresistible draw. Even old curmudgeons will grudgingly have to admit that the show's pretty sweet.

The first tip-off that this is a kiddie show is the fact that it's the only attraction at Universal with its own stroller parking lot. And it's usually full. After the young guests have availed themselves of Mom and Dad's valet parking service, they enter through a gate into Barney's park, complete with a bronze Barney cavorting in an Italianate fountain.

When the show begins, we are all ushered into a stand-up pre-show area where Mr. Peekaboo and his gaudy bird friend Bartholomew put on a singing, dancing warm-up act that wouldn't be complete unless the audience got splashed. Then, using our imaginations, we pass through a misty cave entrance sprinkled with star dust to enter the main theater.

Inside is a completely circular space cheerfully decorated as a forest park at dusk. Low benches surround the raised central stage, but old fogies may want to make for the more comfortable park benches against the walls. The sight lines are excellent no matter where you sit, although Mr. Peekaboo reminds us that once we've chosen a seat we must stay there for the entire show.

The show is brief and cheery and almost entirely given over to singalongs that are already familiar to Barney's little fans. Barney is soon joined by Baby Bop and B.J. and the merriment proceeds apace, complete with falling autumn leaves, a brief snowfall, and shooting streamers. By the end, the air is filled with love — literally.

One particularly amusing point is that the stage crew has little to clean up after the show. The kids are remarkably efficient in policing up the fallen leaves and streamers. Now if only we could get them to do that back home!

True star that he is, Barney stays behind after the show for a well-organized meet and greet session with his young admirers that lets each tyke have a special moment and a photo with the lovable guy. A few of the kids seem overawed to be so close to this giant vision in purple.

The theater audience empties out into **Barney's Backyard**, which is the day-care center of your dreams. Here, beautifully executed by Universal scenic artists, is a collection of imaginative and involving activities for the very young, from making music to splashing in water, to drawing on the walls. For parents who are a bit on the slow side, there are signs to explain the significance of what their kids are up to. A sample: "Young children have a natural inclination towards music [which] encourages the release of stress through listening and dancing." Duh!

Barney's Backyard is where little kids get their revenge. Whereas many rides in the park bar younger children on the basis of height, here there are activities that are off limits to those over 48 inches or even 36 inches. Kids will love it. Grown-ups will wish there were more of it.

Tip: This wonderful space has a separate entrance and you don't have to sit through the show to get in here. Keep this in mind if the family's youngest member needs some special attention or a chance to unwind from the frustrations of being a little person in a big person's amusement park.

Woody Woodpecker's Nuthouse Coaster

Rating:	* * *
Type:	A kiddie roller coaster
Time:	About 1 minute
Our Take:	A thrill ride for the younger set

Woody Woodpecker's Nuthouse Coaster is described as a "gentle" children's roller coaster, knocked together by Woody from bits of this and that, running through a nut factory. The eight cars on the "Knothead Express" are modeled after nut crates; they run along 800 feet of red tubular steel track supported by bright blue steel poles, which are in turn held together with knotty boards and rope.

The ride features some mild drops and tilted turns but it shouldn't prove frightening to any child who meets the 36-inch minimum height requirement, although there have perhaps been some none-too-happy grandparents.

Curious George Goes To Town

Rating: ✶ ✶ ✶ ✶ ✶
Type: A water-filled play area
Time: Unlimited
Our Take: It will be hard to drag kids away

Woody's KidZone turns into a water park in this elaborate play area themed after the illustrated books about George, the playful monkey, and his friend The Man in the Yellow Hat. Expect your kids to get sopping wet here and enjoy every minute of it.

The fun begins innocently enough with a small tent housing a play area for very young children. Nearby is one of those padded play areas with jets of water shooting up from the ground in random patterns. Little ones still in diapers love it. But the main attraction lies a few steps farther along, in the town square. On opposite sides stand the Fire Department and the City Waterworks, dubbed "City H2O." On the second floor balcony, five water cannons let kids squirt those below, and high above is a huge water bucket that fills inexorably with water and, with the clanging of a warning bell, tips over, sending a cascade of water into the square below as kids scramble to position themselves under it for a thorough and thoroughly delightful soaking.

Behind the facades of this cartoonish town square lies a two-level, kid-powered, waterlogged obstacle course. All sorts of cranks, levers, and other ingenious devices give kids a great deal of control over who gets how wet. Most kids take to it with fiendish glee. The concept isn't unique to USF, but the version here is one of the best in recent memory.

When your kids are ready for a change of pace, they can repair to the **Ball Factory**, behind the town square. This cheerfully noisy two-level metal structure is filled with thousands of colored soft foam balls. The noise comes from the industrial strength vacuum machines that suck balls from the floor and send them to aimable ball cannons mounted on tall poles or to large bins high overhead. Some vacuums send balls to stations where kids can fill up mesh bags with balls they then take to the second level balcony to feed into the ten "Auto Blasters" that let them shoot balls at the kids down below. It's a scene of merry anarchy and many adults quickly get in touch with their inner child and become active participants in the chaotic battle raging all about. Those ball bins, like the water buckets outside, tip over periodically, pummeling eager victims below and replenishing the supply of balls.

This is one attraction that can keep kids happily occupied for hours on end. It will also appeal to the older kids in your family who might find some of the other offerings in Woody Woodpecker's KidZone too "babyish." It's not unusual to see ever-so-hip young teens thoroughly enjoying themselves as they splash about with their younger siblings.

Tip: Bring a towel and a change of clothes for the kids if the weather's cool. If you want to avoid getting wet, follow the marked "dry path" to the Ball Factory. This is also a good activity to schedule just before you leave the park, either for the day or for a nap-time break.

Selected Short Subjects

Character Meet and Greet

Here's your chance to meet and mingle with some of Hollywood's cartoon heavyweights. That's right, Woody Woodpecker, Curious George, and the rest of the gang. They show up periodically in the circular plaza at the entrance to KidZone to do a little song and dance, meet their adoring public and, yes, sign autographs. Don't expect much in the way of scintillating conversation, however; they're the strong silent type.

The cartoon animals from *Madagascar* also make separate appearances in front of the *Animal Actors* amphitheater.

Appearances take place on a fairly continuous basis from about midday on a schedule listed in the 2-Park Map. It's hard to predict who you'll see on a given visit, because the stars take turns making these outdoor appearances.

Eating in KidZone

KidZone Pizza Company

> **What:** Food stand with outdoor seating
> **Where:** On Exposition Plaza, next to Universal's Cartoon Store
>
> **Price Range:** $

This walk-up fast-food counter serves up a restricted menu of quick snacks. Personal-sized cheese and pepperoni pizzas, chicken fingers with fries, chef salads, and assorted tropical coolers are available. This stand is generally open from about midday to four o'clock.

If you're looking for something a bit more substantial, or a place to eat in air-conditioned comfort, take the short stroll to the International Food and Film Festival in World Expo (see below).

Shopping in KidZone

▉ E.T.'s Toy Closet

Surprisingly perhaps, there's not a huge amount of shopping here. **E.T.'s Toy Closet** is the small shop you must pass through as you decompress from your visit to E.T.'s home planet. There are plenty of E.T. toys and such, but perhaps your best bet is a souvenir photo of your child on a bike with E.T. in the basket and a huge silver moon as backdrop. Don't forget the Reese's Pieces!

Cuddly plush toys and gaily decorated children's wear are on offer at **Universal's Cartoon Store** where the stock changes rapidly and features everything from Woody Woodpecker to SpongeBob SquarePants to Shrek. **The Barney Shop** is just what it says, a small stock of Barney-related clothing, toys, games, books, and DVDs.

Tip: Parents can avoid exposing their children to the temptations of this shop by exiting through one of the side doors of Barney's Backyard.

 WORLD EXPO

The theme of World Expo is a typical World's Fair Exposition park. The result is a display of contemporary architecture and design that manages to be at once very attractive and rather characterless, although the buildings look quite zippy at night. Fortunately, people don't come here to muse on aesthetics.

The Simpsons Ride

Rating:	* * * * +
Type:	Simulator thrill ride
Time:	4.5 minute ride, with 10 minutes of preshows
Our Take:	A wild and witty spin through Springfield

Welcome to Krustyland, the Krustiest Place on Earth! Krusty the Clown is opening his theme park's "All-New Thrilltacular Upsy-Downsy Spins-Aroundsy Teen-Operated Thrill Ride," and you can join the Simpson family as the first suckers — um, lucky winners — to try it. Krusty's criminal nemesis, Sideshow Bob, has been spotted in the vicinity, but not to worry: as Homer says "they won't kill you in a theme park as long as you've got a dime in your pocket."

Over the last 20 years, Matt Groening's *The Simpsons* has grown from crudely animated interstitials on FOX's *Tracy Ullman Show* to the world's most popular animated family. Thankfully, their translation to the theme-park world hasn't come at the expense of their satirical edge. From the queue video (featuring classic clips of "Itchy and Scratchy Land" and "Duff Gardens," along with sharp new skits) to the cliche-skewering signage (Ride "Captain Dinosaur's Pirate Ripoff"), this attraction pulls no punches in biting the corporate hand that feeds it.

Once inside the carnival-colorful building, you'll wait among midway booths staffed by Apu ("$100 Tacos for $100"), Patty and Selma ("Finders Keepers, Losers Weepers"), and other characters. You'll be separated into groups of eight and directed to a "funhouse" holding room, where you'll see a gruesomely hilarious safety warning before boarding the ride.

The Simpsons Ride retains much of the basic flight-simulator infra-structure of *Back to the Future: The Ride (BTTF)*, the attraction it replaced. The vehicles face a mammoth, curved movie screen that completely fills your line of vision and represents the true genius of this ride concept. Other simulator-based rides (like the *Jimmy Neutron* ride here at USF) use a movie screen that serves as a window to the outside of your spaceship or other vehicle. With this concept, however, you are outside and the environment wraps around you. The illusion is startling, not to mention sometimes terrifying. (Look up as the ride starts for a vertigo-inducing effect.)

In reality, the movement of the simulator's stilts is surprisingly modest. You never actually move more than two feet in any direction. But try telling that to your brain. The kinetic signals sent by your body combine with the visual signals received from the screen to convince you that you are zooming along at supersonic speeds, making white-knuckle turns at dizzying angles.

The new ride improves on its predecessor with high-resolution digital projectors and new tactile and olfactory effects. Though still very turbulent, *Simpsons* is noticeably less jarring than *BTTF*, which had a reputation as a neck-wrecker. Best of all, the writing and voice acting (with nearly the entire original cast except Harry Shearer's Burns and Smithers) are worthy of an episode from the TV show's best seasons. Die-hard fans of the ground-breaking *BTTF* can take solace in a Doc Brown cameo in the queue, and the knowledge that USF is still home to Orlando's best simulator-based ride.

The best seats in the house: The best way to experience this attraction is from the front row of the middle car in the middle level of the dome. Ask the attendant at the point where the line splits for Level 2, then ask the next attendant for Room 6. You may need to wait longer, but it's worth it: you'll experience less distortion of the image, and reduce any tendency toward motion sickness. Sit in the front row of the car for comfort, especially if you are tall.

Tip: The Express line leads directly to Level 2.

Men In Black: Alien Attack

Rating: * * * *
Type: Interactive ride with laser weapons
Time: 4 minutes
Our Take: This one gets addictive

Men In Black, the ride, is a bit like stepping inside a life-size video arcade game, with the element of competition thrown in just to make things interesting. The experience begins when you visit "The Universe and You," a science exhibit left over from the New York World's Fair of 1964. Soon you discover that it's just a cover to enable you to apply for admission to the elite corps of MIB. You are not alone and the wait can get lengthy. Fortunately, snaking your way through the MIB building is an entertaining experience and devotees of the films will find much familiar here. A lengthy and amusing orientation video featuring Rip Torn and Will Smith is worth watching even when there's no line. Farther along, a training film starring two amusingly retro cartoon characters, Doofus and Do-Right, provides safety instructions for the testing vehicles that await you.

Tip: If you don't mind having your party split up, look for the single rider line after your first trip through. It is invariably much shorter than the main line and a real time saver.

Eventually, you are assigned to a vehicle with five other recruits. At each seat is a laser gun and a personal scoreboard that keeps track of hits. You are cruising through a target range, testing your marksmanship, when an urgent bulletin announces that a Prison Transport full of nasty space bugs has crash landed in the middle of Manhattan. At once, you are reassigned to a dangerous but exciting mission. You and another team are dispatched, side by side, to do battle with the aliens through the dark and gritty streets of a cartoon New York.

What follows is a few minutes of chaotic fun. Aliens in every imaginable buggy shape pop up from garbage cans and taxi hoods, from around corners and in shop windows. It's a super-sized sci-fi version of those old shooting galleries down at the boardwalk. Your job is to zap them before they zap you. When the bugs score a hit, your vehicle is sent into a tailspin.

At one point, you discover that aliens have infiltrated the vehicle of the other team and you must fire at your own comrades. Finally, your MIB trainer (Will Smith from the movie) appears on a giant screen to warn you that a particularly nasty bug is bearing down on you. Suffice it to say that it's big enough to swallow two MIB training vehicles. Gulp!

Tip: The guns auto-fire, so hold down the trigger the entire time; you'll score higher and avoid finger cramps. And hit the same target multiple times to boost your score.

The vehicles are not simulators but they do allow for sudden swoops and 360-degree spins, which are both thrilling and discombobulating. And while the two vehicles depart at the same time and cruise along side by side for most of the ride, their progress can be affected by the direct hits scored by the aliens. As the battle progresses, every rider builds an individual score based on their success in targeting the enemy (you will see the tiny red dots of the laser guns dancing on the alien targets); the individual scores contribute to the overall team score. There is a sneaky way to significantly increase your score that you'll have to discover on your own.

Tip: The maximum possible score is 999,999 and, yes, it can be done.

At ride's end, both vehicles are once again cruising side by side as Will Smith appears on another screen to announce which team came out ahead. The combined scores of each vehicle are posted for all to see. Then, Smith breaks the news on how your team did: Galaxy Defender, Cosmically Average, or Bug Bait.

In a final clever touch, Smith uses his neuralizer to erase your memory of the whole experience and you emerge to discover that you have just completed your visit to "The Universe and You," which turns out to be about the possibility of life in outer space. "Are we alone?" the sign asks. "Of course we are," is the reassuring answer.

MIB is a lot of fun and it's hard to imagine anyone having serious complaints. Video game addicts will probably want to ride again and again to improve their scores. Obviously there is at least some skill involved in wielding the laser guns because individual scores in a vehicle can vary by as much as several hundred thousand points. On the other hand, the experience is so chaotic that it is hard to know how well you are doing or get the kind of visual feedback that would help you fine tune your aim.

The best seats in the house. Riders on the outside of the vehicles (i.e., in the seats that are the farthest from the loading platform) have the first view of targets and greater freedom of motion for aiming.

On the way out, you can pause to purchase a photo of your laser-gun-wielding team in the training vehicle.

Note: This ride requires that you stow all your belongings in nearby electronic lockers that are free for a short period of time but charge a hefty fee if you overstay your welcome. For more information, see *Good Things To Know About...Lockers* in *Chapter One.*

Selected Short Subjects

▊ RobOasis

In the *Men In Black* plaza, on the way to KidZone, is this clever advertisement for Coca Cola. Here a tiny alien who is something of a Coke fiend ("Take me to your liter!") sits in a tiny space ship and prattles on about his Earth mission. To either side are niches in the shape of old-fashioned glass Coke bottles. Step in and have your entire body suffused with a fine misting spray of cool water. A fun free refresher for a hot day.

Eating in World Expo

There's only one real restaurant in World Expo, but that doesn't mean there aren't a lot of places to get something to eat. Kiosks pop up seasonally as the weather and the crowds dictate and there are some permanent outdoor refreshment stands in the broad plaza outside the *Men In Black* building.

■ International Food and Film Festival

What: A multicultural cafeteria

Where: On Exposition Boulevard, near the *Animal Actors* stage

Price Range: $ - $$

This is as fancy as it gets in World Expo. This large, loud cafeteria-style food emporium is divided into sections by cuisine. You can choose among Italian, American, Asian, or Ice Cream (our favorite nationality). Entrees like Chicken Parmesan and Mediterranean Tuna Salad are a notch or two above typical fast-food quality. Desserts are also available at the walk-up ice cream counter, which is located outside near the entrance to the restaurant. Be aware that some sections may be closed when you visit. Only soft drinks are served here.

Video monitors scattered around the large seating area plug Universal films. On the walls are posters advertising movies, some of them in their overseas, retitled versions.

Shopping in World Expo

The **Kwik-E-Mart,** Homer's favorite convenience store, stands outside the exit of *The Simpsons Ride.* On sale are all the expected souvenirs from Springfield, from T-shirts and DVDs to "Flaming Moe" energy drinks. The tongue-in-cheek signage plastered inside and outside the store ("Today's Merchandise at Tomorrow's Prices!") is an attraction in itself. If you get thirsty for an ice-cold *Squishee,* a stand outside sells the sweetened slush.

The **MIB Gear Shop** is a spacious, high-ceilinged shop that sells clothes for MIB agents. Everything from T-shirts to sweatshirts is in the black, white, and orange color scheme MIB agents seem to prefer, and all at moderate prices. You will also find some sleek MIB glassware, mugs, and cups along with a wide variety of action figures, sunglasses, and toys tied into the movie. There are even a few books on the movie and its characters. For an "out of this world" treat, try the freeze-dried "alien" ice cream (better yet, don't).

On Exposition Boulevard, outside the International Food and Film Festival, you will find several tent-like structures housing some of Universal Studios' most attractive souvenirs. Under one tent, as many as four caricaturists hold forth, billed as **Expo Art**, turning out devastatingly accurate portraits for remarkably reasonable prices. (You'll find more caricaturists in San Francisco/Amity.)

SAN FRANCISCO / AMITY

Juxtaposing California's San Francisco and New England's Amity might seem jarring at first, but in the movies anything is possible. In fact, the two areas are quite separate and the designers have done a good job of finessing the transition from one to the other; the double-barreled name for this "set" is more a matter of convenience than anything else.

San Francisco/Amity is distinguished by the presence of *Jaws*, the wonderfully scary boat ride. The San Francisco part is also packed with eating places, some of them quite nice indeed.

Fear Factor Live

Rating:	* * +
Type:	Amphitheater show
Time:	30 minutes
Our Take:	The TV show comes to life

For big fans of reality television shows, this live version of the now-canceled NBC show may make for great live entertainment. Six contestants, who have been preselected prior to each show, compete in three events. Contestants are ruthlessly eliminated and forced to take the "Walk of Shame" until the two finalists square off in a multipart test of nerves, climbing ability, and guts. The stunts are not for sissies, involving as they do considerable heights, "carnivorous" eels, and other assorted nastiness. Most impressive is the final challenge, which features two tilted convertibles raised to the rafters; contestants must climb onto the water-slicked hoods to retrieve flags attached to the grilles.

Note: If you'd like to be a contestant, you must present yourself in front of the attraction an hour and a quarter prior to the show. Your chances seem to be enhanced if you are an adult, reasonably good looking, and in better than average physical shape.

For those of us who don't meet any of these qualifications, there's still hope. Volunteers are drawn from the audience to fill a variety of roles. Some (kids, mostly) fire water cannons (remember those water-slicked car hoods?)

81

and other fiendish devices designed to make the main contestants' jobs even harder. Others are given challenges (like confronting creepy-crawlies and drinking yucky concoctions) that might make them wish they'd thought twice about volunteering.

Note: This show is only performed "seasonally," which means at times of peak attendance. It may be gone for good by the time you visit.

Jaws

Rating:	* * * *
Type:	Water ride
Time:	5 minutes
Our Take:	A scare-fest for kids of all ages

Welcome aboard, as Captain Jake takes you on a sightseeing tour of peaceful Amity harbor. As the waiting line snakes toward the dock, you get your first inkling that something might be amiss. Television monitors broadcast an appropriately hokey local news show about the strange doings in Amity, complete with interviews with the real Sheriff Brody (who complains that Arnold Schwarzenegger would have been a much better choice than Roy Scheider to play him in the movie).

The conceit, of course, is that you are in the real town of Amity and that the blockbuster film *Jaws* was not fiction but fact-based. One not unwelcome by-product of the film is that the sleepy town is now a major tourist draw, allowing Captain Jake to make a good living as the best — make that the only — sightseeing company offering visitors tours of the island.

This is a water ride and, as you are informed several times before embarking, you will get wet. Some people just don't seem to believe it. One of the extra added amusements of this ride is watching fastidious tourists take out a tissue and carefully wipe off the damp seats before sitting down. Don't bother. There's a lot more where that came from. If you come to the park in the winter, when temperatures can be on the cool side, you might want to consider protecting yourself with a cheap plastic poncho.

As your tour boat is about to leave the dock, your friendly but cocky guide shows off a grenade launcher for effect. He tells us that, since the great white was killed way back in '74, Amity's been pretty peaceful. He points out Sheriff Brody's house on the left and then heads out of the harbor.

This being a Universal ride, it doesn't take long for things to go ominously amiss. A crackling, fragmented radio transmission from Amity 3, a returning tour boat, is a clear signal that danger lies ahead, but the guide assures us nothing's wrong. A turn around a rocky promontory reveals the other tour boat shattered and sinking on our left. A huge dorsal fin breaks the surface, we feel a slight bump as Jaws passes beneath us, and the thrills begin.

The best seats in the house. Where you sit can make a difference on this ride. Inveterate thrill seekers will not be satisfied with anything but the outside seat, whichever side it's on. On balance, the left side offers the most thrills, especially the furnace blast of a gas depot explosion. The right side has the best view of Jaws' entrance into the boathouse. Probably the best seat is the far left of row five. Since Jaws rises from the water a few times, those on one side of the boat will have a slightly obstructed view of his appearances on the other side. The obvious solution is to take this ride more than once. Early risers, who get to the park before the gates open, can usually cycle through the ride several times before the lines become too daunting. *Jaws* is even better after dusk when additional fire effects are turned on.

While there is a certain shock value to be derived from the element of surprise and the fire effects can be intense, this ride is not truly scary. At least for most grown-ups. Little ones may disagree. The shark, while a masterpiece of clever engineering, always betrays its latex and aluminum origins, at least close-up. As a result, much of your enjoyment will depend on the acting talents of your guide. Still, this doesn't detract from the fun, especially the first few times. As you take your third, fourth, and fifth turns around the harbor, you'll probably find yourself deriving equal enjoyment by looking behind you to see shattered sets automatically reconstructing themselves in preparation for the next boatload of happily terrified tourists.

Disaster!

Rating: * * * +
Type: Show and ride
Time: 25 minutes, ride portion is 3 minutes
Our Take: Best for the ride

Disaster! takes the "Ride the Movies" slogan to its logical extreme. Here, the ride *is* the movie and everyone who rides it is a star. Well, okay, everyone who rides it is an extra. There are chills and thrills in store, but first you have to go through some mildly amusing silliness to put you in the mood.

The experience begins with a visit to Disaster Studios, an "independent, boutique" studio, the creation of disaster flick genius, Frank Kincaid. Kincaid is quite the Renaissance man, writing, directing, and producing shoestring-budget disaster epics like *Baboom, Fungus,* and *300 Knots Landing,* which is about a plane crash apparently.

Once inside, you discover you have stumbled into a casting call. One of Mr. Kincaid's lackeys is looking for a few willing victims... er, *volunteers* to serve as actors and stunt people for Kincaid's next blockbuster. There are parts for a young child, 10 to 12, a "gardening grandma," a "hunky" guy (who usually winds up being anything but), and assorted other types, so if you're interested in being part of the action, you probably have as much of a chance of being selected as the next guy.

Then it's on to the next room, for the best part of the pre-ride show. Here we meet Mr. Kincaid himself, played by a subdued, but still bizarro, Christopher Walken. Through a bit of technological magic called "Musion" that will have you scratching your head and asking, "How'd they do that?" Kincaid (or at least a holographic simulation of him) strides on stage and interacts with his assistant.

Kincaid treats us to a brief lecture on his "secret" rules of disaster films ("The annoying guy always dies") and announces his next magnum opus, *Mutha Nature,* a global warming eco-disaster flick starring Duane "The Rock" Johnson as a heroic park ranger battling evil corporate villains.

In the third room, the volunteers picked earlier are put to work filming bits and pieces that will later be edited into the final film. "Time is money," Mr. Kincaid points out, so these bits are shot in an ultra-fast-paced illustration of "green screen" techniques, but minus any explanation of the what and why, it may seem a bit confusing. Perhaps in the age of DVD special features, it's assumed there's no mystery left to movie-making. The big news, however, is that Mr. Kincaid has decided to cast all of us in the grand finale to his film. With that, the audience is ushered in to the final phase of the *Disaster!* experience.

This is the part most people come for, a simulated earthquake aboard San Francisco's BART (Bay Area Rapid Transit). The train (with open sides and clear plastic roof) pulls out of the Oakland station, enters the tunnel under the Bay, and soon emerges in the Embarcadero station. A voice over the train's P.A. system instructs you to scream for the camera as the earthquake reaches eight on the Richter scale and the Embarcadero station begins to artfully fall apart. Floors buckle and ceilings shatter. The car you're in jerks upward, while the car in front of you drops and tilts perilously. Then the entire roof caves in on one side, exposing the street above. A propane tanker truck, caught in the quake, slides into the hole directly toward us. The only thing that prevents it from slamming into the train is a steel beam, which impales the truck and causes it to burst into flames. Next, an oncoming train barrels into the station directly at us, but the buckled track sets it on a trajectory that narrowly misses us. And it's still not over. What looks like the entire contents of San Francisco Bay comes pouring down the stairs on the other side.

All too soon, the terror is over and the train backs out of the station, returning us to "Oakland." As it backs out, we are treated to a trailer for *Mutha Nature*, into which have been inserted the scenes shot earlier, to humorous effect. *Disaster!* has retained the most exciting elements of the former *Earthquake* attraction and refreshed the tired preshow portions with fun, if somewhat frantic, results.

Tip: The exuberant performance of the sign-language interpreter, presented at selected shows, is a treat whether or not you are hearing-impaired.

The best seats in the house. The train holds about 200 people and is divided into three sections. The first section (that is, the car to the far left as you enter the BART station), has its seats facing backwards. The other two sections have seats facing forward. This arrangement assures that people in the first section won't have to turn around to see most of the special effects the ride holds in store. The front of each section has a clear plastic panel but the view is somewhat obstructed. Avoid the first two rows of a section, if possible. Probably the best view is to be had in the middle of the second car. The major attraction for those sitting on the right (as the train enters the tunnel) is the flood, which can get a few people wet. The more spectacular explosion of the propane tanker and the wreck of the oncoming train are best viewed from the left. As always, the outside seats are the primo location.

Beetlejuice's Graveyard Revue

Rating:	* * *
Type:	Amphitheater show
Time:	20 minutes
Our Take:	Best for teens and pre-teens

Beetlejuice began his career as the eponymous obnoxious "bio-excorcist" (played by Michael Keaton) of Tim Burton's breakout film. After his stint as a streetside performer on USF's New York set proved popular, he was "discovered" by Universal Studios and given his own amphitheater show. The addition of a set, pyrotechnics, and what sounds like several million dollars worth of sound equipment hasn't changed the show's basic appeal, just made it louder.

The set is a jumble of crumbling castle walls, complete with a mummy's sarcophagus and a more modern coffin. The "plot" is nonexistent. Beetlejuice, your host with the most, emerges from the mummy's tomb in a burst of fireworks that is literally blinding.

He immediately gets to the business at hand, summoning the Wolfman, Dracula, Frankenstein, and the ever lovely Bride of Frankenstein from their ghostly lairs for your listening pleasure. It looks at first like it will be a real horror show — an Andrew Lloyd Webber opera! Fortunately, Beetlejuice steps in and before your very eyes — well, behind a wall of smoke actually — the cast changes into suitably hip attire. Then they begin, appropriately enough, to wail.

The premise is wafer thin and the classic Universal monsters theme goes completely out the window when, presumably to even out the gender distribution, two girls named Hip and Hop are added to the lineup. But what the show lacks in sophistication and coherence, it more than makes up for in energy and noise. The sound volume is guaranteed to wake the dead. The tender-eared and the old at heart should consider themselves suitably forewarned.

The choreography is straightforward, energetic, and more than a little suggestive. Anyone heretofore sheltered from modern pop concerts will find it a suitable introduction to the genre.

Tip: The latest incarnation of this show is a little less raunchy. Much will go over the heads of little ones, but parents should be advised of the innuendo nonetheless.

The best seats in the house. There are really no bad seats for this one. An interesting seating choice would be next to the pit in the center of the house, where the sound and light techies run the show. If your kid has dragged you to the show for the fifth time, you can amuse yourself watching these wizards ply their high-tech trade. Seating is pretty much first-come, first-served, although at peak periods attendants may direct you to a seat to speed the flow.

Selected Short Subjects

■ The Amity Boardwalk

Between *Disaster!* and *Jaws* is a winding stretch of road that offers up a typical New England boardwalk as a child might see it — bright and shining. Of course, the originals are a lot shabbier and far more weather-beaten, the games a bit more threadbare, but never mind. This is the movies, after all, and with the genius of the best set designers Universal has to offer, everything should be perfect.

Here you can try your skill at knocking over plastic glasses with a whiffle ball, tossing a softball into a farmer's milk can, or playing skee-ball. If you fancy yourself a superhuman, try ringing the bell with a mighty blow of your sledgehammer. You can also test the skill of the Amazing Alonzo, who bets you that he can guess your weight or age. Games cost several dollars and, as with the seaside attractions they mimic, the odds are heavily weighted toward the house. Universal, however, makes it easier to win at least something and the prizes, while modest (or ugly, depending on your mood), are a cut above those you'll find along, say, the Jersey shore.

Eating in San Francisco/Amity

The San Francisco/Amity area enjoys the distinction of having the most eateries of any of USF's six sections, thanks largely to the leisurely way it snakes along the lagoon. Here, in the order you encounter them as you proceed from World Expo around the lagoon to New York, are your choices:

■ Boardwalk Snacks

What:	Funnel cakes and ice cream at picnic tables
Where:	Along the Amity boardwalk
Price Range:	$

This stand sells funnel cakes with a variety of toppings that include apples, strawberries, and chocolate. Everything is topped off with whipped cream. Soft serve ice cream is also available as are beer and soft drinks.

All seating is outdoors at weathered picnic tables. Venture around behind the snack stand and sit by the lagoon for one of the nicest views in the park and the chance of a breeze on a hot day.

■ Midway Grill

What:	Outdoor snacking at picnic tables
Where:	Along the Amity boardwalk, amid the pitch and skill games
Price Range:	$

The sign says "Hot dogs * Sodas * Fries" and the menu, courtesy of Coney Island's famous Nathan's, is scarcely more elaborate than that, although the dogs come in several varieties — Reuben, Chicago, Chili, and

87

Slaw — and kids can get corn dog nuggets. This is the only place at Universal to get Nathan's signature "crinkle cut" fries served with every platter. Walk up to the window and carry your snack to a nearby picnic table.

Amity Fried Chicken

What:	Outdoor snacking at picnic tables
Where:	Along the Amity boardwalk, amid the pitch and skill games
Price Range:	$

Another walk-up stand, this one serving chicken baskets and fish and chips, along with soft drinks and beer.

San Francisco Pastry Company

What:	Small pastry and coffee shop
Where:	Across from *Disaster!*
Price Range:	$

Right at the entrance to Lombard's stands this tempting alternative. It features most of the pastries and sandwiches you found at the Beverly Hills Boulangerie in Hollywood as well as coffee, cappuccino, and soft drinks. There are no tables inside and a small outside seating area, so many customers will have to take their snacks to one of the scenic spots along the nearby waterfront.

Lombard's Seafood Grille

What:	Elegant restaurant evoking Fisherman's Wharf
Where:	On the lagoon, across from *Disaster!*
Price Range:	$$ - $$$

Lombard's is a full-service restaurant boasting the most elegant decor at Universal — and the best food. The main dining room exudes an industrial-Victorian aura, with brick walls, filigreed iron arches and tapestry-covered dining chairs. The room is dominated by a huge, square, centrally located saltwater fish tank like something Captain Nemo might have imagined. Windows on three sides look out over the lagoon. All in all, the atmosphere is charming.

The food here, which is strong on seafood, is excellent, beautifully presented, and our favorite at USF. Appetizers cost $5 to $8 and range from simple bisques and chowders to a sumptuous shrimp cocktail. For the main course, the grilled, blackened, or herb-crusted Catch of the Day option ($16) can't be beat. Other entrees ($11 to $13) reflect the diverse cuisine of San Francisco and include fish and chips, a San Francisco Stir Fry, Tomato and

Basil pasta, and ravioli. There are also salads ($9 to $13) and sandwiches ($10 to $12), including a Boursin steak sandwich and a decent burger.

The wine and cocktail menu is as enticing as the food. Wines by the bottle are mostly in the $25 to $40 range, although you can splurge on a $190 bottle of Dom Perignon. Wines by the glass ($6 to $9) are more afford-able, as are the martinis and specialty cocktails ($6 to $10).

For dessert, the same miniature sweets served at Finnegan's and IOA's Mythos are also offered here, at $1.75 for each sugar-stuffed "shot." They're fine finishers, but fans of Lombard's gone-but-not-forgotten "San Francisco Foggy" brownie and ice cream concoction may leave unsatisfied.

There is a children's menu offering kid-friendly fare for about $7 per entree. Reservations can be made by calling (407) 224-3613.

▮ Chez Alcatraz

What:	Outdoor drink stand
Where:	On the lagoon, across from *Disaster!*
Price Range:	$

This seasonal stand is a great little bar in warm weather, serving up a variety of frozen drinks.

▮ Richter's Burger Co.

What:	Fast-food burger joint
Where:	On the lagoon, across from *Disaster!*
Price Range:	$

That's Richter as in scale, and just in case you didn't get it the first time, one glance at the damaged interior of this warehouse-like structure will let you know that the theme here is pure earthquake. It's a fun environment in which to chow down on standard burger fare.

The Big One is a burger or cheeseburger served with "a landslide of fries," while the San Andreas is a chicken sandwich. The Fault Line is an "all-natural gardenburger" with cheese, and The Richter Scale salad comes with chicken breast. Frisco shakes, chocolate and vanilla, are offered.

The decor is fun and imaginative, and worth more than a passing glance. At the back, you'll find tables with a lagoon view and a balcony offer-ing a great bird's-eye view of the New York end of the lagoon.

Shopping in San Francisco/Amity

Shopping here is a mixed bag. The **San Francisco Candy Factory** is another place selling scoop-it-yourself candy at inflated prices along with other goodies like coated apples and fudge. **Salty's Sketches** offers much better value in the form of Universal's expert caricaturists, who will immortalize your goofy grin for posterity. These artists must all have studied under the same master because their styles are almost identical and the quality of the renderings excellent. And the cost is also surprisingly moderate given the high quality of the finished product. (You'll find more caricaturists in World Expo.)

Tucked into an old wooden lighthouse (look up as you enter), **Quint's Surf Shack** celebrates the surfer lifestyle in clothes. For women, there is a good selection of brightly colored and quite attractive beach and resort wear. There is less for men, but it's also quite nice. The prices seem fair and occasionally you can pick up a genuine bargain. By the time you reach this part of the park, you may have realized what a good idea it is to cover your head in the Florida sun. Quint helps out with a good selection of hats for both sexes.

The vest-pocket **Oakley** shop sells high-end sunglasses and watches, most of them bearing the ultra-hip Oakley brand for astronomical prices. (There's a price to be paid for being on the cutting edge of fashion.) They also offer shoes and backpacks, just in case you have any money left.

NEW YORK

Compared to some others on the lot, the New York set seems downright underpopulated — with attractions, eateries, and shops, that is. Whole streets in New York are given over entirely to film backdrops. Gramercy Park, Park Avenue, the dead end Fifty-Seventh Street that incongruously ends at the New York Public Library, and the narrow alleys behind Delancey Street contain nary a ride or shop. These sets, however, provide some wonderfully evocative backgrounds for street shows and family portraits, especially the library facade, with a collection of familiar skyscrapers looming behind it. They also include some clever inside jokes for those familiar with the movie industry. Check out the names painted on the windows of upper story offices along Fifth Avenue and see if you can spot them.

Of course, New York does have attractions, including the blockbuster *Revenge of the Mummy* and *Twister* (although oddly enough, neither of the films involved is set in the Big Apple).

Revenge of the Mummy

> **Rating:** ****+
> **Type:** Indoor roller coaster and dark ride
> **Time:** About 4 minutes
> **Our Take:** A brilliant blend

The *Revenge of the Mummy* starts innocently enough. It seems Universal is in need of more extras for this new film and you are lucky enough to be passing by as they solicit volunteers. (Don't get your hopes up. *Revenge of the Mummy* is not a real film, it's just a polite fiction for the sake of the ride.)

As you enter the queue line, it looks like one of those "The Making Of..." displays that Universal mounts from time to time. Props and set pieces are scattered about, all carefully labeled. On video monitors, director Steven Sommers, star Brendan Fraser, and others on the crew give chatty interviews about the making of the film, dropping ominous references to ancient curses and strange happenings. A recurring character in these vignettes is Reggie, a hapless gofer who keeps losing his anti-Mummy amulet to Hollywood big wigs.

Then the queue line takes a sharp turn through a narrow passageway and things become truly strange. It appears you are in the tomb of Imhotep where the usually cheerful ride attendants have started acting strangely.

There's no more video and the queue line now looks remarkably like a real Egyptian tomb in the Valley of the Kings at Thebes and something in the air seems to bring out the evil in your fellow tourists. Press a glowing scarab and you can startle folks elsewhere in line with a frightening blast of air and watch the result on a video monitor. Oddly, there's nothing to indicate whether this is supposed to be a movie set or the real thing, whether you're still in 21st century Orlando or back in the 1930s.

Up a rickety wooden staircase, past a massive sculpture of Anubis, the god of the Underworld, you finally reach the loading platform for the ride. Once again, there's no explanation of why you are being asked to board the 16-passenger, four-abreast cars, or what lies ahead. The ride vehicles appear to have been built by U.C. & Sons of London, England, back in 1925 to make tomb exploration easier (although it seems possible that "U.C." stands for Universal Creative).

The best seats in the house. The front row provides the best view of the dark ride elements, and they're worth checking out. Coaster fans, however, will find that the far left seat in the back row offers the most "air" (that feeling of being lifted out of your seat on the ride's drops). For most folks, any seat will deliver the thrills they seek.

Tip: Eyeglass wearers should note that water effects in the ride (more pronounced in the front) can wet their glasses and blur their vision.

Like the queue line, the ride itself starts deceptively. It's not too far removed from those gentle "dark rides" at a certain family park complex down the Interstate. But you're still in that nasty Imhotep's retirement home and before long things get dicey. You turn a corner and there's Reggie again, all wrapped up for Mummy take-out, warning you to turn back.

Imhotep himself appears rather dramatically and looking decidedly the worse for wear after several millennia of entombment. "With your souls, I shall rule for all eternity," he bellows, which sounds like a great slogan for a modern-day political campaign.

Around the next bend, you are given a stark choice: Get with the program and receive riches beyond imagination or resist and die a hideous death. Your cries of "I'll take the gold! I'll take the gold!" go unheeded and the ride begins in earnest.

Tip: Check the early scenes of the ride for some subtle references to *Kongfrontation*, the ride the *Mummy* replaced. It's Universal's very own version of "hidden Mickeys."

At this point, the curse of the Mummy takes hold, and our description stops so as not to reveal too much about what follows. Universal bills this as a "psychological thrill ride" and it does, indeed, mess with your mind. Suffice it to say that the ride morphs into a supercharged roller coaster experience that takes place largely in near darkness. There are a couple of never-been-done-before elements that make this ride truly startling and absolutely unique. And, of course, what would a Universal ride be like without a little pyrotechnics? In short, if you think this will be just another indoor roller coaster ride, think again. The Mummy himself puts it nicely: "Death is only the beginning."

Thanks to linear induction technology, you will go from zero to 45 miles per hour in less than two seconds, pulling a full G, and for much of the ride you will be at or above that speed as you zip up and down through a series of sharp turns past visual effects that remind you that the Mummy and his unholy minions are still breathing hotly down your neck.

Tip: Those who balk at mega-coasters like *The Hulk* and *Dragon Challenge* over at Islands of Adventure are still encouraged to give *Revenge of the Mummy* a try. Because the ride is so smooth, it is only slightly more intense than *Spider-Man* at IOA. If you can handle Disney coasters like *Thunder Mountain* and *Space Mountain*, you'll survive this one. You'll just have more fun.

Note: This ride requires that you stow all your belongings in nearby electronic lockers that are free for a short period of time but charge a hefty fee if you overstay your welcome. For more information, see *Good Things To Know About...Lockers* in *Chapter One.*

As you exit, check the souvenir ride photos to see the clever way in which the ride vehicles have been articulated (split in two) so they'll hug the track better and enhance the thrills.

All in all, this ride is a major success that further cements Universal's reputation for being on the cutting edge of ride technology. The roller coaster elements certainly deserve the highest marks. However, connoisseurs, who look on theme park rides as an art form, will note some narrative lapses and anticlimactic effects that keep the ride from full five-star status.

Twister ... Ride It Out

Rating:	* * * +
Type:	Stand-up theater show
Time:	15 minutes
Our Take:	Amazing in-your-face special effects

Here is an attraction that will almost literally blow you away. Based on the hit film of the same name, *Twister* is a theater show without seats that leads you through three sets for a payoff that lasts all of two minutes. But what a two minutes it is!

The journey begins as you snake though a waiting line in Wakita, Oklahoma, around large props from the film. You are entertained by two disk jockeys ("the storm chasers of rock and roll") from WNDY ("windy") who spin peppy rock songs with appropriately stormy titles. You will be kept cool by large fans that blow a fine water mist over the crowds. As you draw closer to the Soundstage on which the real adventure unfolds, the entertainment gives way to videos of actual tornadoes, some of which are really scary.

The line may seem formidable, but don't despair. This show can handle 2,400 people each hour, so the line moves fairly quickly. Once inside, the show follows a familiar three-part format. In the first chamber, themed as the prop room for the film, you watch a video in which the vivacious Helen Hunt and an oddly wooden Bill Paxton set the scene. If you missed the movie, this segment gives you the information you need to understand what the film and this attraction are all about.

The second chamber is themed as the ruined interior of Aunt Meg's house from the movie. Trees and the front end of an automobile protrude through the ceiling, where a string of video monitors continue the introduction process. There is barely any "edutainment" in this attraction, but what little there is happens here. We get a brief explanation from Bill and Helen of how "dangerous" it was to act in front of the film's niftier effects.

Then it's on to the final chamber where the "real" show happens — live, in-person, and right before your eyes. You enter a set where you stand on a three-level viewing area under the deceptive protection of a tin roof. In front of you is the Wakita street that runs past the Galaxy outdoor movie theater where a "Horror Night" double feature of *The Shining* and *Psycho* is being shown. The street is deserted, but no sooner is everyone in place than all heck breaks loose and the inanimate objects before you take on a scary life of their own.

The best seats in the house. You will have a great experience here no matter where you stand. However, die-hard thrill seekers will want to be as close to the action as possible. Stay to the right as you are ushered into this final chamber if you want to stand in the front row. Most people hug the railing, but you can form a second row and make your way to dead center if you wish.

You've probably already figured out that you'll be living through the vortex of a twister. Some of the effects are versions of what you may already have seen while riding *Disaster!*, and the final funnel effect sometimes fizzles. But first-time viewers always get a big kick out of the explosive ending.

Tip: This is a wet, if not precisely soaking, experience. A poncho might be in order if you're really fussy. Otherwise, you probably will find the sprinkling fun, even refreshing. Interestingly enough, one seems to get wetter in the back row than in the front.

Selected Short Subjects

■ Arcades

Why would anyone pay good money to get into Universal Studios Florida and then waste their time in a video arcade? The Arcades in New York never seem to lack for customers, so some people seem to have an answer to that question.

■ The Blues Brothers

The Dan Ackroyd-John Belushi routine that made a better *Saturday Night Live* sketch than it ever did a movie is immortalized in this peppy street show, which currently holds forth from a makeshift stage on Delancey Street.

The warm-up comes courtesy of a belting blues singer whose gospel-tinged renditions of blues standards are a show in and of themselves. Then, backed by a live sax player and a recorded sound track, Jake and Elwood goof and strut their way through a selection of rock and blues standards, winding up with a rousing, extremely high-decibel version of "Soul Man."

The genial performers, who are look-alikes only to the extent that one is tall and lanky and the other short and stout, do the material justice, and Jake's hyperkinetic dance steps are a highlight of the show. If you like your rock straight and unadulterated, you should enjoy it.

Performances are listed in the 2-Park Map brochure, but Jake and Elwood take no chances; they cruise the studio backlot in their funky revamped cop car avidly promoting the show. During the holiday season a special Christmas version is performed, featuring "Snow Man" and "Santa Claus is Coming to Town."

Eating in New York

■ Finnegan's

What:	Irish pub and sit-down restaurant
Where:	On Fifth Avenue across from *Revenge of the Mummy*
Price Range:	$$

Finnegan's has two parts and two personalities. The first is a full-fledged Irish pub complete with live entertainment and walls crowded with beer and liquor ads and offbeat memorabilia. Cozy up to the antique bar and order a yard of ale if that's your pleasure, or choose from a classy selection of domestic and imported beers. Guinness stout, Harp lager, and Bass ale are available on draught. Hard cider and wine are also available. Happy hour specials (typically $3.50 domestic beer and well liquor, $4.50 imports) are available from 4 p.m. to 7 p.m. daily.

The other half of Finnegan's is a full-service restaurant hidden behind the false facades of the New York lot. The decor here is pared down and perfunctory, reflecting the room's other identity as a movie set. Fortunately, the food is anything but pared down or perfunctory. The theme is Irish and British Isles, with generously sized entrees to match. Appetizers (in the $6 to $8 range) include "Irish Chicken Stingers," Cornish pasties, and Scotch eggs.

Among the entrees ($11 to $13, with sirloin steak at $22), Irish Times fish and chips is traditional, right down to the newspaper it's served in. The shepherd's pie is a juicy souvenir from the Emerald Isle, topped with perfectly browned mashed potatoes. There's also bangers and mash (sausage and mashed potatoes), Irish stew, and (of course) corned beef and cabbage. All entrees are accompanied by hearty steamed vegetables in a light nutmeg-tinged sauce.

For lighter appetites, there are sandwiches in the $10 to $12 range, and salads at $5 to $12. Mini-desserts served in tall skinny shot glasses are $1.75. Bet you can't eat just one! By the way, these are the same desserts-in-a-glass served over at Mythos in Islands of Adventure.

Reservations can be made by calling (407) 224-3613.

■ Louie's Italian Restaurant

What:	Cafeteria-style Italian restaurant
Where:	At the corner of Fifth and Canal, near the lagoon
Price Range:	$

Louie's is a remarkably successful re-creation of the ambiance of New York's Little Italy section — tiled floors, plain tables, and cafe chairs. The only hint you're at Universal Studios is the cafeteria style serving area and the odd ceiling with its jagged edges and movie lights that remind you that the restaurant can do double duty as a film set.

The fare is standard Italian and just the basics. Cheese, pepperoni, and vegetable pizza is served by the slice or whole pie. Entrees include spaghetti and meatballs and fettuccine alfredo. Caesar salad and meatball subs round out the menu. There is imported Italian beer and wine as well as Bud and Bud Lite. In one corner of the restaurant, there is a counter selling gelato and Italian ice.

The quality is above average, as well, making Louie's our favorite USF cafeteria. Louie's is quite large and makes a good place to duck in out of the sun or rain for a rest.

Across from Louie's, under the "Games and Amusements" marque, is a **Starbucks** serving coffee, cappuccino, and pastries, as well as a **Ben & Jerry's** serving ice cream sundaes and smoothies.

Shopping in New York

New York is an international city and the shopping here reflects that. Re-calling Gotham's heyday as a largely Irish city, **Rosie's Irish Shop** sells a variety of Irish imports, including pricey Aran sweaters. There are also much less expensive souvenirs, many bearing pithy Irish sayings.

Sahara Traders is the shop you pass through after your escape from *Revenge of the Mummy*. Here you can pause to pick up your candid Mummy ride photos. In the shop itself, you will find the requisite Mummy T-shirts and an assortment of ghastly looking Mummy figures for the seri-ously disturbed child. More attractive are figurines based on ancient Egyp-tian originals and some nice books on Egyptology. On the other hand, you can also get a perfectly silly shiny gold and black pharaoh's hat.

The cleverly named **Aftermath** forms the exit to *Twister*. There are plenty of *Twister* souvenirs here, including more mugs than in most shops. Reflecting the film's farm land setting, many of the items for sale are in-spired by cows and pigs. Other than that, there is a wide variety of *Wizard of Oz* and Universal Studios souvenirs.

PRODUCTION CENTRAL

Production Central is modeled on a typical film studio front lot. Essentially, it is a collection of soundstages and has a resolutely industrial feel to it. But with recent additions injecting some architectural pizzazz, this area now has visual interest to match its entertainment value.

Hollywood Rip Ride Rockit

Rating: * * * * +
Type: Music-themed steel coaster
Time: About 2 minutes
Our Take: The next generation of Aaaargh!

Towering over the soundstages, smashing through the New York firehouse facade, and snaking its way toward CityWalk, the *Hollywood Rip Ride Rockit* has literally changed the face of Universal Studios Florida forever. Billed as "the most technologically advanced coaster in the world," this first Floridian installation from innovative European designer Maurer Söhne boasts statistics to make any speed freak salivate. It's the tallest (167 feet) and one of the fastest (65 mph) coasters in Orlando, and features a number of unique, newly engineered elements.

The experience begins in a flatscreen-festooned queue near the Blue Man Group theater, where "edgy" animated characters introduce themselves as the camera crew for your new music video. The seven 12-passenger cars are just as high-tech, with on-board video and sound systems, and color-changing LEDs that put on a carnival lightshow as they swoop overhead. Even the boarding process has been upgraded: a moving walkway keeps cars continuously loading, minimizing wait times.

Once in the car, you'll use a seat-mounted display to select a soundtrack from one of five musical genres, including "Classic Rock/Metal" (ZZ Top, Limp Bizkit), "Country" (Dwight Yoakam, Kenny Chesney) and "Rap/Hip-Hop" (Black Eyed Peas, Kanye West). With 30 songs to choose from, everyone should be able to find something they'll like screaming along to.

Tip: If you press the *Rip Ride Rockit* logo for 10 seconds a hidden menu of "bonus tracks" will appear. Type in any 3-digit number (our fave is 902). There's even a "Pocket Rockit" iPhone app available to tell you all the codes!

Once your music selection is made, you begin the ride by ascending a "record-breaking" vertical lift (lying flat on your back!) in only 17 seconds, then dive into a 103-foot "non-inverting" twisted loop dubbed a "Double-Take" above the plaza stage. Other maneuvers take you spiraling through the *Twister* queue facade, "crowd surfing" over waiting guests, and skirting the edge of CityWalk. The twisty track is deceptively disorienting (and surprisingly silent); you'll be back in the station before you know what hit you.

During the ride, while your chosen song is delivered to your eardrums at up to 90 decibels courtesy of custom in-seat speakers, 14 digital cameras along the track (plus 6 in each train) capture your every shriek. You may purchase packages with still photos ($16 to $20) and personalized music videos ($30 to $40) in a freely web-sharable format after you return to earth. (Bonus tracks do not appear on souvenir videos due to licensing restrictions.)

Rockit isn't as intense an experience as the *Incredible Hulk*, but delivers more kick than *Revenge of the Mummy*. It's too wild to be considered a "family coaster" (especially in the bumpy back seats) but the lack of upside-down inversions makes it a good bet for tweens ready to graduate to grown-up thrills. The best news for coaster purists (or worst for the weak-kneed) is that there are no over-the-shoulder restraints, only a large curved lap bar that holds you firmly in place while allowing big doses of out-of-your-seat airtime. Unfortunately, inconsistent operations make the line move slowly, and an uncomfortable amount of side-to-side shaking keeps *Rockit* from reaching its full potential.

Tip: *Rockit* is the hottest ride at Universal Studios and it doesn't currently offer Universal Express, so do it first thing in the morning and/or use the single rider line (if available).

Note: *Rockit* has a minimum height requirement of 51" (130 cm) and a height maximum of 6'7" (201 cm).

Jimmy Neutron's Nicktoon Blast

Rating:	* * *
Type:	Simulator ride
Time:	5 minutes
Our Take:	For younger thrill seekers

If you had kids in the early 2000s (or were a kid), you are likely familiar with James Isaac "Jimmy" Neutron, the pre-pubescent whiz kid whose popular Nickelodeon TV show was inspired by the 2001 full-length animated film, *Jimmy Neutron: Boy Genius.* Jimmy Neutron was Nick's first CGI (computer-generated) cartoon and, as the film and this attraction attest, the animators are very good indeed at what they do.

Despite the kiddie-orientation of *Jimmy Neutron,* this ride is not kids' stuff — at least in terms of the wallop it packs. If you are shaken up or made queasy by simulator rides, approach this one with care. It features some bone-jarring, inner-ear-discombobulating effects.

Tip: There is a row of stationary benches in the front for little ones and those who wish to forego the thrill ride aspect of the show. This section has a separate entrance with virtually no line, even at busy times. You are very close to the screen here, however, making for somewhat distorted viewing, which might induce the queasiness you are trying to avoid. If you choose this option, try to sit as close to the center aisle as possible.

As you are ushered into the antechamber to this ride, Jimmy and his nerdy buddy Carl appear on overhead screens to show off Jimmy's new Mark IV rocket, the fastest ever built, along with earlier versions including the "slightly unpredictable" Mark I. But before Jimmy can get very far into his presentation, Ooblar the Yokian, Jimmy's nemesis in the film, appears to steal the Mark IV, with the ultimate goal of copying it and using it to enslave the earth. Obviously, Jimmy must give chase and, just as obviously, we must tag along in that unpredictable Mark I.

The hangar containing our vehicles is actually a movie theater divided into twelve eight-seat sections. Each section is actually a simulator car, a cousin of the high-tech simulators used to train airline pilots. It hovers a few feet off the ground, like a box on stilts, and moves and tilts in sync with the on-screen action. It may only move a foot or so in any direction, but try telling that to your mind. For all it knows, you are hurtling through space with Jimmy at supersonic speeds.

When the show begins, the screen in front of us becomes the door to the hangar and when it opens we are off on a light-speed chase to overtake Ooblar and retrieve the stolen spacecraft. After a discombobulating tour of Nicktoons Studios, we crash through some sort of space warp to the Yokian Planet and the throne room of King Goobot, who in a Yokian gesture of welcome tries to feed us to Poultra, a cross between a chicken and a fire-breathing dragon. After a hair's-breadth escape, we make it back to earth, splashing into Bikini Bottom, home to SpongeBob SquarePants. Eventually, Ooblar is vanquished, the Mark IV is retrieved, and the planet is saved.

It's all great fun, but don't be too surprised if you find the action hard to follow, especially if you are unfamiliar with the Nick lineup of shows and the

Jimmy Neutron film. The sound track is loud, multi-layered, and muddy and much of the dialog is impossible to understand. Kids, it must be noted, don't seem to mind this minor narrative glitch. Adults can amuse themselves looking for fleeting cameos from Ren & Stimpy and a certain Tibetan spiritual leader.

The best seats in the house. As the line approaches the entrance to the antechamber, it divides in two. By choosing the left lane, you will wind up toward the back or middle of the theater. If you position yourself in the middle of the group in the antechamber, you stand a good chance of ending up in the middle of the theater. Probably the most advantageous spot is in the middle of the house in the last or next-to-last row. From there, you get the best, least distorted view of the screen.

After the show, the audience files out through an "interactive area," a large open space with a number of "stations" where kids can email an e-card to a friend, try their hands at being the director or sound effects wizard on a cartoon show, or play games based on Nicktoon trivia.

Photo op: The first stop to your left as you exit the theater is set aside for photo ops with SpongeBob SquarePants, who appears on a schedule listed in the 2-Park Map.

Tip: The interactive area can be entered at any time through the Nick-stuff Store. So, if you are on a tight schedule, you might want to skip this feature. You can always come back later in the day after you have visited your must-see attractions.

Shrek 4-D

Rating:	* * * * +
Type:	Theater show
Time:	25 minutes
Our Take:	Another boffo 3-D extravaganza

Welcome back to Duloc, that magical kingdom where everything is perfect — or would be if it weren't for all those pesky fairy tale characters that Lord Farquaad tried to do away with. If you remember the film (and if you don't, don't worry), Shrek sent Lord Farquaad to his eternal rest while rescuing and falling love with the beautiful Princess Fiona.

But it's hard to keep a good villain down, it seems, and as we enter Duloc we find ourselves in a dungeon antechamber where Pinocchio and the Three Little Pigs are being tortured under the direction of the ghost of Lord Farquaad. On the "Dungeon Cam" we see the gingerbread man tacked down to a torture table awaiting an even worse fate. Apparently, we're next.

In a very funny preshow we learn, courtesy of the Magic Mirror from the old Snow White tale, that the evil Lord still carries a considerable torch for the lovely Fiona, who is now off on her honeymoon with Shrek and Donkey. (Not most people's idea of the perfect honeymoon perhaps, but there you have it.) The preshow also does an excellent job of reprising the plot of the film for those who were foolish enough to miss it.

The ghost of Farquaad vows to steal Fiona and make her his spirit bride and, just to cover all the bases, decides to torture us for information as to her whereabouts.

Tip: Sidle to the right as you wait in the first chamber and take the time to read the instructions for "Duloc Express," a witty send-up of Universal's own Express Pass Plus system.

The next stop is a spacious, 300-seat 3-D theater where the story continues on film. The 15-minute film that follows would be a minor masterpiece of 3-D animation just by itself. But the clever designers of this show have added so many little extras that *Shrek 4-D* ends up in a virtual dead heat with *T2* as the top 3-D theater attraction in all of Orlando.

Best of all are the seats. They aren't quite simulators, but let's just say they make the tale unfolding on the screen a truly moving experience. There we see Shrek and Donkey trying to plot a course to the Honeymoon Hotel when Farquaad's henchman, Thelonius, appears and kidnaps Fiona. The chase that follows packs enough thrills and cliffhangers (literally) for a full-length action film and involves not one but two fire-breathing dragons. Good prevails, Fiona is saved from a watery death, and in true fairy tale fashion everyone lives happily ever after. Except Farquaad.

Both the preshow introduction and the film do a wonderful job of poking fun at the conventions of films based on fairy tales, theme park attractions, and theme parks themselves, making *Shrek 4-D* Orlando's most subversive attraction. And it must be therapeutic for theme park employees to be able to visit an attraction where guests are actually warned, "Cell phone users will be flogged. Flash photographers will be burned at the stake. Enjoy the show!"

Selected Short Subjects

▌ Music Plaza

The Hollywood Bowl-styled stage that sits at the foot of *Hollywood Rip Ride Rockit's* signature loop is home to Universal's seasonal concert series.

The 2,400-square-foot performance space features eco-friendly lighting equipment and a bone-shaking sound system. Performers range from to-day's Top 40 to oldies acts; recent guests have included Jordin Sparks, Rob Thomas, Pat Benatar, and Chicago. Some concerts, like those during Mardi Gras, are included in your regular admission, while others (including the "Rock The Universe" Christian music events) require a separate ticket. Popular artists can fill up the 15,000-square-foot astroturf viewing lawn hours early, so unless you're a die-hard fan, just wait until showtime and find a spot in the New York area in sight of the 20-foot-high projection screens.

Donkey's Photo Finish

Just across the street from the *Shrek 4-D* exit, you will find a rustic stable facade where you can get your picture taken with everybody's favorite noble steed, Donkey. Shrek shows up, too, from time to time. While Shrek is the usual theme park costumed character, Donkey is a clever animatronic who sticks his head out of his stable door and, thanks to an unseen performer doing an uncanny Eddie Murphy imitation, ad libs to hilarious effect with guests and passersby. Just eavesdropping is a great way to kill time.

You can snap photos with your own camera, but if you've left yours back at the hotel, there is a photographer on hand to oblige. You can pick up (and pay for) the photos later at the On Location shop in The Front Lot.

Eating in Production Central

Classic Monsters Cafe

What:	Buffet restaurant
Where:	Across from *Twister*
Price Range:	$-$$

Those glamorous ghouls of our collective black-and white subconscious take center stage in an eatery filled with souvenirs from zany sci-fi movies like *Abbott and Costello Go To Mars* and chillers like *Frankenstein, The Mummy,* and *Dracula.* The Creature from the Black Lagoon even floats in a big tank in the "Swamp Dining" room. Amazingly enough, they have resisted the seemingly irresistible temptation to use terms like Monster Meals, FrankenFries, and Mummy's Pasta on the menu.

Salads, some quite fancy, are popular, as are the pasta dishes. Wood-fired pizzas come in cheese and pepperoni, and chicken dishes come with roasted potatoes, onions, and fresh corn. Draft beer is available in addition to the usual assortment of soft drinks and desserts.

Outside, a kiosk dubbed **Bone Chillin' Beverages** serves up harder stuff, including mixed drinks and slushies. There's nothing stopping you from bringing these more potent potables inside to enjoy with your meal.

The food is served "buffeteria" style in Frankenstein's laboratory, which makes you wonder if eye of newt is among the condiments. You can take your pick of several dining areas — Space, Crypt, Swamp, and Mansion Dining — each with a different theme and all packed with life-sized statues, props, and photographs. Universal Studios' early success was fueled by its inventive horror movies, and this gleefully ghastly gastronomic goulash is a fitting celebration of that bygone era.

Note: This restaurant is only open seasonally.

Shopping in Production Central

You will enter **Shrek's Ye Olde Souvenir Shoppe** in a good mood because you will be exiting from the immensely entertaining *Shrek 4-D* attraction. It houses the usual assortment of Shrek-ified souvenir fare, from T-shirts to plush dolls of all the principal characters. Petite green "ogre ears" like the ones sometimes worn by the ride attendants make a nice fashion statement (so much nicer than those large clunky round black ears worn by the fashion-challenged) and they're cheap, too. There is also a line of princess apparel, and accessories including tiaras, cone-shaped hats, purses, and (for the casual princess) T-shirts.

Tip: Check out the mirror behind the cashier.

The *Jimmy Neutron* ride empties out into **Nick Stuff**, a brightly decorated toy and souvenir shop, where SpongeBob SquarePants outshines Jimmy and his pals. Wearables include socks, T-shirts, sweats, sandals, and p.j.s at prices ranging from the minuscule to the moderate. Expect merchandise showcasing the latest Nick hit to be featured when you visit.

EXTRA ADDED ATTRACTION

In the spirit of those old-time Saturday matinee specials, Universal serves up a special treat just before the park closes on those sultry summer evenings. It's designed to send you off into the evening toward CityWalk in a good mood and it succeeds pretty well.

Universal 360: A Cinesphere Spectacular

Rating: * * * *
Type: Multimedia extravaganza
Time: 15 minutes
Our Take: Best for the fireworks

Those four large globes you saw floating in the lagoon all day come to life at night, just before park closing, in this seasonal show that runs only when the park is open late. As the sky darkens, they look quite lovely as projectors inside fill them with scudding white clouds and blue sky, all of which is reflected in the water below.

When the show begins, the globes become circular movie screens (hence the 360 of the title) on which a kaleidoscopic survey of Universal film history is projected. Covering "almost a century" of Universal movies, the clips range from silent classics like *The Hunchback of Notre Dame* (that's Lon Chaney under all that hideous makeup) to recent studio releases like *Frost/Nixon* (that's Frank Langella under all that hideous makeup).

The film editors, who collaborated with director John Landis, have assembled the film clips in a series of thematic montages: action movies open, followed by patriotic and inspirational films, horror flicks, comedies, romances, and epics. Some find it hard to discern a throughline to all this, but what the show may lack in coherence it more than makes up for in comprehensiveness. The rapid-fire selections range from Hellboy to Hitchcock and from Gregory Peck to Rowdy Roddy Piper. The screens (all four show exactly the same clips) are filled with monsters and mobsters, aliens and astronauts, comedy and carnage, heroes and the Holocaust. Fireworks punctuate key screen moments, ingenious projections appear on the walls

105

of buildings around the lagoon, and laser lights pierce the night sky, creating fun effects in the smoke from the fireworks.

It's unlikely you'll be able to identify every movie and every star represented (we sure couldn't) but you'll probably come away with a renewed appreciation of just how many films Universal has produced over the years and how many of them were first-rate.

The show seems to come to a touching end with E.T.'s famous line, "I'll be right here," suggesting that all these films reside forever in our collective memories. But then John Belushi appears in a clip from *Animal House* to say, "Over? Who says it's over?" which cues a razzle-dazzle, slam-bang finale that fills the sky overhead with fireworks. Considering that Universal sits in the middle of a residential neighborhood, it's a pretty amazing display.

The best seats in the house. First, understand that you will probably be standing for this show, although some people find places to sit, especially on the rocks on the World Expo side of the lagoon. The most comprehensive view is from the smoking section behind Richter's Burgers, which sits directly below the show technicians' control booth. Standing near Bull's Gym, where the New York set meets Production Central, offers a fun view of all four globes and an excellent perspective on the fireworks finale. Another good option is the second floor balcony above Lombard's Seafood Grille. A late meal at Lombard's and a friendly server can probably open the right doors. From here you have an especially nice view of the facade of the *Men In Black* building, which is completely filled with projections at points in the show.

Note: This show is only presented on nights when the park is open late, which means during the summer, at Christmas time, during Spring Break, and at other times of peak attendance.

CHAPTER THREE:

ISLANDS OF ADVENTURE

Billed as "Orlando's next-generation theme park," Islands of Adventure has certainly raised the competitive bar with its assortment of cutting edge attractions, thrill rides, and illusions. And in 2010, thanks to an certain boy wizard, Orlando's "next big thing" became even bigger.

Islands of Adventure is located right next door to Universal Studios Florida, just a five- or ten-minute stroll away. Despite the proximity, Islands of Adventure is not just more of Universal Studios. It has a separate identity and, with some notable exceptions, its attractions draw their inspiration from very different sources from those in its sister park.

Guests reach Islands of Adventure through the Port of Entry, a separate themed area that serves much the same function as the Front Lot at Universal Studios Florida. Through the Port of Entry lies a spacious lake, dubbed the Great Inland Sea. Artfully arranged around it are six decidedly different "themed areas" — Seuss Landing, The Lost Continent, The Wizarding World of Harry Potter, Jurassic Park, Toon Lagoon, and Marvel Super Hero Island. The "islands" of Islands of Adventure are not true islands, of course; but the Great Inland Sea's fingerlike bays set off one area from the next and the bridges you cross to move from one to another do a remarkably good job of creating the island illusion. The flow of visitors is strictly controlled by the circular layout. If you follow the line of least resistance (and it's hard not to), you will move through the park in a circle, visiting every island in turn.

There are a number of themes, if you will, that differentiate Islands of Adventure from Universal Studios Florida (and from other Central Florida theme parks, too, for that matter):

Roller coasters. Islands of Adventure introduced to Orlando some heavy hitters in the increasingly cut-throat competition for bragging rights in the world of high-end steel coasters. *Dragon Challenge* in The Wizarding World of Harry Potter features twin coaster tracks that intertwine and come within inches of collision, while the *Incredible Hulk Coaster* on Marvel Super Hero Island zaps you to the top of the first drop with what they say is the same thrust as an F-16 jet.

Pushing the envelope. Universal's designers take obvious pride in "next generation" rides and attractions that will be like nothing you have experienced before. As just one example, the *Spider-Man* ride takes standard motion simulator technology, drops it into a simulated 3-D world right out of *T-2*, puts it on a moving track, and spins it through 360 degrees along the way. *Harry Potter and the Forbidden Journey* further ups the ante by adding in-your-face animatronics and a first-of-its-kind ride vehicle.

More for the kids. While Islands of Adventure provides plenty of the kind of intense, adult-oriented thrill rides for which Universal Studios became famous, it makes a special effort to reach out to kids. Seuss Landing is almost exclusively for the entertainment and enjoyment of younger children. Toon Lagoon will appeal to slightly older kids, Marvel Super Hero Island is the perfect place for adolescents to scare themselves to death, and Harry Potter has legions of young (and not-so-young) fans.

More themeing. Although it hardly seems possible, Islands of Adventure is even more heavily "themed" than its sister park and many other parks. What that means is that the park designers have made a concerted effort to stretch the theme of each island into every restaurant, every shop, indeed into as many nooks and crannies as possible. With Potter's arrival, the already excellent themeing has achieved a whole new level of detail.

Music. Islands of Adventure is the first theme park to feature originally composed soundtracks — one for each island — just like a movie. Of course, music is nothing new in theme parks, but what is both new and exceptional at Islands of Adventure is the way the music is integrated into the park experience. It swells as you enter each island, changes gradually as you move from one part of the island to another, and as you cross to another island, blends seamlessly into the next island's theme. The effect is pervasive yet unobtrusive, so much so that many people may not even be aware of what a special achievement it is.

Eating in Islands of Adventure

Islands of Adventure's best-kept secret is the food. Those who truly care about the taste and quality of what they put in their stomachs and who despair of eating well in a theme park will find much to celebrate here.

Mythos, the full-service restaurant in The Lost Continent, is an award-winning dining experience that would be a credit to any cosmopolitan city. Its presence in a theme park is cause for wonderment. There are annual passholders who come to the park just to have dinner. The food at Islands of Adventure's other full-service restaurant, Confisco Grille, while not up to the level of Mythos, is also very good.

The fast food in the park is a cut above the norm, too. Best of all, given the obvious quality of the food, the prices are no more than you would expect to pay for far less adventuresome cooking at other theme parks.

Shopping in Islands of Adventure

Much of what can be said about the shopping in Universal Studios Florida can be repeated for the shopping experiences offered in Islands of Adventure. However, a number of things are worth noting.

The Middle Eastern bazaar section of The Lost Continent offers a number of shops run by some very talented artisans. Look here for the kind of gifts that won't scream "bought in a theme park!" Look, too, in Port of Entry for unusual folk sculptures and decorative items.

As writers, we take a certain pleasure in seeing so many books for sale in Seuss Landing, even if they are children's books. And speaking of the child in us all, the treasure trove of comic books to be found in Marvel Super Hero Island is nothing to look down your nose at. Finally, the Wizarding World sets a new standard for theme park shopping with unique merchandise sure to have Potter fans panting.

Again, keep in mind the wisdom of saving your shopping for the end of the day. The Islands of Adventure Trading Company in Port of Entry has a good selection of souvenirs representing all of the park's islands, including a sampling of Potter products. There's even a Universal Store in CityWalk, which means you can shop for souvenirs days after your tickets to the parks have expired. You can also shop by phone by calling (877) 318-2732.

Good Things To Know About...

Here are some notes that apply specifically to Islands of Adventure. General notes that apply to both parks will be found in *Chapter One: Planning Your Escape*.

▮ Dining Passes

It is actually possible to eat at Mythos, IOA's top-tier restaurant, without paying admission to the park. Here's how it works: Make a reservation at Mythos (see "Reservations," below) and then stop at the "Will Call" window, to the right of the ticket booths at the front entrance to the park. Tell them you have a reservation at Mythos and want a "Dining Pass." They will provisionally charge your credit card for one-day passes for everyone in your party. You then have 2 1/2 hours from the time of your reservation to eat and return to Guest Services. In addition, they require that you return within 30 minutes of the time you pay your check at Mythos (the time will be stamped on your credit card receipt). When you return and show your receipt, they will tear up the credit card slip; overstay your welcome and you will be charged for a one-day pass. If you find yourself running late at Mythos, alert your server to the situation and the restaurant will run interference for you with Guest Services.

If you have a pass to the park, you can use this system to invite guests to lunch. If you've been freeloading with family or friends during your Orlando vacation, this is a great way to say "thank you." It's also a good way to dazzle business associates. Although the Dining Pass program was designed specifically with Mythos in mind, you can use it to visit Confisco Grille as well, if you ask.

▮ First Aid

There is a first aid station in Port of Entry, just past the turnstiles, in the Open Arms Hotel building. A second first aid station will be found tucked away in the bazaar area near the Sindbad theater in The Lost Continent (number 8 on the IOA map in this chapter).

▮ Getting Away From It All

Each of the islands has a park-like, attraction-free section tucked away near the shores of the Great Inland Sea. They seem to have been designed as venues for private parties and corporate events. They are little visited by most guests and offer a terrific opportunity to escape the madding crowd. They also boast excellent views across the Sea to other islands. On days when the park is open past sunset, they are surprisingly private and quite romantic places to snuggle up with that special someone.

▮ Getting Wet

Islands of Adventure has some great water-themed rides. They offer plenty of thrills but they pose some problems for the unprepared. Kids probably won't care, but adults can get positively cranky when wandering around sopping wet.

The three water rides, in increasing order of wetness, are *Jurassic Park River Adventure, Dudley Do-Right's Ripsaw Falls,* and the absolutely soaking *Popeye & Bluto's Bilge-Rat Barges*. Fortunately, these three wonderful rides are within a short distance of each other, allowing you to implement the following strategy:

First, dress appropriately. Wear a bathing suit and T-shirt under a dressier outer layer. Wear shoes you don't mind getting wet; sports sandals are ideal. Bring a tote bag in which you can put things, like cameras, that shouldn't get wet. You can also pack a towel, and it might be a good idea to bring the plastic laundry bag from your hotel room.

Plan to do the rides in sequence. When you're ready to start, peel off the outer layer, put it in the tote bag along with your other belongings, and stash everything in a convenient locker. You can use the all-day lockers in Port of Entry, but a more convenient choice is the bank of small lockers at the entrance to the *Jurassic Park River Adventure*. These lockers cost $2 an hour. The all-day lockers are more spacious but will cost you $8. You decide.

Once you've completed the circuit of rides, you will be very, very wet, especially if you have gone on some of the rides more than once. You now have a choice: If it's a hot summer day, you may want to let your clothes dry as you see the rest of the park. Don't worry about feeling foolish; you'll see plenty of other folks in the same boat, and your damp clothes will feel just great in the Florida heat. In cooler weather, it's a good idea to return to the locker, grab your stuff, head to a nearby restroom, and change into dry clothes. Use the plastic laundry bag for the wet stuff.

Another option is the "Haystack" full-body dryer outside *Bilge-Rat Barges*. A family of four can fit inside the big orange closet and be blasted with hot air for $5.

The alternative is to buy an Islands of Adventure rain poncho (they make nice souvenirs and are usually available at most shops) and hope for the best. This is far less fun and you'll probably get pretty wet anyway.

▌ Height Restrictions and Other Warnings

Due to a variety of considerations, usually revolving around sudden movements and the configuration of lap restraints, a few rides will be off-limits to shorter (typically younger) guests. Here is a list of rides that have minimum height requirements:

High in Sky Seuss Ride	34 in. (86.4 cm.)
Flight of the Hippogriff	36 in. (91.4 cm.)
Pteranodon Flyers	36 in. (91.4 cm.)
Spider-Man	40 in. (101.6 cm.)
Jurassic Park River Adventure	42 in. (106.7 cm.)
Popeye & Bluto's Bilge-Rat Barges	42 in. (106.7 cm.)
Dudley Do-Right's Ripsaw Falls	44 in. (111.8 cm.)
Forbidden Journey	48 in. (121.9 cm)
Doctor Doom's Fearfall	52 in. (131.1 cm.)
Incredible Hulk & Dragon Challenge	54 in. (137.2 cm.)

The rides in Seuss Landing require that children under 48 inches tall be accompanied by an adult.

Another problem may be encountered by taller and heavier guests. *Forbidden Journey*, the roller coasters, and *Doctor Doom's Fearfall* employ state-of-the-art harness-like contraptions to make sure that you don't go flying off into space. Unfortunately, not everyone fits into them. Anyone with a chest measurement over 50 inches may have difficulty fitting into the harness and at 54 inches (137.2 cm.) you can pretty much forget about it. Height is less of a problem (they say basketball players have ridden) but some extremely tall individuals may also be out of luck. The rides in question provide a sample seat outside so you can check to see if you'll fit. These, by the way, also offer great photo ops.

▌ Reservations

Mythos and Confisco Grille both accept priority seating reservations. During busier periods you may spot a small kiosk in Port of Entry where you can make reservations. If you're really planning ahead, the central reservations number is (407) 224-9255. They will take reservations up to 30 days in advance.

▌ Single Rider Lines

To help shrink long lines, some rides open single rider lines when things get busy. You will find single rider lines at *Incredible Hulk, Doctor Doom's Fearfall, Spider-Man, Ripsaw Falls, Bilge Rat Barges, Jurassic Park River Adventure,* and *Forbidden Journey.* Operation of single rider lines is solely at the discretion of the lead ride attendant, so don't count on this time-saving ploy.

▌ Special Diets

The map in the 2-Park Map has a special symbol for restaurants serving vegetarian meals. Confisco's and Mythos can provide kosher meals with 48 hours advance notice. Call Food Services at (407) 363-8340 to make arrangements. These restaurants may also be able to accommodate other special dietary needs, such as low-carb regimens. Call the reservations number above a few days ahead to discuss your needs.

▌ Special Events

Islands of Adventure has fewer special events than Universal Studios Florida next door, but that may change in the future as Universal looks for ways to expand on the enormous popularity of the Wizarding World of Harry Potter.

Grinchmas. December sees Seuss Landing transformed into a winter wonderland, complete with Seussian holiday decor and a *Mannheim Steamroller*-scored musical show starring the Grinch himself, who proves to be a delightful (if parentally incorrect) host.

Treasure Hunt: Your Day at Islands of Adventure

Thanks to the wildly popular Harry Potter, seeing all of Islands of Adventure in a day is a lot harder than it used to be. That might change in the months and years ahead, as the initial excitement over Harry subsides, but we're not making any bets. Of course, the definition of "all" will be different for everyone. For example, many people will have no interest in subjecting themselves to the intense thrills of the roller coasters, *Doctor Doom*, or *Forbidden Journey.* Teenagers, young singles, and those without children can probably skip the interactive play areas (although they're pretty nifty and worth a peek).

Those who are want to see literally everything Islands of Adventure has to offer can still probably come pretty close in a single day, especially if they are willing to arrive early and step lively. If you pay for Universal Express

Plus passes or enjoy the front-of-the-line privileges of staying on site, then seeing it all is much more manageable.

Doing Your Homework

This assignment is not mandatory, but those who have not seen the original Jurassic Park should really rent the DVD before visiting Islands of Adventure. This easy-to-handle research project will add to your enjoyment of what the designers have achieved in IOA's Jurassic Park.

If you have not yet introduced your small children to the magical world of Dr. Seuss, this is an excellent excuse to do so. A knowledge of *The Cat in the Hat*, *If I Ran the Zoo*, and other Seuss books will make their visit to Seuss Landing a whole lot richer, and reading from the books is a great way to pass the time on those long car trips to Florida.

And of course, reading the seven-book Harry Potter series, and seeing the accompanying movies, are mandatory to get the most out of the Wizarding World. You can certainly enjoy the rides and shops without prior Potter knowledge, but at a minimum you'll enjoy the wealth of detail much more if you've at least seen the first film.

What To Expect

Islands of Adventure has many of the same kinds of attractions as Universal Studios Florida, with some notable exceptions. As at Universal Studios Florida, your first step is to consult the **2-Park Map** brochure, which you can pick up as you enter the park or in many shops throughout the park. It has a great map of the six "islands," each of which will be discussed in detail in the sections that follow. Here are some general observations about what's in store for you:

Rides. The rides here come in all shapes and sizes, from relatively tame kiddie rides to slam bang simulators and coasters. They also vary widely in terms of "throughput" — the number of people they can accommodate per hour. *Pteranodon Flyers*, for example, has a minimal throughput, while *Cat in the Hat* processes a surprising number of riders each hour.

Roller Coasters. Coasters spawn long lines, although the ones at Islands of Adventure are so intense that sometimes the wait to ride is surprisingly brief. Both coasters have separate lines for the daring few who want to ride in the front row; for these folks the wait is often lengthy.

Amphitheater Shows. These operate on a fixed schedule listed in the 2-Park Map. Generally, seating is not a problem.

Theater Shows. Only *Poseidon's Fury* falls into this category and even that's not an exact fit.

Displays and Interactive Areas. There are three separate interactive play areas for children; all of them can captivate your kids for hours on end. Keep that in mind when planning your touring schedule. The displays in the *Discovery Center* in Jurassic Park, while also enthralling for many children, are less likely to eat up considerable chunks of time.

All the Rest. Islands of Adventure has many more places to get away from the crowds than does its sister park. In fact, if you have a multi-day pass, you might want to bring a good book one day and just chill out along the shore of the Great Inland Sea.

Not-So-Buried Treasure

If you have limited time to spend in Islands of Adventure, or if you simply choose not to run yourself ragged attempting to see it all, here are our selections for the best the park has to offer:

Harry Potter and the Forbidden Journey. Quite simply the best ride we've ever been on, and the current state-of-the-art in thrill ride technology. Don't miss it.

Spider-Man. The park's former top attraction has been dethroned by *Forbidden Journey*, but is still a can't-miss mix of high-tech wonders

The Roller Coasters. Those who can tolerate the cutting edge coaster experience (and you know who you are) will want to ride both *The Hulk* and *Dragon Challenge* — several times. Absolutely awesome.

Popeye & Bluto's Bilge Rat Barges. A soaked-to-the-skin (but very clean) raft ride.

▌ Runners-Up

Here are a few more suggestions that aren't at the very top of our list but are well worth considering:

Cat in the Hat. This kiddie ride manages to be both traditional and cutting edge.

Jurassic Park River Adventure. River boats, raptors, and a hair-raising splashdown.

Dudley Do-Right's Ripsaw Falls. IOA's take on the themed flume ride is a cut above most in this genre.

Seuss Landing and Camp Jurassic. Even if you don't go on the kiddie rides, you should at least take a slow stroll through this these over-the-top wonderlands to marvel at the design.

Mythos. This is a restaurant, not a ride, but that doesn't mean the experience is any the less thrilling. Repeat visitors may notice some falling off, but if you order wisely Mythos still serves up some of the best food to be had in any theme park in the country And the eye-popping interior design makes even a cheeseburger a special experience.

The One-Day Stay

If you have time, you should avoid trying to cram this wonderful park into a single day; multi-day passes and the Orlando FlexTicket offer excellent value and the luxury of a more leisurely pace. Realistically, however, one day is all many visitors have. In this case, if you are staying at one of the resort hotels, the preferred access (and early admission to the Wizarding World) your room key affords will save you enough time that you won't have to plan your visit to the park like a military campaign. The same can be said (although to a lesser extent) for the paid Universal Express Plus passes.

However, the arrival of Harry Potter has completely rewritten all the rules for theme park attendance. On Opening Day, June 18, 2010, tens of thousands lined up beginning before 5:30 a.m., resulting in an eight-hour-long line that snaked around the entire park and out into CityWalk. At press time, enormous crowds are still streaming in, regularly resulting in two- to four-hour waits to enter the Wizarding World area, and hour-plus queues once inside to enter the rides and shops. By the time you visit, the intense interest will likely have abated somewhat, but IOA will remain the hot ticket in town for the foreseeable future.

If you are a die-hard Potter partisan who has traveled to Orlando primarily to visit his world, you'll want to join the diehards at dawn. Arrive at the park as early as humanly possible, at least 60 to 90 minutes before the official opening time. If there is a crowd, you will be routed clockwise to the land through Marvel, Toon Lagoon, and Jurassic Park (i.e. "the long way around"); otherwise, exit Port of Entry to the right through Seuss Landing, making a left at Green Eggs and Ham, and cross the bridge to Lost Continent. Once inside the Wizarding World, head straight for Ollivander's Wand Shop, followed by *Forbidden Journey*, the roller coasters, and the remaining shops. Once you've sated your thirst for Butterbeer, explore the rest of the park counter-clockwise from Jurassic Park to Seuss Landing.

Islands of Adventure

Harry Potter

Seuss Landing

The Lost Continent

Port of Entry

Entrance

Jurassic Park

Marvel Super Hero Island

Toon Lagoon

N
W E
S

0   250   500   750   1,000
Feet

Seuss Landing

1. The Cat In The Hat
2. If I Ran the Zoo
3. Caro-Seuss-El
4. One Fish, Two Fish, Red Fish, Blue Fish
5. The High in the Sky Seuss Trolley Train Ride

The Lost Continent

6. Poseidon's Fury
7. The Mystic Fountain
8. The Eighth Voyage of Sindbad Stunt Show

The Wizarding World of Harry Potter

9. Dragon Challenge
10. Flight of the Hippogriff
11. Forbidden Journey

Jurassic Park

12. Jurassic Park Discovery Center
13. Jurassic Park River Adventure
14. Camp Jurassic
15. Pteranodon Flyers

Toon Lagoon

16. Dudley Do-Right's Ripsaw Falls
17. Popeye & Bluto's Bilge-Rat Barges
18. Me Ship, The Olive

Marvel Super Hero Island

19. The Amazing Adventures of Spider-Man
20. Doctor Doom's Fearfall
21. Storm Force Accelatron
22. Incredible Hulk Coaster

If the above sounds more like boot camp than vacation to you, here's a better way to see it all with less stress. Note that this plan works best when the park is open past sunset (ideally 10 p.m. or later).

1. Arrive at the park at least 30 minutes prior to the official opening time. As soon as the gates open, proceed to the *Spider-Man* ride. Go straight to the end of Port of Entry and turn left. Hard-core thrill seekers should then ride *Hulk* and *Doctor Doom*, preferably in that order. If lines are short, you may want to take the opportunity to ride *Hulk* twice. Using single rider lines can speed things up considerably.

2. Now head through Toon Lagoon to ride *Popeye & Bluto's Bilge-Rat Barges*, followed by *Dudley Do-Right's Ripsaw Falls*, assuming you don't mind getting wet. It's enticing to leave these soakers until later in day, but in hot weather you'll face a long wait by early afternoon (unless you have Universal Express or are a resort guest).

3. Ride the *Jurassic Park River Adventure*.

4. At this point, it may be close to noon and time to take stock. Take the bridge near the *Jurassic Park Discovery Center* to the Lost Continent. *Poseidon's Fury* is a good choice for midday since the queue is indoors and mercifully air-conditioned. Also, check the schedule for the *Sindbad* show, and consider lunch at Mythos.

5. Afternoon is also good time to explore Seuss Landing. Don't skip *The Cat in the Hat*, and enjoy any other rides if the wait is short.

6. Two to three hours before closing time, walk through Lost Continent into The Wizarding World of Harry Potter. By now the early-morning Potter fans have pooped out, and crowds should be much more manageable. Stroll through the village, and then ride *Dragon Challenge, Flight of the Hippogriff,* and *Forbidden Journey.* Visit Ollivander's if the line ahead of you is under an hour. Save your shopping for closing time, since the stores stay open later than the attractions.

Again, those who are temperamentally averse to the giant coasters and intense thrills like *Doctor Doom* will find it much easier to take in all of Islands of Adventure in a day. But as we noted earlier, coaster lovers may be pleasantly surprised at how short the lines are, especially at slower times of the year, because these giants scare off a lot of people. The exception is the line for the first row, which is often lengthy.

The One-Day Stay With Kids

Many kids, especially those who are tall enough to avoid the height restrictions listed earlier, will be perfectly happy going on all the rides, in which case the strategy outlined above will work just fine. However, if you have children who are too short or too timid to tackle the thrill rides, you can adopt a much different strategy.

1. If your Potter-crazy child won't pay attention to anything else in the park once they've spotted Hogwarts' spires, bite the bullet and get there at the crack of dawn. Better yet, if you have park-to-park tickets see USF in the morning and save your first IOA visit for evening. Visit Ollivander's and ride *Flight of the Hippogriff* (ask for a seat near the front). Then walk through the *Forbidden Journey* queue but use the "baby swap" to bypass the ride if your kid is under 48" or spooked by spiders and skeletons.

If you decide to pass on the early-morning Potter patrol, you should make *Pteranodon Flyers* your first priority — assuming, of course, you feel your child will enjoy it. This ride takes only two people at a time per vehicle and does not accept Universal Express Plus, so the line gets very long very quickly.

Otherwise (and if your child is over 40 inches tall), do *Spider-Man* first. Most kids will have no problem with this one, although some of their adult guardians may. After that, you can relax and take your time.

2. Take a trip to Seuss Landing for those who won't find it too "babyish." However, even kids who consider themselves too "sophisticated" for most of Seuss will get a kick out of *The Cat in the Hat* ride. Your first ride in Seuss Landing should be the *High in the Sky Seuss Trolley Train Ride*, because of its slow loading time.

3. You can pretty much pick and choose after that, using the height restrictions listed earlier and your child's preferences to guide you. Despite the cartoon violence, *Sindbad* is a fun show for kids; and don't miss the *Mystic Fountain* in front of the stadium entrance.

4. When you need a break, steer your kids to an age-appropriate play area: *If I Ran the Zoo* and *Me Ship, The Olive* for younger children, *Camp Jurassic* for older ones.

5. Save the Wizarding World for late in the day when the thickest crowds have dissipated.

Note: Whichever plan you follow, be sure to pick up a copy of the 2-Park Map as you enter the park.

■ PORT OF ENTRY ■

The towering lighthouse with the blazing fire at the top, modeled after the ancient lighthouse of Pharos in Alexandria, Egypt, marks the gates to Islands of Adventure and the beginning of your adventure. This striking structure is only the most obvious of the metaphors used in an eclectic blend of architecture and decor that evokes the spirit of wanderlust and exploration. At the base of the lighthouse a series of sails, like those on ancient Chinese junks, shade the ticket booths for the park.

Through these gates lies Port of Entry, a sort of storytelling experience that combines evocative architectural motifs and haunting music to build your anticipation as you enter more fully into the spirit of discovery. Universal's scenic designers have outdone themselves on this one. To centuries old Venice, they've added images of Istanbul, a soupçon of Samarkand, a touch of Timbuktu, and a dash of Denpassar to create a ravishingly beautiful example of fantasy architecture. Hurry through in the morning if you must, but if you are among the last to leave the park, you should really linger in Port of Entry and drink in the atmosphere.

As you marvel at the architectural details and the exquisite care with which the designers have "dressed" this sensuous streetscape, pay attention to the sounds that swirl around you. In addition to the chatter of your fellow adventurers, you will experience one of IOA's "next level" touches. Like all the other islands in the park, Port of Entry has its own specially composed soundtrack that unfolds as you walk along, drawing ever closer to the Great Inland Sea. But there are other inspired aural touches as well, like the muffled conversations from dimly lit upper-story windows hinting at intrigue and adventures unknown. It's a very special place.

Tip: See if you can find the gambling hall, dance studio, former fire department, and jail-broken prison.

Port of Entry serves some more mundane purposes as well. Before you pass through the gates you will find, on your left, a pale green building that houses Group Sales. If you are the leader of a group of 20 or more, this is the place to pick up your tickets. To the right of the ticket booths, you will find a Guest Services walk-up window marked "Will Call." Stop here if you have arranged to have tickets waiting for you. Nearby is the only **ATM** in Port of Entry, so if you are in need of ready cash, make sure to stop here before you enter the park. Other ATMs are found in The Lost Continent, The Wizarding World of Harry Potter, and Marvel Super Hero Island.

Once past the ticket booths and the entrance turnstiles, you will find a spacious semicircular plaza. Directly ahead of you is a large stone archway. Behind the fantastic facades of the buildings to either side are a variety of Guest Services functions.

▮ To the left of the archway are . . .

Restrooms. Because there are some things you don't need to carry on your adventures. Nearby are phones and phone card vending machine.

Lockers. There are four bays of electronically controlled lockers here. Rental fees are $8 for the day for smaller lockers and $10 for family size, both with in and out access. The machines accept both bills and credit cards.

Stroller & Wheelchair Rentals. "Reliable Rentals" has a large sign outside informing you that all the jinrickshaws, gliders, submersibles, and tuk tuks are either out of service, decommissioned, hired, or, in the case of the time machine, "stuck in the 6th century." Fortunately they still have strollers ($15 for singles, $20 for doubles), wheelchairs ($12), and electric convenience vehicles ($50) for rent. Slightly more elaborate strollers, called "kiddie cars," feature a kid's steering wheel and cup holders and rent for $18 and $23 respectively. All prices include tax. A $50 refundable deposit is required for wheelchair and electric convenience vehicle (ECV) rentals, or you can leave your drivers license or a credit card imprint.

▮ To the right of the archway are . . .

Guest Services. Questions or complaints? The cheerful folks here can help you out. Annual passes can also be obtained here.

Lost & Found. Don't give up on that lost item. There's a very good chance a fellow tourist or a park staffer will find it and turn it in. Check back the next day, too, just in case.

First Aid. This is one of two first aid stations in the park. The other is in The Lost Continent, near the Sindbad Theater.

Now that you have replenished your wallet, stowed your excess gear, and rented your strollers, you step through that crumbling stone archway incised with the thrilling words "The Adventure Begins" and start your journey toward the Great Inland Sea and the magical islands that ring it.

Port of Entry's main (and only) street is given over to a variety of shopping and eating establishments. As you stroll along, don't be surprised if someone tries to talk you into a photographic souvenir of your visit; this is, after all, an exotic marketplace bustling with hawkers. There's no charge to have your photo snapped; at the end of the day, you can stop into De Foto's (see below), survey the results, and make your decision.

At the far end of this market street, under another crumbling archway that's being propped up by a jury-rigged contraption of giant planks and chains, the street opens out into another broad plaza on the shore of the Great Inland Sea. Amid the souvenir kiosks that dot the plaza, look for a large signboard that can help you plan your itinerary. The board is electronically linked to the attractions throughout the park and updates regularly with the current waiting times for the all the rides. If no wait time is posted, that means that the ride is temporarily out of commission.

Tip: Roughly opposite the Backwater Bar (see *Eating in Port of Entry,* below), is a secluded park-like snarl of rock-shielded walkways along the edge of the Inland Sea. At the end, on a point of land jutting into the water, you will find a little-visited hideaway that is wonderfully romantic at night.

Eating in Port of Entry

Whether you're on the way in, on the way out, or just breaking for lunch, there's both good food and fast food to be had in Port of Entry.

Tip: Visit the thatched-roof kiosk across from Cinnabon by the Inland Sea to make reservations for any restaurant in the theme parks or City-Walk.

▌ Croissant Moon Bakery

What: Sandwiches, pastries, and coffee
Where: On your right as you enter, under the second archway
Price Range: $

Every theme park needs a place, strategically located near the entrance, to serve those who thought they'd save some time by skipping breakfast only to arrive at the park starving to death. Croissant Moon Bakery opens when the park does and its popularity tends to overwhelm its minuscule indoor seating area and the small number of outdoor tables. There are two separate lines here, starting from opposite ends of the deli-like counter, and both serve exactly the same fare.

For breakfast, there are muffins and such along with the house's own branded coffee. Better yet, treat yourself to one of the pastries, pies, or cakes that are served here. Many of them are exceptional. Or pick up an "On the Run Continental Breakfast" (coffee, fruit cup, and your choice of muffin or Danish) for $6.

Later in the day, try the Port of Call sandwich platters. Peppered roast beef, smoked turkey, and honey-glazed ham are served with potato salad and fresh fruit, while hot, pressed paninis come with pasta. Soup and salads are also available.

▋ Confisco Grille

What:	Full-service restaurant with flair
Where:	On the waterfront plaza
Price Range:	$$ - $$$

The simple wooden chairs are painted green and blue and there are no tablecloths. But don't let the casual atmosphere fool you. Confisco Grille is a full-service sit-down restaurant that serves up a limited but imaginative menu that draws on far-flung culinary influences.

Part of the fun is the decor, vaguely Mediterranean with Turkish accents, that asks you to imagine you are in the Port of Entry Customs House. The place is lit by hanging lamps in a variety of styles and decorated with bizarre items, like a stegosaurus skull, confiscated from would-be smugglers.

But the real fun is the food. The Adventure Starters ($5 to $10) are described on the menu as "a perfect way to start your adventure." Take the hint and treat the table to nachos or Confisco Fries, which are served with a variety of dipping sauces. Also worth noting in this section of the menu is the Explorer's Vegetable Pizza, which crowns the Italian favorite with a medley of healthful toppings.

Burgers are done well here, too, with the bacon cheddar version a standout. Other sandwich choices ($9 to $11) include a toasted Italian ciabatta, a Tex Mex wrap, and a club sandwich. Entrees and pastas ($12 to $18) are a mixed bag, with the House Specialty Pad Thai noodles a bit on the bland side, but the Penne Puttanesca is worth trying. Entree-sized salads ($11) get high marks, too. Wines are served by the glass and the bottle. Kids can order from the "Little Travelers Menu" ($6 to $7).

Don't forget to leave room for one of the desserts, because they are terrific. The selection changes from time to time, but recent offerings included strawberry cheesecake, tiramisu, and a yummy chocolate banana bread pudding, served with vanilla ice cream (all around $5).

Perfect for lunch, Confisco might make a good choice for a light dinner on days when the park is open late. (Check Confisco's closing time on your way in. It's been known to close earlier than the park itself.)

The adjacent **Backwater Bar** is too upscale to be a perfect replica of the kind of tropical dive where lonely adventurers come to drink away their memories of that low-down cheap saloon singer they loved and lost in Rangoon, but it will do in a pinch. It also makes a convenient staging area for those waiting for a table in Confisco, not to mention those who see no reason to interrupt their drinking with food. While the bar itself is small, there's a large outdoor seating area, a great place to survey the passing scene while getting a buzz on.

Note: Confisco offers a **Character Breakfast** featuring Spider-Man, Cat in the Hat, and other characters, along with a very nice breakfast buffet from 9:00 to 10:30 a.m. ($18 adults, $12 children). These events are "seasonal," which means they happen on a variable schedule. Recently, that meant most Sundays and Thursdays, plus Fridays during busy months. For more information about what's happening during your visit or to make reservations call (407) 224-4012 or email diningreservations@universalorlando.com.

▌Cinnabon

What:	Gooey pastries
Where:	Across from Confisco, on the waterfront
Price Range:	$

Another outpost of the well-known national chain (the other is in City-Walk), this walk-up stand sells classic Cinnabon pastries in a variety of styles and quantities. Drinks range from plain milk to a fancy mochalatta chill. All seating is outdoors.

▌Arctic Express

What:	Ice cream, funnel cakes, and waffle cone sundaes
Where:	Right next to Cinnabon
Price Range:	$

The Arctic theme seems a bit out of place here, but the "Fabulous Funnel Sundae" and "Wonderful Waffle Sundae" it serves will take your mind off any seeming contradictions. A variety of toppings and accompaniments are offered, including strawberries, apples, and chocolate sauce. You can also get soft serve ice cream in sugar or waffle cones, a root beer float, or the usual soft drinks, coffee, and milk. Service is from walk-up windows and all seating is outdoors.

Tip: Take your food from these two stands and eat it on a bench in the park by the water. It's a bit hidden, but keep looking. It's worth it.

Shopping in Port of Entry

As you would expect of any great city along the ancient Silk Road, the main street of Port of Entry is lined with shops and bazaars filled with traders offering trinkets and treasures from near and far. Most of these emporiums have one or more entrances opening onto the street but be aware that they form one continuous space inside, so they offer a cool and convenient refuge from the broiling sun or driving rain to those entering or leaving the park.

Islands of Adventure Trading Company is the largest of the shops in Port of Entry and it occupies most of the left-hand side of the street as you walk toward the Great Inland Sea. As the name suggests, you will find here a broad selection of souvenirs representing all the islands in the park. It's the usual array of logo-ed T-shirts and trinkets, everything from key chains, to mugs, to jackets and sweaters (in season), most with IOA logos. This store stocks the best selection of Harry Potter merchandise outside of the Wizarding World, so do your shopping here if the Potter shops are too crowded.

Past the Islands of Adventure Trading Company is **Ocean Trader Market**, a bazaar reminiscent of a Middle Eastern souk, its sides open to the street and shaded with tent-like canopies. Inside is a selection of offbeat handicrafts from around the globe. There is some attractive wooden folk sculpture as well as crafts from around the world, most of it reasonably priced. You should be able to find the kind of unusual decorative objects that make a nice addition to your living room or a gift for a friend back home. Also on offer here are various items of lightweight, brightly colored summer clothing for the ladies and a few shirts for the guys.

Across the street is a string of shops that open one onto the other. The nearest to the park entrance is **DeFoto's Expedition Photography**, the place to stop for film supplies and a variety of disposable cameras. You can even replace the camera you brought with you if the spirit moves you and pick up some nice photo albums and frames while you're at it. De Foto's also offers sunscreen and suntan lotion, just in case you forgot to bring some along. This is where you can view and purchase any photos of you and your family taken by those strolling photographers in the park.

Island Market and Export is a sweets shop selling overpriced candy, while at the **Port of Entry Christmas Shoppe** it's Christmas in July, or any other month for that matter, at this small shop selling tasteful ornaments for the tree and the yuletide hearth.

Near the park exit sits **Port Provisions.** This tiny open-air shop straddles the exit and provides a last chance to pick up something small. It also offers a limited selection of sale merchandise that's worth checking out by those in search of a bargain.

SEUSS LANDING

Probably best described as a 12-acre, walk-through sculpture, Seuss Landing adds a third dimension and giddy Technicolor to the wonderfully wacky world of Theodor Geisel, a.k.a. Dr. Seuss, whose dozens of illustrated books of inspired poetry have enchanted millions of children.

Universal designers have gone to great lengths to evoke the out-of-kilter world of the Seuss books, avoiding straight lines and square corners wherever possible. Buildings curve and swoop and sometimes seem to be on the verge of toppling over. Much of the architectural detail looks as though it was sculpted out of some especially thick cake icing and is now gently melting in the Florida sun. Even the foliage is goofy. Many of the wacky, twisted palm trees that dot the landscape were created by the fierce winds of Hurricane Andrew and loving transplanted here by Universal's grounds staff. The rest had to be painstakingly trained to create that Seussian look.

In its own cheerful, candy-colored way, the fantasy architecture here is just as successful and just as impressive as that in Port of Entry. Even if you have no interest in sampling the kiddie rides on offer here, you will have a great deal of fun just passing through.

If I Ran The Zoo

Rating:	* * *
Type:	Interactive play area
Time:	Unlimited
Our Take:	Fabulous fun for toddlers

This interactive play area is based on the charming tale of young Gerald McGrew who had some very definite ideas of what it takes to create a really interesting zoo. There are three distinct areas, each of which allows little ones a slightly different interactive experience. The first is filled with peculiar animals that appear over the hedges when you turn a crank or laugh when you tickle their feet. Little adventurers can also slide down the tunnels of Zamba-ma-tant and crawl through the cave in Kartoom in search of the Natch before reaching a small island surrounded by a wading pool. There they'll be able to control bouncing globs of water and trap their playmates in cages made out of falling water. In the final area kids can stand over a grate where the Snaggle Foot Mulligatawny will sneeze up their shorts. Then they can squirt a creature taking a bubble bath, only to get sprinkled themselves when the critter spins dry.

All told, there are 19 different interactive elements to keep your child giggling all the way through this attraction. Kids will dart about eager to try them all, which may be one reason the "Zoo Keeper Code of Conduct" at the entrance warns, "Keep track of adults, they get lost all the time."

The Cat In The Hat

Rating: * * * *
Type: "Dark ride"
Time: 3.5 minutes
Our Take: Kiddie ride with a little zip

Dr. Seuss's most popular book tells the tale of what happens when two kids, home alone, allow the cat of the title to come in for a visit. Step through the doors beneath that giant red and white striped top hat and you will get your chance to relive the adventure.

This is a "dark" ride but perhaps one of the brightest and most colorful you'll ever encounter. You and your kids climb into cars that are designed like miniature six-passenger sofas and set off through a series of 18 show scenes that re-create the story line of the book. Just don't expect the static tableaux of the older generation dark rides.

One of the nicer touches on this one is something that Universal describes as "a revolving, wallpaper-peeling, perception-altering 24-foot tunnel." Brace yourself for a few quick swoops, sudden turns, and maybe a 360-degree spin.

Along the way, the ride does a remarkably good job of telling the story of the book. The fantastic animated sculptures of the cat and his playmates, Thing 1 and Thing 2, spin and twirl while furniture teeters and topples. The wise fish, who is the tale's voice of reason, cries out warnings and ignored advice until, miraculously, all is set to rights before Mom gets home. Kids familiar with the book will be delighted and those who aren't will doubtless want to learn more. This is a must-do for little ones, although a few very timid tykes still may find the swoops and spins of the ride vehicles (which were greatly toned down in 2010) a bit startling .

While you probably won't care, this ride employs never-before-available computer systems to control the flow of 1,800 guests per hour and activate the innumerable special effects along the way.

One Fish, Two Fish, Red Fish, Blue Fish

Rating: * * *
Type: Flying, steerable fish
Time: 2 minutes
Our Take: Good, wet fun

Here's an interesting twist on an old carnival ride. You know, the one where you sit in a little airplane (or flying Dumbo) and spin round in a circle while your plane goes up and down. On this ride, based on the Seuss book of the same name, you pilot a little fishy. While you can't escape the circular route of the ride, you can steer your fish up or down.

Supposedly, if you follow the directions encoded in the little song that plays during the ride ("red fish, red fish up, up, up; blue fish, blue fish down, down, down"), you can avoid being doused by the water coming from a series of "squirt posts" that ring the perimeter. There are three verses to the song and, it seems it actually is possible to stay dry for the first two by following directions. The third verse, however, tells you that all bets are off and that your guess is as good as the next fellow's. It is the rare rider who gets through the ride without getting spritzed. Not that most people care. In fact, it looks like some kids do just the opposite of what the song counsels in the hope of getting Mom and Dad soaked.

Note: On cold days, and sometimes in the cooler morning hours, the ride does not spray water on the riders, which will probably come as a relief to parents and a disappointment to little ones.

This ride is very nicely designed, with perfectly adorable little fish cars and an array of Seussian characters serving as the squirt posts. Presiding over the center of the circle is an 18-foot-tall sculpture of the Star Belly Fish from the book.

Caro-Seuss-El

Rating: * * * +
Type: Old-fashioned carousel with Seuss figures
Time: About 1.5 minutes
Our Take: For carousel lovers and little kids

This ride marks yet another design triumph. The old-fashioned carousel has been put through the Seuss looking glass and has emerged as a towering, multicolored confection. In place of old-fashioned horses are marvelously imaginative Seuss critters with serene smiles plastered across their goofy faces. Even if you have no interest in actually riding the thing, it's worth the time it takes to stop and admire this imaginative whirligig in full motion.

The *Caro-Seuss-El* is billed as the world's first interactive carousel. Here kids can ride on the back of a beautifully sculpted Seussian animal like Cowfish from *McElligott's Pool* or the Twin Camels from *One Fish, Two Fish*. There are seven different characters and a total of 54 mounts on the 47-foot diameter ride. The interactive part comes when you pull back on the reins and watch your steed's head shake, his eyes blink, his tail wag. A special loading mechanism for wheelchairs allows the disabled to experience the ride from their own rocking chariots.

High in the Sky Seuss Trolley Train Ride

Rating: * * *
Type: Aerial train ride
Time: 3 minutes
Our Take: A pleasant new perspective on Seuss Landing

Based loosely on Dr. Seuss's anti-discrimination parable about Sylvester McMonkey McBean and the Sneetches, this brief excursion over Seuss Landing is designed for the kiddies but offers rewards for their adult companions.

Cute and colorful five-car, 20-passenger trolleys tootle along two separate tracks, each traveling a slightly different aerial route. In addition, each train has two different audio tracks, which adds up to four different experiences. This is definitely one your child will want to ride multiple times. Mom and Dad won't mind the repetition because there's plenty to see.

The train to your right as you enter the platform has the more interesting route, as it passes though the Circus McGurkus restaurant before heading out over Seuss Landing. Most of the trip is in the open air on loopy swirling tracks that take you on a bird's eye tour of this magical land. If you weren't impressed by the design of Seuss Landing after strolling through, this ride will change your mind.

Note: This is a gentle ride, but it is "high in the sky" so those with a fear of heights might want to give it a pass.

And all the rest...

There are nooks and crannies of Seuss Landing that are easy to miss. These are not major attractions, to be sure, but if you take a fancy to this whimsical land, or if you have a young Dr. Seuss fan in tow, they might be worth seeking out.

Just through the woozy archway that marks the entrance to Seuss Landing from Port of Entry you will find, on your right, **McElligott's Pool**, a pretty little pond with a waterfall, some charming statuary, and some interloping ducks who have made it home. Just past this area, next to the Cats, Hats & Things shop, in a private courtyard with its own kid-sized entrance arch, lies **Horton's Egg**. Climb atop the spotted egg (a sign invites volunteers to do so) for a great **photo op**.

The **Street of the Lifted Lorax** is a small walk-through area next to the *Caro-Seuss-El*. It retells the story from Dr. Seuss's book, *The Lorax*, the moral of which is "Protect the environment!"

From time to time, there is a **Seuss Character Meet and Greet** held at the Seuss book shop (times will be listed in the 2-Park Map. And don't forget to be on the lookout for the cat of *The Cat in the Hat*, who makes frequent personal appearances on the street. He is fond of sneaking up on unsuspecting tourists and will gladly pose for photos.

A "Grinchmas" musical show is staged in the area between *The Cat in the Hat* and *One Fish, Two Fish* ; the actors are talented but the tone is closer to the vulgar Jim Carey film than the sweet storybook and sixties cartoon. The rest of the year you may find a storyteller or balloon-blower here.

Finally, if you are hurrying through Seuss Landing, you can save a few seconds by turning left at Green Eggs and Ham and following the path that circles behind the shops. This takes you through a broad open area next to the Inland Sea and beneath the tracks of the *Trolley Train Ride* and lets you out a few paces from the bridge that leads to The Lost Continent, thereby avoiding the crowds that throng Seuss Landing's colorful main drag.

Eating in Seuss Landing

The eateries in Seuss Landing give new meaning to the term "fun food." The exteriors and interiors are every bit as ingeniously designed as the rides, with the same loopy, drooping, and dizzy details. Dining here is strictly casual, with brightly colored plastic utensils.

Note: The charmingly designed **Green Eggs and Ham Cafe**, which served the signature "Green Eggs and Hamwich" (scrambled eggs, thin slices of ham, and a touch of pureed parsley for color) has been shuttered for some time, with no indication if it will ever reopen.

Circus McGurkus Cafe Stoo-pendous

What: Large indoor cafeteria
Where: Across from the *Caro-Seuss-El*
Price Range: $

Under that enormous droopy big top is this humongous fast food emporium themed to a fare-thee-well with circus imagery a la Dr. Seuss. This is one of the most delightful restaurants in all of Islands of Adventure — clever, colorful, comfortable, and imaginative as all get out.

To one side are two complete cafeteria lines; to the other a series of booths disguised as a circus train transporting a weird variety of Seuss creatures, like the Amazing Atrocious, "a beast most ferocious." In between is a spacious seating area under the twin big tops from which swing a nutty trapeze artist and a spinning mobile of Seuss characters. Periodically, a train from the *High in the Sky Seuss Trolley Train Ride* chugs by overhead bearing a load of happy passengers.

The food is designed with kids in mind, which means personal-size pizzas, both pepperoni and cheese, and various pasta dishes served with bread sticks. Grown-ups might prefer the Chicken Caesar Salad or the Fried Chicken Platter. A kids' menu features pasta and chicken meals, and deserts include Dippin' Dots ice cream.

At one end of the room you'll see a zany pipe organ that is sometimes played during peak season. There is limited seating just outside the doors if you'd prefer to dine al fresco.

Hop on Pop

What: Ice-cream stand
Where: Across from All the Books You Can Read
Price Range: $

The enormous ice cream cone that decorates this walk-up stand says it all. Most delicious is the Brownie Sundae in a waffle bowl. The promisingly named Sundae On A Stick turns out to be a standard, chocolate-covered ice cream bar studded with sprinkles or nuts. Plain old waffle cones are also available with various toppings.

There is no seating but you can take your goodies around the corner to the Green Eggs and Ham outdoor seating area or even head across the street and into Circus McGurkus to eat in air-conditioned comfort.

■ Moose Juice Goose Juice

What:	Frosted smoothies at an outdoor stand
Where:	On your left as you exit to Lost Continent
Price Range:	$

On closer examination, Moose Juice turns out to be a "turbo tangerine" fruit drink and Goose Juice is sour green apple. Either drink can be had fresh or frozen. Cookies, churros, pretzels, and soft beverages are also available.

Shopping in Seuss Landing

It is impossible to miss the cheerful **Cats, Hats & Things** if you take the *Cat in the Hat* ride, but even if you don't, you might want to pop in for a quick look. Here you'll find plenty of souvenirs and clothing commemorating the famous cat, as well as Things 1 and 2. You'll also find the actual book that inspired the ride. A perennial favorite is the Cat's trademark striped stovepipe hat.

Tip: If you visit the shop, don't forget to take a peek into the quiet back courtyard that houses Horton's Egg (see above).

The **Mulberry Street Store** is the megastore of Seuss Landing, with its very own kid-sized entrance, and the tag line "Gizmos, Gadgets, Goodies Galore" pretty much sums it up. Here you'll find a large selection of Seuss wear for everyone in the family from the littlest tykes all the way to the grown-ups, who will find cotton p.j.s in their sizes. There are toys, nice jackets decorated with Seuss characters, and lots of infants' clothing, as well as games, books, and backpacks. Among the more intriguing gifts are some lovely limited-edition, hand-pulled Seuss lithographs and other artwork at prices approaching $1,000.

Photo Op: Outside, you can pose as part of a police escort that's whizzing by a reviewing stand filled with Seuss Landing dignitaries.

Even though it's called **Dr. Seuss's All the Books You Can Read**, most of the space here is given over to clothing, mugs, and plastic glasses. Fortunately, there are a few books and this happy, kid-scaled place is a great way to introduce your little ones to the magic of Seuss and reading in general. Books range from small single volumes to fairly expensive collections. You'll find videos, DVDs, CDs, and cloth and non-toxic plastic baby books. The shop offers some kid-sized places to sit down and read.

Finally, **Snookers & Snookers Sweet Candy Cookers** is yet another overpriced candy emporium redeemed by the presence of some wonderfully whimsical Seuss mugs and plastic glasses.

THE LOST CONTINENT

From the color and fantasy of Seuss Landing, the intrepid adventurer plunges into the mystery of The Lost Continent. Cross a wooden bridge to the sound of mystical windchimes, and enter a land of ancient myth.

Photo Op: The first thing you see, when you enter from Seuss Landing, is a statue of an armor-clad griffin. This grim guardian has become a favorite spot for tourists to pose for that "I was at Islands of Adventure" shot.

As you approach the Lost City, you glimpse over a craggy boulder an enormous hand holding an equally enormous trident. Only when you have walked a little farther do you realize that the boulder is an enormous head of the god Poseidon and what you are seeing are the remnants of a very large and very ancient statue that fell down eons ago. Just opposite is a brooding extinct volcano, with the faces of titans carved in its flanks. It hides Mythos, perhaps the most eye-popping restaurant in any Orlando theme park.

The grand scale and attention to detail in the architecture of The Lost Continent is exceeded only by the adjoining Wizarding World. It's rare that theme park visitors pause just to take pictures of buildings but it happens here all the time. Add to the visual splendor what many people consider to be one of the finest restaurants in any theme park in the world and The Lost Continent becomes a small but special island indeed.

Tip: A barely themed wooden bridge leads from near Mythos to the *Discovery Center* in Jurassic Park. This "temporary" addition, built during construction of the Wizarding World, allows you to bypass the Potter area when it's overpopulated. Look for it to remain as long as the crowds do.

Poseidon's Fury

Rating:	* * * +
Type:	Special effects extravaganza
Time:	About 25 minutes
Our Take:	Chaotic fun, but not everyone's cup of tea

Behind the ruins of Poseidon's statue lies his enormous temple, now cracked and crumbled by earthquakes, where his devotees once worshipped. Before entering, take a moment to drink in the scene. This is yet another of the park's triumphs of fantasy architecture. The scale alone is awe-inspiring. Check out the huge feet of Poseidon's now tumbled statue and the towering trident that stands nearby. Marvel at the once-gorgeous mosaic floors now running with water diverted from its ancient course by long-ago earthquakes. Stare up at the towering facade, its massive columns seemingly ready to topple at any moment. The art direction that has created not just the iconography of an ancient and imaginary religious cult but its language as well is truly impressive.

With understandable trepidation, we step inside to something of a disappointment — a cool, dimly lit, snaking passageway. The overall design and the fragmentary murals on the crumbling walls are vaguely Minoan in appearance, but other than the flickering lights, some hard-to-read signage from "Global Discovery Group," and the ominous music, there's nothing here to hint at what lies ahead, certainly no advancing "plot line" to keep visitors informed and entertained as the line inches forward.

When we reach the front of the queue line, we hear a static-filled walkie-talkie transmission: "Get out of the temple! If you can hear my voice, get out of the temple!"

Then we are greeted by Taylor, a very young and very nervous volunteer assistant to ace archaeologist, Professor Baxter. The prof seems to have disappeared along with everyone else on the dig while Taylor was on a lunch break. Too bad, because the professor had announced the discovery of a "secret message" but disappeared before he could tell anyone what it was. Taylor, played by a young guy or gal, gamely carries on with our tour of recent temple excavations.

The first chamber, which Taylor tells us is the Chamber of Sacrifices, contains an altar and ancient wall paintings documenting an epic struggle. Legend has it that a high priest of the temple, the dumbly named Lord Darkenon, seized power from Poseidon, sparking a battle in which all perished, and that the spirits of those combatants still haunt the ruined temple. There is another terrified transmission from Professor Baxter, and then all the lights go out.

Taylor grabs an ultraviolet lamp for illumination and in so doing reveals a hidden message written on the frieze that circles the chamber. Fortunately, the ancient Greeks had the foresight to write the message in English so Taylor can read it aloud. This turns out to be a big mistake because reading the message aloud awakens the spirit of Darkenon, who is no one's idea of a gracious host.

We don't want to spoil it for you, so suffice it say that your journey will take you into an even spookier chamber and finally into the middle of a pitched battle between Poseidon, who uses water as his weapon, and Lord Darkenon, who responds with fire. We're talking heavy artillery here, with more than 350,000 gallons of the wet stuff and 25-foot exploding fireballs.

We should note that this attraction has its detractors. Some people find the story line confusing and, in the heat of the battle, some of the dialogue does get hard to hear. Others just don't seem that impressed with the effects. The "water vortex" that was once the attraction's highlight has been disabled for over a year at press time. The substitute lighting effects may be more "green," but are not nearly as effective. For many people, their enjoyment of the show will depend on how long they have waited to see it.

The best seats in the house. The entire show is experienced standing up. In the second and third chambers, the audience stands on a series of steps set in a semicircle, with a guardrail on each level. In the first two chambers, it really doesn't matter where you stand.

For the final battle scene, however, you will have a good deal more fun if you are in the very first row. It seems like most people instinctively climb the steps, not realizing that you can actually stand in front of the first guardrail, on ground level so to speak. That means that you can simply walk to the front as you enter. Despite being almost on top of the action, you won't get terribly wet, although some of those towering explosions of water find their way into the audience.

The Eighth Voyage of Sindbad

Rating:	* * * +
Type:	Amphitheater show
Time:	About 20 minutes
Our Take:	Slapstick stunts and explosions galore

In a 1,750-seat theater we get to witness the eighth voyage of the legendary Sindbad (seven just weren't enough). This is a live-action stunt show that attempts to rival the Indiana Jones show over at that other movie studio park (no, not Universal) but is betrayed by the worst-written script in town.

Here Sindbad sets off on yet another search for riches untold, encountering along the way the inevitable life-threatening perils. It's an action-packed spectacular that features six "water explosions" and 50 — count 'em, 50 — of Universal's trademark pyrotechnic effects, including a 10-foot-tall circle of flames and a 22-foot-high fall by a stunt person engulfed in flames.

Sindbad and his trusty but talkative sidekick Kabob (as in "Shush, Kabob!") have traveled to a mysterious cavern filled with treasure and the bones of earlier adventurers. Here the evil sorceress Miseria holds the beautiful Princess Amora in thrall and only the Sultan's Heart, an enormous ruby with magical powers, can free her. It's Sindbad to the rescue, but first he must battle Miseria for the Sultan's Heart and the ultimate power that goes with it.

Sindbad fights valiantly on the Princess's behalf. But this is no wimpy maiden in distress. Amora is a princess for the postmodern age, with hair of gold and buns of steel, who can hold her own against evil monsters, thank you very much. Together, the three heroes battle the forces of evil in its many grisly guises and (we don't think we're giving anything away here) eventually triumph.

Sindbad's set alone, with its dripping stalagmites and crumbling pirate vessels, is stupendous. The show takes advantage of every inch of it, including the wrecked prow of an ancient ship that seems to have run aground in the very middle of the audience, and the stunts are all energetically executed by the athletic cast. Unfortunately, the dialogue is packed with clumsy one-liners and pop-culture anachronisms that drag the production down. The result is a dazzling but depressingly dumb display best enjoyed by children and non-English speakers.

The best seats in the house. If you enjoy getting wet, there are two "splash zones" in this show, one toward the front to the right of the audience and the other in the middle, to the left of the wrecked prow that juts into the seating area. Otherwise, every seat gives a good view of the action, which has very thoughtfully been spread all over the enormous set. Sitting a few rows back, just to the right of the wrecked prow, offers a particularly good perspective on the action, including some bone-crunching fights that happen almost on top of you.

Another good choice is the last row in front of either of the two arched entrances on the left and right. These seats give you a great panoramic view of the action, have a back rest, and offer a quick getaway at show's end. Another bonus, if you're sensitive to sound: the open archways behind you let the sound out instead of bouncing it back at you.

And all the rest ...

The Middle Eastern bazaar section, sometimes referred to as Sindbad's Village, houses a number of carnival-style games, much like those found along the Amity Boardwalk in Universal Studios Florida, just decorated different-ly. Also like those games, there must be some reason why people feel drawn to them, we just haven't figured it out yet.

Far more entertaining than another game of ring toss is the mysteri-ously smoking and bubbling **Mystic Fountain** that sits in front of the cen-tral entrance to the Sindbad show's amphitheater. Once just an interesting added touch to the fun of Lost Continent, the fountain has been elevated to the rank of a full-fledged attraction in the park map. It would appear to be dedicated to some ancient and mysterious oracle, to judge by the open-mouthed face sculpted into it. Indeed, this fountain even talks to you. Al-though it seems friendly enough, beware. Its hidden agenda seems to be to get you very, very wet.

Eating in The Lost Continent

The Lost Continent boasts the best restaurant in Universal Orlando's two theme parks — Mythos, which is among the better restaurants to be found in the theme parks of the world. For those who take a strictly utilitarian ap-proach to food, there are walk-up stands offering a quick and filling bite.

▉ Mythos Restaurant

What:	Fine dining
Where:	Opposite *Poseidon's Fury*
Price Range:	$$ - $$$

This upscale restaurant is the feather in Islands of Adventure's culinary cap. In keeping with the unspeakably ancient theme of the island, it is housed (if that's the right word) in an extinct volcano with water cascading down its weathered slopes. Step inside and you've entered a sea cavern whose sinuous walls have been carved out and smoothed by centuries of surging waves. Eerie yet soothing music tinkles through the air. In the main dining room, the cavern's roof vaults skyward and a large windowed opening gives out onto the lagoon and a spacious outdoor seating area. Subterranean streams run between the handsome seating areas, with seats upholstered in regal purple. The walls take on the shapes of long-vanished gods and their spirit minions. The effect is only a step or two this side of awesome. Decor like this is a hard act to follow, and you find yourself wondering if the food can rise to the level of your heightened expectations.

Not to worry. The cuisine produced under the direction of executive chef Steven Jayson and chef de cuisine Mark Wachowiak pays homage to the hallmarks of contemporary cuisine — intriguing combinations of ingredients and flavors, dazzling presentations — and still manages to taste, well, just plain yummy. Mythos' menu is not as ambitious today as it was at opening when whole roasted lobster was featured, but it still serves up consistently superior fare. The menu changes occasionally, so this menu description won't be exhaustive but will hopefully whet your appetite.

Soups and Appetizers ($5 to $10) always include the Chef's Signature Pizza of the Day. These are thin-crusted masterpieces that blend traditional cooking methods (there is a spectacular wood-fired pizza oven in clear view of the dining area) and eclectic ingredients that change with the seasons. One appetizer that has proven a perennial is the Tempura Shrimp Sushi, a miniature work of art served with a wasabi and soy drizzle. The soups are nothing short of ambrosial.

Salads ($6 to $14) range from deceptively simple bowls of mixed baby greens to elaborate entree-sized extravaganzas featuring chicken, shrimp, or fish. Pastas ($11 to $16) are meals in themselves. Be sure to ask about the "Pastabilities" selection, which changes regularly and allows the chef to show off a bit.

Entrees ($10 to $19) range from a not so humble cheeseburger with smoked applewood bacon to some very well-executed specialty sandwiches and wraps. The beloved Chicken a la Oscar and Balsamic Chicken are gone, but you can almost guarantee that the list of entrees will include Cedar Plank Bay of Fundy Salmon, Bistro Fillet with Truffle Butter, or Blueberry Pistachio Crusted Pork, all excellent. In addition to the pizza, the menu always includes a Risotto of the Day (often interesting, but sometimes underdone). You can add a small soup or salad to an entrée for $3. There is a kids' menu ($6 to $11) featuring simple dishes for the less sophisticated gourmet.

Tip: Ask if the chef has any off-menu specials (besides the pizza, risotto, and wrap, that is). From time to time, the chef will experiment with new dishes or whip up something to use up ingredients left over from last night's banquet. Many times these specials are more adventurous than items on the regular menu. We've never been disappointed. Gourmets take note!

After one of these terrific meals, desserts are generally a let down. Fortunately, there is the Warm Chocolate Banana Gooey Cake, which is spectacular and probably the only dessert worth ordering. The others are "mini-desserts" ($1.75 each) served in skinny shot glasses; they are the same ones served at Finnegan's and Lombard's in USF and are merely so-so.

The restaurant features an intelligent and reasonably priced wine list of American varietals along with some imports ($24 to $65). Many are available by the glass; feel free to ask for guidance. For something more potent, try the Potion of the Gods or a Mythos Martini (about $7). They also have their own brand of beer.

The restaurant seats 180 with an additional 50 seats outdoors, many of them sheltered by the overhanging volcano. Try for an outdoor seat if open on a balmy night.

Reservations are taken at Islands of Adventure's central reservations number, (407) 224-9255, but try the restaurant's direct line at (407) 224-4534 to feel like a regular. Mythos is only open from 11:00 a.m. to 3:00 p.m., although hours are extended during busy periods (Spring Break, mid-July through August, and the Christmas season).

Note: See *Good Things To Know About. . . Dining Passes,* above, for information on how to dine at Mythos without paying for park admission.

And after you've finished dining, it's just a short stroll to either the *Incredible Hulk* or the *Dragon Challenge* roller coasters. This could be the best meal you'll ever lose!

■ Fire Eaters Grill

> ***What:*** Walk-up fast food stand
> ***Where:*** Near *Poseidon's Fury*
> ***Price Range:*** $

This stand offers "walking sandwiches," which is good because the nearby outdoor seating is limited and not very well shaded. The fare is vaguely Middle Eastern and on the spicy side, featuring Grilled Gyros and both Chicken Fingers and Fiery Hot Chicken Stingers. Crispy chicken salads, chilli cheese dogs, and cheeseburgers round out the menu. There are cookies for dessert and plenty of ice cold soda and beer to wash it all down.

■ Frozen Desert

> ***What:*** Walk-up ice cream stand
> ***Where:*** In the bazaar area near the Sindbad Theater
> ***Price Range:*** $

In addition to Frozen Mirage Swirls in cup and goblet sizes, this ice cream stand also offers a Sultan's Sundae of vanilla and pineapple swirl topped with fresh pineapple. Somewhat more traditional is the Treasure Chest Sundae of vanilla and strawberry. You can create your own delight by choosing from a selection of Turban Toppings.

Shopping in The Lost Continent

Some of the best shopping at Islands of Adventure is to be found in the Lost Continent, especially if your taste runs to one-of-a-kind craft items.

The **Treasures of Poseidon**, near the exit of *Poseidon's Fury*, sells a grab bag of T-shirts, sandals, and (oddly enough) a variety of live plants.

In the *Sindbad* area, the **Coin Mint** features hand-minted medallions of bronze, silver, or "gold layered silver," made to order while you watch by an artisan who's garbed in Renaissance clothing and speaks in a simulation of a British regional accent. The master minter uses a heavily weighted guillotine-like device to slam the designs onto discs. The tented shop also sells chains in sterling silver and crystal pendants. Nearby, **Historic Families** offers classy coats of arms and accessories for the serious family historian. Especially nice are the elaborate hand-embroidered versions with two coats of arms designed to commemorate a marriage. And in case the marriage doesn't work out, the shop also sells daggers and swords. Things can get pricey here.

Entering the atmospheric tent that houses **Star Souls** transports you to a time before 900 numbers and the Psychic Friends Network. Here one of several fortune tellers will reveal your past and delve into your future — for a price. You can choose from sessions of various lengths for $15 to $75. Kids are welcome too. There always seems to be a line of willing seekers here.

Too timid for tattoos? The new-agey designs at **Mystic Henna Body Art** are painted on with henna and last anywhere from a few days to a few weeks before fading into memory. The **Pearl Factory** sells Japanese cultured pearls in a variety of settings at prices that start at about $29 and go up to $5,000 for a black Tahitian pearl necklace. For $16 you can pick an oyster and, if you like the pearl you find inside, have it set in a variety of gold settings for a modest fee.

The Middle Eastern bazaar section of The Lost Continent has other specialty shops that change from time to time, including one offering "Free Magic Shows" similar to the ones on Hollywood Boulevard in Universal Studios. Thus their omission here.

THE WIZARDING WORLD OF
■ HARRY POTTER ■

In 2007, Universal Orlando rocked the attraction industry by announcing a partnership with Warner Brothers and author J.K. Rowling to bring her mega-selling series about a United Kingdom conjuring academy into three-dimensional reality. Insiders speculated that securing the notoriously reticent Rowling's cooperation (in a deal that granted her unprecedented levels of artistic control over the project) could be the kind of coup that might finally allow Universal to beat Disney at its own game.

After three years of eagerly observed construction, the Wizarding World of Harry Potter premiered to the public on June 18, 2010, in a star-studded opening ceremony that was broadcast globally. Millions of Potter-maniacs, whose money helped make the books and films into a $15 billion dollar franchise, held their breaths in anticipation. Could this new section of Islands of Adventure possibly live up to the wonders they experienced on page and screen? Well, the verdict is in, and it is a resounding "Yeeesss!"

From the moment you step under the stone archway into Hogsmeade Village (beneath a sign reading "Please Respect the Spell Limits"), you will be completely enveloped in this enchanted universe. The word "immersive" is ubiquitous in the themed-entertainment business, but nowhere else on earth is its application more apt. When you walk into the Wizarding World, you don't feel like you've just entered another area in an amusement park; you've seemingly been transported into the charmingly archaic Scottish hamlet where Harry and his friends relax on winter holidays, down to the worn cobblestone streets and sparkling snow-capped eaves. Everywhere you look, from the Hogwarts Express train belching steam to the exquisitely detailed storefront windows, you'll find an overabundance of exacting detail that makes this area – which was carved from the former "Merlinwood" section of Lost Continent, as well as some previously unused nearby acreage – seem far richer than its 20-acre size might suggest. Simply put, this is the most visually dense attraction in any park, Mouse-made or otherwise, with the possible exception of Tokyo DisneySea in Japan.

Universal may have somewhat oversold the scope of the expansion by initially referring to it as a "park within a park." The area is similar in size to the other "islands," and no separate admission is required. And return visitors to IOA will remember the area's re-purposed roller coasters, which may explain why they always have less of a wait than the other Potter attractions.

141

Still, the area is enormously popular, with dedicated Potter devotees waiting hours in the hot sun just to enter their hero's home.

However, the Wizarding World's greatest asset is also its Achilles' heel: the authentically intimate scale of the streets and stores. Unlike many other oversized epic fantasies, the Potter books and films depict a more human-scaled world of congested markets and narrow alleyways. Confines here are just as cramped as Rowling imagined, which is great for preserving the illusion but poor for pedestrian management.

In order to keep this compact area from being overwhelmed by eager visitors, Universal will "pulse" small groups of visitors into the land only as earlier guests depart. On busy days, the queue to enter the area may stretch from Jurassic Park through Toon Lagoon to Marvel, with guests issued numbered tickets to prevent line-jumping. If faced with a line to enter, we instead recommend waiting until late afternoon or evening to visit, when crowds are thinner and nighttime illumination makes the area even more entrancing.

If you aren't already a Potter-head, you'll want to pick up at least the first few novels or films to better appreciate the area, which is currently focused on the first four "years" in the seven-book series. Even if you're merely a Muggle with no prior Potter interest, the beauty and wit you'll find here may inspire you to start reading once you return home.

Except for a few celebrity "Imagineers" like Disney's Tony Baxter and Joe Rohde, theme park designers are largely anonymous. But if any attraction ever proved that this is an art-form like any other, Wizarding World is it and artists deserve credit for their creations. So, to the ride designers (Mark Woodbury and Thierry Coup), art directors (Oscar-winner Stuart Craig and Alan Gilmore, who recreated their work from the films), and show directors (Mike Aiello, Lyle Moon, Anitra Pritchard, and Patrick Braillard), a well-earned round of applause.

Harry Potter and the Forbidden Journey

Rating:	* * * * *
Type:	Next-generation dark thrill ride
Time:	About 30 minutes for the tour, 4 minutes for the ride
Our Take:	The best theme-park ride in the Western Hemisphere

As you emerge from Hogsmeade and round the corner, you'll catch sight of an awe-inspiring vision: the majestic spires of Hogwarts Castle, home to the ancient school where Harry and his schoolmates learn the ways of wizardry. Perched high atop a craggy cliff face, the edifice is actually an empty shell perched atop a massive camouflaged show building, but thanks to clever use of forced perspective it appears even larger and more impos-ing, if less colorful, than Cinderella's digs down the road.

Tip: Duck into the first cliff crevice for a glimpse behind the scenes.

Pass between the school's stone gates (which mystically glow with the attraction's name at night) and enter the castle dungeon to begin your ad-venture.

Tip: If a line extends outside the castle, it may be for the lockers, lo-cated to the right of the entrance. If you don't have any loose belongings, proceed past the line to the left.

Note: This ride requires that you stow all your belongings in electronic lockers located immediately inside the entrance. They are free for a period of time that varies with the queue length, but charge a hefty fee if you over-stay your welcome. Be aware that wand boxes may not fit in the lockers, though you may use the "baby swap" as a "wand swap." For more informa-tion, see *Good Things To Know About...Lockers* in *Chapter One.*

Tip: There is a small pouch in the back of each rider's seat, just big enough for your keys, wallet, and cellphone or compact camera. Don't for-get your belongings when your journey ends!

Forbidden Journey is actually comprised of two attractions in one. The first is the queue, cleverly disguised as an elaborate walking tour of Hog-warts, which has opened its doors to non-magical Muggles like yourself for the first time in its ten-century history. (For serious continuity nerds, your visit occurs on a day "frozen in time" outside of the Potter canon, sometime between the events of *Goblet of Fire* and *Half-Blood Prince.*) Waiting in line is rarely considered entertainment, but here is the exception; with more details and effects than most entire attractions, this surpasses Disneyland's *Indiana Jones Adventure* as America's most impressive holding pen. If you were to walk slowly through the queue with no one ahead of you, examining the artifacts and watching all the effects, it would take almost thirty min-utes. The production values are high enough that even those uninterested in the ride should still experience the castle tour.

Tip: "Single Riders" will start their tour in the final chambers, skipping 90% of the castle queue, so be sure to take the standard line your first trip through. Universal Express (if available) utilizes a line that experiences al-most all of the magical effects, including a private portrait gallery.

Warning: Spoilers Ahead!

The tour begins in the dungeon, where you'll see screen-accurate repro-ductions of artifacts like the "One-Eyed Witch" and "Mirror of Erised," and pass by the "Potions Classroom" where Neville Longbottom can be heard being upbraided yet again for his ignorance. Emerge from the dark dungeon into the sunny greenhouse, where Professor Sprout's magical herbs, like hanging pitcher plants and mandrakes (thankfully silent), are raised.

Note: If the extended queue outside the greenhouse is in use, anticipate at least an hour wait before entering the air-conditioned interior.

Once inside the castle corridors, you will spend twenty to thirty minutes exploring some of Hogwarts' most iconic locations. Begin by passing a series of ancient-looking statues, including one of the school's architect, and the regal stone griffin that guards the Headmaster's office. Next you'll encounter a portrait gallery, featuring one of Universal's most startling effects: paintings that move and speak, appearing even up close to be oil on canvas instead of video projections. The four founders of Hogwarts (Godric Gryffindor, Rowena Ravenclaw and Helga Hufflepuff, and the never-before-seen Salazar Slytherin) greet you and bicker about the presence of Muggles inside their school.

Next, you'll enter the spectacular set of Headmaster Dumbledore's office, exactingly reproduced from the films, right down to the Pensive in the corner. Dumbledore appears (played by actor Michael Gambon in a startlingly real upgrade of *Disaster!*'s "Musion" hologram effect) welcomes you, warning that "the time may come when you must chose between what is right, and what is easy." Oh, and look out for Hagrid's pet dragon, which has apparently gotten loose again.

Exiting the office, you encounter the Defense Against the Dark Arts classroom, festooned with skeletal beasts and other occult artifacts, where you are promised a multi-hour lecture on Hogwarts history. Luckily, Harry Potter himself (played by Daniel Radcliffe), along with his friends Ron (Rupert Grint) and Hermione (Emma Watson), materialize on a balcony above you from beneath their Invisibility Cloak (another amazing Musion). They invite you to play hooky with them, skipping the boring lecture in favor of a game of Quidditch (the series' flying-broom-based sport). Soon you are swept past the "Fat Lady" portrait that guards the Griffindor Common Room into the lounge's comfy confines, where a trio of new paintings prepare you to board the "enchanted benches" that will take you on your adventure.

The final step in your preparation comes courtesy of an animatronic Sorting Hat, who delivers the safety spiel in rhyming verse. Finally, you enter the floating candlestick-filled Room of Requirement, which doubles as the boarding area. Four guests at a time step onto a two-stage moving sidewalk (similar to Disney's *Haunted Mansion*) and are fastened side-by-side into one of 40-odd golden, high-backed benches, that flow by in a constantly

Above: The funnies come to life. (Toon Lagoon)

Left: A velociraptor is born. (Jurassic Park)

Below left: Spidey drops in for lunch. (Port of Entry)

Below right: Like they say, you will get wet. (Toon Lagoon)

Above: Getting off to a good start on the Hulk. (Marvel Super Hero Island)

Right: There are surprises lurking in those bushes. (Jurassic Park)

Below: Dudley Do-Right and pals get their own Mt. Rushmore. (Toon Lagoon)

Above: Hogwarts Castle throws open its doors to Muggles.

Left: Are you in need of a wand?

Below: A typical Hogsmeade street scene, complete with butterbeer.

(All photos from the Wizarding World of Harry Potter)

Above: The Hogsmeade Express has arrived.

Right: Wizards shop, too.

Below right: Food fit for a wizard at the 3 Broomsticks.

Below left: Let's get Sirius.

(All photos from the Wizarding World of Harry Potter)

Above: Jimmy Buffett's Hemisphere Dancer touches down outside Margaritaville. (CityWalk)

Left: The world's largest Hard Rock Cafe. (CityWalk)

Below: Blue Man Group brings avant garde weirdness to Universal. (CityWalk)

Top: A complimentary water taxi takes you to ...

Above: ... Portofino, Italy. (Portofino Bay Hotel)

Right: Relax in high style at the Villa Pool. (Portofino Bay Hotel)

Above: A guitar fountain graces the entrance. (Hard Rock Hotel)

Left: Desserts at The Kitchen. (Hard Rock Hotel)

Below left: Universal Orlando's hippest pool. (Hard Rock Hotel)

Below right: Frogs stand guard at Islands Dining Room. (Royal Pacific Resort)

Universal Orlando Resort © 2010

Above: Elephants frolic in the lobby courtyard. (Royal Pacific Resort)

Right: Memorabilia adds fun to Jake's American Bar. (Royal Pacific Resort)

Below: Recreating the tropical glamour of a bygone era. (Royal Pacific Resort)

Universal Orlando Resort © 2010

moving stream. The purple seats feature overhead restraints similar to a roller coaster, but with a curved handlebar to grip, and partitions that prevent you from looking at other riders.

With John Williams' theme music twinkling in your seat-mounted speakers, you glide sedately sideways until Hermione scatters some "Floo powder" over you. All at once your feet lift off the ground as you lean backwards, flying up through a network of chimneys, and floating into the castle's towering Observatory. Next, you are summoned by Harry and Ron, riding by on their broomsticks, and you plunge through the window after them, skimming precariously along Hogwarts' rocky foundations. Catching up with the boys, who assure you they haven't lost anyone on these "dodgy" devices yet ("this week, anyway"), you are confronted with Hagrid's missing dragon. Putting your Quidditch match on hold, you hide from the creature inside the creaky old Covered Bridge; you can spot his massive wing beating against the windows, and scorch-marks appear on the walls. Suddenly the floor collapses, dropping you eye-to-eye with the fire-breather, who delivers a warm blast of steam in your face. That sends you spiraling down into the Forbidden Forest, lair of Aragog the enormous Acromantula and his web-spitting kin.

Before you say we've given it all away, that's barely the first third of the adventure! Before you're done, you'll be whacked by the Whomping Willow, watch a Quidditch play up-close, and see a Dementor suck your soul right out of your body. It's a dark, discombobulating, and often startling experience that will leave you breathless (and moist). Naturally, all ends well, with cheering throngs in the Great Hall, a wizardly admonishment to "tuck your elbows in," and a final tumble down the Floo Network back the room where you began.

End of Spoilers!

After your journey, all that remains is to tumble downstairs into Filch's Emporium (see Shopping below), check out your souvenir photo, and sprint to rejoin the line, no matter how long it is. *Forbidden Journey* is the only ride Seth has gleefully waited an hour for immediately after having just waited an hour.

The Best Seats in the House: All four seats on each bench are excellent, but the middle two give the least-distorted view of the curved screens. The "front" seat (far left when seated) gets the biggest "boo" scares, while the "back" seat (far right when seated) experiences the most motion.

How did Universal Creative create this masterpiece? By starting with the template they pioneered with *Spider-Man*: motion-simulator seats moving through a seamless blend of physical effects and projection screens.

This time, they upgraded the sets from *Spider-Man's* comic-book styliza-tion to fully sculpted environments that seem to extend in all directions, then stuffed them with animatronic monsters that aggressively lunge within feet of your face. As for the video, it ditches the 3-D (the glasses would go flying), but makes up for it with high-definition footage featuring the film stars, projected onto vision-encompassing domes (think smaller-sized *Simpsons* screens, mounted on a clever carousel contraption that gives ev-ery car a sweet-spot perspective).

What elevates *Forbidden Journey* above those predecessors is the KUKA Robocoaster, a world-exclusive new technology that takes an indus-trial robotic arm and for the first time mounts it on a moving track. The result is not a roller-coaster. There are no sustained speeds, big drops, or upside-down moments. Nor is it a traditional simulator. With your legs dangling free, you have an unprecedented feeling of "floating" that will have you flat on your back and leaning dynamically from side to side. The motion is extraordinarily smooth, never jerky or jarring, though its intensity will be disorienting to those prone to motion sickness. Then again, many will find temporary queasiness a fair price to pay for this kind of exhilaration.

Most amazing is the way that this next-generation underpinning is completely invisible to the rider. As long as you keep your head back in your seat as instructed, you'll never see the arm holding you aloft. Nor will you see any other ride vehicles, making it seem like a uniquely personal adven-ture. That is an amazing feat when you consider that a new vehicle can be dispatched every seven seconds.

Tip: After your first few times through, try sitting in an outside seat and leaning slightly forward for insight on how the magic happens.

Just because *Forbidden Journey* is the new attraction champion of Or-lando (and possibly the world) doesn't mean it's perfect. The trip is dizzyingly chaotic, and the bare-bones plot boils down to a greatest-hits mishmash of memorable action moments from the films. The projected sequences seem somewhat blurry, likely due to your extreme proximity to the screen and the rapid movement of the action. And a few of the spooky animatronics appear unconvincing after repeated rides. But these are minor quibbles that don't detract from this being a five-star attraction in the truest spirit of that score.

One issue that may keep some away are size restrictions imposed by the safety restraints. Though the ride utilizes an over-the-shoulder harness sim-ilar to standard looping coasters, some visitors with larger chest, tummy, or thigh dimensions may have difficulty getting the locking mechanism to give the "three clicks" required. While the safety restrictions are justified by the unique forces the ride places on you (unlike a coaster there is no centrifugal force to pin you in your seat), some people who would not be considered obese may find themselves denied due to their proportions.

Universal has not issued any official measurement requirements beyond the 48" minimum height, and they point out that basketball star Dwight Howard rode safely. But informally we've heard of 300-pound weight and 52" torso/waist maximums. As a rule of thumb, if you are able to ride the coasters without needing the special double seat-belts, you should be okay. If you have any doubt, test out the sample seats outside the attraction entrance. Even if you get the "green light" outside, you may be retested before boarding. Don't take it personally, the attendants are only looking out for your safety, and Univeral says it is working on making the ride accessible to more people.

Tip: An alternate stationary loading platform is available for those needing to transfer from a wheelchair, or anyone physically unable to navigate the moving belt. Just ask an attendant for assistance.

Forbidden Journey fuses emotionally engaging characters, astounding images, and unprecedented physical sensations in a near-ideal package. It redefines the term "ground-breaking" in relation to ride technology, and should be experienced by anyone physically able to handle the "dramatic aerobatics." If you're anything like us, you'll be sprinting back (through the much-shorter Single Ride line) every chance you get. And if you aren't, there's no shame in taking the "chicken exit" and skipping the ride, because the castle tour alone is worth the wait.

At press time Universal Express is not available on the ride, so visit first thing or after sunset to avoid a lengthy wait in the heat.

Dragon Challenge

Rating:	* * * * +
Type:	Twin roller coasters
Time:	1.5 minutes
Our Take:	Aaaargh!

An easily overlooked stone archway marks the entrance to this immense inverted steel roller coaster, hidden behind the stone wall through which the Hogwarts Express appears to emerge. Actually, two separate roller coasters lurk back there, travelling along separate but closely intertwined tracks that diverge and then converge to terrifying effect.

Note: This ride requires that you stow all your belongings in electronic lockers located immediately outside the entrance, in a shelter disguised as a train station. They are free for a period of time that varies with the queue length, but charge a hefty fee if you overstay your welcome.

This coaster (formerly known as *Dueling Dragons*) is themed after the first of three tasks comprising the "Triwizard Tournament," the wizarding competition seen in the fourth Potter tale, *Goblet of Fire*. Begin by walking the meandering path toward the small (compared to Hogwarts) castle ahead. Along the way, you'll pass banners supporting Harry Potter and his competitors Fleur Delacort and Victor Krum (though Cedric Diggory goes unmentioned), and the Weasley's flying Ford Anglia, which has crashed into a nearby tree. Pass into the stone structure and you enter the Champions's Tent, where the Goblet of Fire stands spewing an otherworldly blue flame. Further ahead, you'll find the Triwizard Cup itself on a pedestal, a trio of golden dragon eggs, and a chamber filled with flickering floating candles. Those who remember the wonderfully macabre theming of the *Dueling Dragons* queue will be disappointed by the labyrinth of featureless stone walls that follows, but eventually you will be asked to turn left toward the red "Chinese Fireball" or right to the blue "Hungarian Horntail." While waiting for your coaster, look up at the shadowy dragons battling above the ruined ceiling.

This is an inverted coaster, which means that the cars, completely dressed to look like dragons, hang from a track over your head. Your feet dangle in the air below your seat. When the cars are fully loaded the passengers look as though they are hanging from the dragons' claws. Then it's off on a ninety-second ride over a lake that is actually shaped like a dragon, a fact that few people who ride this attraction are likely to notice.

The two coasters share the same lift to the top of the first drop, but then the Chinese Fireball peels off to the left as the Hungarian Horntail swoops to the right. After that, their separate trips are carefully synchronized so that, as they loop and swirl their way around, they meet in mid air at three crucial moments. A computer actually weighs each coaster and then makes the appropriate adjustments to get the timing just right. Perhaps the scariest close encounter comes when they come straight at one another on what is obviously a head-on collision course. At the last moment, they spin up and apart with the dangling feet of the riders coming within a foot or two of each other at nearly 60 miles per hour. At another point, both coasters enter a double helix, spinning dizzily around one another. All told there are three near misses in the 50 seconds or so it takes to travel from the first drop to the point where the coasters slow down to reenter the castle. If you've ever asked yourself what could be more terrifying than the current generation of high-speed steel roller coasters, ask no more.

Some people find this ride so extreme, the motion so violent, and the experience so short that they can't decide whether they liked it or not. Indeed, you'll notice many people exiting in stunned puzzlement.

Tip: If you'd like to get a preview of this ride, look for the exit. It's to your left as you face the entrance. A short way up, you will find a viewing area behind a high metal fence; most likely a number of departing riders will have paused here for another look. This vantage point gives you a pretty good view of the twin coasters' routes. For those who have no intention of ever strapping themselves into this coaster, it's a pretty entertaining attraction in of itself.

It's also possible to enter the queue line itself for a peek. Just a short way in is a spot where you can witness two of the ride's close encounters up close. You'll actually feel the wind rush through your hair as the coasters spiral past. If this dissuades you from venturing farther you can turn back.

The best seats in the house. The first row is the clear choice for the thrill seeker. Otherwise, the outside seats in each row give a better view (if you have your eyes open!) and are less likely to induce motion sickness. Seats farther back in the vehicle offer a different ride experience, partly because you can't see what's coming and partly because the back rows snap about with a bit more zip. Finally, the left hand track is more "aggressive" than the right one; that is, it has a few more spins to it and moves a bit faster at some points. Overall, our favorite seats are the first row inside on the Hungarian Horntail, and the last row outside on the Chinese Fireball.

Tip: *Dragon Challenge* is the only ride with a "re-ride" door. If the wait is less than 15 minutes, ride attendants will open this door and let you get back on immediately.

Flight of the Hippogriff

Rating:	* * * +
Type:	A junior roller coaster
Time:	About a minute
Our Take:	Best for the view of Hogsmeade

Just past Hogsmeade Village and just before you enter Hogwarts Castle, you'll find a stone monolith marking the entrance to this cute coaster. Formerly known as *The Flying Unicorn*, the ride was re-themed around one of the favorite pets of Rubeus Hagrid, Hogwarts' "care of magical creatures" instructor. Eager riders wind around Hagrid's pumpkin patch and stone hut on the fringe of the Forbidden Forest, listening as the gentle giant instructs us on the proper way to approach the proud Hippogriff.

We board one of the two 16-rider trains, which appear to be made of woven wicker, and are urged to bow respectfully to the life-size animatronic eagle/horse that sits nodding in its track-side nest. After a slow climb to the first drop, which provides a spectacular view of the Wizarding World and beyond, the coaster glides briefly through a series of dips and swoops before returning to the wooden hut that serves as the station.

Smaller kids will delight in the gentle ride from the slower front seats, but even adults have been know to squeal when sitting in the surprisingly zippy back rows. Though the "Vekoma Junior" track is similar to Woody Woodpecker's coaster next door in USF, the *Hippogriff* is 400 feet longer, 15 feet taller, and 7 m.p.h. swifter. Striking vistas and rich themeing make this a worthwhile spin even for childless grown-ups.

Ollivander's Wand Shop

Rating: * * * *
Type: Small-scale show
Time: About 5 minutes
Our Take: A charmingly magical moment not to be missed

A mysteriously levitating wand in the window marks this Hogsmeade storefront, behind which hides the sleeper attraction everyone will be talking about back home. Though it doesn't even appear on the park map, people line up for hours to enter this Rowling-approved franchise of the famous Diagon Alley purveyor, "maker of fine wands since 382 BC."

Groups of twenty-odd guests are allowed at a time into the tiny shop, its towering shelves stocked with dusty boxes. The kindly proprietor greets you, and selects one or two lucky customers (almost always children) to test out a wand. As Potter followers know, wands have embedded in their cores various magic substances like unicorn hair or a phoenix feather, and each wand must choose its own master. As the volunteers test the "wrong" wands, a range of disastrous special effects are triggered. Flowers wilt and shelving collapses, requiring the shopkeep to magically repair the damage. Finally, the destined wand is found, as signified by a swirl of light and wind straight out of the cinema.

Afterwards, the volunteers are sent into the adjoining Owl Post store to pay for their new wand (or another of their choosing), and the next group is ushered in. There is no charge to attend or participate in the show, if you want to take your wand home it will run about $30 (see Shopping below).

The entire show lasts about five minutes, the queue can be daunting, and the effects are sweetly simple. But the actors involved are so engagingly "in character" (all with exhaustive knowledge of wand arcana and credible accents) that it's worth the wait, especially if your child is the one selected.

Tip: There are multiple "spells" rigged throughout the shop, so repeat visitors will experience slightly different shows.

And all the rest ...

There are no formally scheduled theater shows within the Wizarding World. Nor are there any actors portraying "Harry Potter" or any other name characters (you'll have to go on the ride to see them). But there are a number of interactive entertainments involving less-famous Potter characters that are worth seeking out.

The **Hogwarts Express Conductor** watching over the train at the area's Lost Continent entrance is more than a living prop for photo-ops. He's a veritable wealth of knowledge about the attraction and all Potter lore; just try to stump him.

Several times daily, one of two performances is presented in front of the pseudo-Celtic, rune-covered monolith across from the friendly frozen snowman. Both are good fun, but operate on an unpublished schedule. No set show times are listed on the park map (yet), but performances usually occur a couple times each hour, so hang around and see what pops up.

The **Frog Choir,** briefly seen in *Prisoner of Azkaban,* is an a cappella choir consisting of four Hogwarts students and two bass-singing toads (psst, they're puppets). The group, led by an emphatically gesticulating conductor, performs beat-box versions of songs from the Potter scores, such as "Hedwig's Theme" and "Something Wicked This Way Comes."

At the **Triwizard Spirit Rally,** the visiting students from the Beauxbatons and Durmstrung show off their school pride. First the lovely French ladies demonstrate their ribbon dancing talents to a classical soundtrack. Then the Russian lads show off their martial arts skills with some fighting-stick acrobatics. Afterwards, everyone poses for pictures.

When you are exhausted from your adventures, seek refuge from the sun in **The Owlery**, a pleasantly shaded area beneath the innards of a rustic clockwork bell tower. Animatronic owls roost in the rafters, depositing realistic droppings on the beams below.

The restrooms, located across from Ollivander's, are an attraction in and of themselves. Not only do you get to dry your hands with those nifty

"Dyson AirBlades," but you can hear the ghostly **Moaning Myrtle** sighing and weeping. If you have young kids you're probably used to hearing a little child cry while you try to pee; for us it was an odd new experience.

But the greatest Potter attraction is the one most likely to be overlooked in the rush to the headliner rides. Each street-facing window, including the ones that front inaccessible facades, contains delightfully detailed dressing and animated illusions. Hidden touches abound, from floating dishes to rolling eyeballs. Here are a just few to keep an eye out for:

The goblin-run bank *Gringotts* has an ATM branch near the back patio. *Spintwitches* sporting goods sells quivering quidditch equipment (spot the runaway Golden Snitch flying in their window). *Tomes & Scrolls* displays living pictures of Gilderoy Lockhart (Kenneth Branagh), while *Scrivenshaft's & Pottage's* stock quills and cauldrons that work by themselves. Inside *Dogweed & Deathcap Exotic Plants* you'll spot a potted Shrieking Mandrake and other freaky flora. *Gladrags Wizardwear* has Heromine's Yule Ball gown, with a tailor-tape cat pawing at its hem. In *Dominic Maestro's* second-story music shop, when the enchanted cello hits a bad note, sheet music flies. And outside the Three Broomsticks, dishes wash themselves!

Eating in the Wizarding World

The Potter stories are filled with exotic foodstuffs and impossible beverages that have had readers salivating for years. In bringing to life the Wizarding World, J.K. Rowling was just as involved with the creation of comestibles as she was with the rides. Executive Chef Steven Jayson worked to ensure everything not only looked, smelled, and tasted as Rowling described, but also met her standards for nutrition. And ingredients for everything had to be shipped to Scotland for her personal approval. That's why you'll find Butterbeer and pumpkin juice to drink, but no corn syrup-based Coke products.

Speaking of Butterbeer, it's the most popular drink on everyone's lips (literally), and every bit as good as you've dreamed. It's a vanilla shortbread cookie flavored soda, with a thick head of butterscotch non-dairy whipped topping. It's sweet but not overbearingly cloying and almost universally adored. The only debate is "cold" vs. slushie-style "frozen." We vote for frozen while standing outside in line, then cold with your meal. A disposable cup will cost about $3 cold and $4 frozen. A 16-ounce souvenir vessel is $10 to $11, and can be refilled for the disposable price.

Tip: It's almost always quicker to get a Butterbeer inside the air-conditioned Hog's Head Pub or Three Broomsticks restaurant than at the scenic cart in the center of Hogsmeade's thoroughfare. Three Broomsticks offers a nine-ounce cup for $2, if you just want a sample.

Pumpkin Juice ($6) is more of an acquired taste. People either love its Thanksgiving pie spices and pulpy texture, or can't take more than a sip. Some say it's better at room temperature. We say the best part is the cute pumpkin-topped bottle. Other unusual drinks available in Three Broomsticks include pumpkin fizz (carbonated pumpkin juice) and non-alcoholic apple or pear cider ($3).

▌ The Three Broomsticks

What: British fare in an enchanted setting
Where: On your left as you enter from Lost Continent
Price Range: $$

Grab a seat inside the tavern where Harry and his classmates unwind after a hard day of supernatural scholarship. The entrance, marked by the namesake trio of broomsticks, may appear deceptively brown and bland, as it is intended to blend in with the surrounding village. But look for subtle magical touches throughout its rough-hewn walls. The design of this wood-timbered restaurant actually inspired the look of *The Half-Blood Prince* film's set, instead of the other way around. So the elaborate catwalks and seemingly endless ceilings appear to have stepped straight off the screen. From time to time, shadows of house elves and delivery owls at work appear on the walls, surrounding you with wizardry while you dine.

The eating experience itself falls somewhere between counter-service and sit-down dining. You'll be directed by a greeter to a numbered cashier, who stands in front of an animated menu, in the style of Potter newspapers. Place your order, then pick up your food from an adjacent counter. You will be shown to an empty table by a staff member who will bus your tray at the end, and even refuse a tip. It's a far more civilized system than elbowing your way around similar quick-service eateries, but it can lead to lines out the door at peak mealtimes.

Tip: If it's not too hot outside, try a table on the back patio with a view of the lagoon.

Menu offerings are as authentically British as any you'll find in a theme park, and tastier in some cases than in many an authentic pub. Shepherd's Pie ($10) is slightly spicy seasoned ground beef and minced vegetables covered with a piped mashed potato crust; it's served with a standard iceberg salad and an un-magical selection of dressings. Cornish Pasties ($8, with salad) take a similar meat filling and stuff it into three small half-moon pastries, sort of like British empanadas. Finally, the Fish and Chips ($12) features three generous pieces of sustainably caught white fillets, fried in an ale-infused batter, and served with wedge-cut potatoes and tartar sauce. More American-oriented entrees include rotisserie smoked chicken ($10), chargrilled ribs ($14) and combo platters ($12), all served with roasted potatoes and corn on the cob. If you've a Hagrid-sized appetite, consider the "Great Feast" ($50 for four, $13 each additional serving), a giant-sized rib and chicken combo platter with salad. Other options include baked potato ($3), split pea or potato leek soup ($6 with salad), or a rotisserie chicken salad ($9). Desserts ($4) include strawberry & peanut-butter ice cream, apple pie, and a chocolate trifle with cake and fresh berries.

In the mornings, a fixed-price breakfast is served for $15 including beverage. Choose from the traditional British breakfast (with black pudding, grilled tomato, and baked beans, a big hit with the Virgin Holiday tourists), Continental (with croissants and jam), American (scrambled eggs, bacon, sausage, potatoes), porridge, pancakes, or Scottish smoked salmon.

Attached to the side of the restaurant is the **Hog's Head Pub**, a gloriously grimy shrine to intoxication. In addition to virgin Butterbeers, there's a fine selection of European brews ($6.50) on tap, including Guinness, Bass, Stella Artois, Newcastle, Boddingtons, and Strongbow. (Bud Light is available for those who refuse to get in the spirit). The featured potable is "Hog's Head Brew" a hoppy dark-amber Scottish ale brewed exclusively for the park. Sadly, the "Firewhiskey" on display isn't drinkable, nor is any hard liquor available (though there is wine behind the bar if you prefer).

Tip: Be sure to slide the barkeep a tip if you want to see the establishment's grizzly namesake (mounted behind the bar beside a brace of shrunken heads) come snorting to life.

Shopping in the Wizarding World

For many, shopping will be as much an attraction in the Wizarding World as the rides. There are no "Toys R Us" action figures or "I Survived" T-shirts here. Instead, everything for sale has been custom-designed down to the packaging to look like it was delivered direct from Harry's world. If you are any kind of fan, be prepared to drop a bundle.

Tip: These tiny shops are often packed during the day, so save your shopping for closing time. A limited selection is also found in Port of Entry's Trading Company and CityWalk's Universal Studios Store.

Zonko's Joke Shop stocks fantastical toys like "Fanged Flyer" toothy frisbees, "Comb-a-Chamelon" color-changing hairbrushes, "Screaming Yo-

Yos" and "Sneakoscope" spinning tops (all around $10), alongside retro playthings like chattering teeth and tin-toy robots. The hottest seller is the "Pygmy Puff" ($20), a stuffed pink Tribble look-alike that gets a bell-ringing naming ceremony with each adoption; don't be surprised if they are out of stock (or "breeding"). The upper reaches of the Oriental-styled red shelves are stuffed with strange creatures, vintage Halloween decorations, and curios like a box of "Portable Swamp." Don't forget to eavesdrop on the Extendable Ears that dangle from the ceiling near the sales register.

Adjoining Zonko's is **Honeydukes Sweetshop,** a pastel candyland that could give Willy Wonka a toothache. Popular items include the "Chocolate Frog" ($10), a solid milk chocolate amphibian that comes with a collectable "famous wizard" trading card, and "Bertie Bott's Every-Flavour Beans" ($10) with tastes including Ketchup, Black Pepper, and Mashed Potatoes. The treacle fudge is too sugary to swallow, but we can vouch for the yummy dark chocolate Peppermint Toads ($8) and cinnamon "Pepper Imps" ($5).

Dervish and Banges specializes in wizarding school supplies, from neckties ($30) and class robes ($100, in sizes from XXXS to XXXL) to Quidditch Bludgers and Golden Snitches. If you admire the hovering brooms tethered to the second-story balcony, you can take home a Firebolt or Nimbus 2000 for $250 to $300 (non-flying models only, alas). And say hello to the Monster Book of Monsters snoozing in his cage, but watch out; he bites when woken.

Owl Post is a small annex of Dervish and Banges that serves as the exit for Ollivander's wand shop, so it quickly becomes claustrophobic. Here guests can purchase their own wand ($30), selecting a reproduction of a favorite character's instrument, or picking one of 13 original designs based on a fanciful 13-symbol zodiac. You can also buy Wizarding World-themed U.S. mail stamps ($15 for 10) and have your outgoing mail stamped with a Hogsmeade postmark (a postal box sits outside the shop). And you can't miss the holographic "Howlers" screaming at passersby from the window.

Filch's Emporium of Confiscated Goods, at the exit of the *Forbidden Journey* ride, is festooned with items reclaimed from rambunctious students, like copies of *Quibbler* magazine, Whammy Rockets, and bottles of Skele-Gro potion. While those props from the films aren't for sale, everything else is, including fold-out Marauder Maps ($70 in a handsome wood and glass case), Sorting Hat puppets ($30), and reproduction Death Eater masks ($100). If you want a T-shirt declaring your allegiance to Bellatrix Lestrange or other baddies, this is the place. Of course, you can also view and purchase souvenir photos of your *Journey* here ($20 for a single print, packages from $30 and up).

■ JURASSIC PARK ■

If you've seen the movie *Jurassic Park*, you will recognize the arches that greet you as you enter. If you haven't, you should make sure to rent the original film from your local video store before coming. Knowing the film will help you understand a lot of the little details of Jurassic Park, including the frequent references to velociraptors.

Here, Universal's design wizards have re-created the theme park that the movie's John Hammond was trying to create before all prehistoric heck broke loose, and the lush and steamy jungle landscape they have devised fits in perfectly with Florida's humid summers.

As in the movie, we are asked to believe that we are in a park containing actual living dinosaurs, some of which are quite dangerous. Periodically, roars are heard, and we've seen more than one child start in terror when an unseen critter growled in the underbrush. Unfortunately, the surprisingly realistic atmosphere has been somewhat disrupted by the boy wizard's arrival. It's understandably difficult to hide a huge honking castle, but hopefully they'll at least give its backside a coat of "go-away green" in the future.

Discovery Center

Rating:	* * +
Type:	Interactive displays
Time:	Unlimited
Our Take:	Best for young dinosaur buffs

This is lifted almost straight from the film and houses a fast food restaurant, a shop and, on the ground floor, a children's "science center," which blends fantasy and reality in such a way that you might have to explain the difference to your more trusting kids. Kids will certainly recognize the huge T-Rex skeleton that perches menacingly on a rock outcropping and pokes its head through to the circular railing on the upper level.

A nursery carefully incubates dinosaur eggs. Nearby, kids can handle "real" dino eggs and put them in a scanner to view the developing embryo inside. Periodically an attendant appears and conducts a deadpan scientific show-and-tell as you watch an adorable baby raptor emerge from its shell.

Closer to reality is an actual segment of rock face from the North Sea area containing real fossilized dinosaur bits from the Triassic, Jurassic, and

Cretaceous eras. A series of clever "neutrino data scanners" let kids move along the rock face looking for dinosaurs. When a fragment is found, the scanner analyzes it and then identifies and reconstructs the dinosaur from which it came. In somewhat the same vein is an exhibit of life-sized dinosaurs that supposedly lets you see the world as the dinosaurs saw it by looking through high-tech viewfinders mounted periscope-style into the model dinosaurs' heads and necks and moving the creatures' heads around (unfortunately, it rarely seems to work properly).

On the zany side is a DNA sequencing exhibit that explains the cloning premise on which the movie is based and then lets you combine your own DNA with that of a dinosaur to create a saurian you. And completely over the top (but a lot of fun) is a quiz show with the rather naughty name, "You Bet Jurassic." Here you and two other tourists compete in a game of dinosaur trivia. But don't get your hopes up; the grand prize is a lifetime supply of Raptor Chow, which is apparently manufactured from losing contestants!

On the back wall of the lower level you'll find a large mural depicting life in the Jurassic era. If you entered the *Discovery Center* from the upper level, you might want to take a peek through the massive double doors in the middle of this wall. They open out onto a spacious park-like terrace that descends to the shores of the Great Inland Sea. This is one of the loveliest open spaces in the park and offers a stunning view back to the Port of Entry and the lighthouse that welcomes arriving guests. With its tropical foliage, it's secluded and romantic at night. Near the dock area once used by boats that ferried guests back and forth from Port of Entry is a bridge leading to the Lost Continent area near Mythos restaurant.

Jurassic Park River Adventure

Rating: ＊＊＊＊
Type: Water ride
Time: 5 minutes
Our Take: Terrific fun

This is the attraction that will draw people to Jurassic Park. The pre-ride warm-up plays it straight. Video monitors in the queue line emphasize proper boarding procedures and ride safety, just as you would expect in the "real" Jurassic Park. The result: it's nowhere near as entertaining as the *Jaws* warm-up at USF.

River Adventure itself is an idyllic boat ride that gives you an opportunity to view from close range some of Jurassic Park's gentlest creatures.

Unfortunately, on the trip you take with 25 other guests, things go very, very wrong. Your first stop is the upper lagoon, where you meet a 35-foot tall mama ultrasaur and her baby. Then you cruise past the park's north forty where you glimpse stegosaurs and the playful hydrosaurs. Too playful, unfortunately.

Before you know it, you're off course in the raptor containment area and on the lunch menu. In a desperate attempt to save you, the boat is shunted into the environmental systems building, that huge 13-story structure at the back of Jurassic Park. It is in this vast, dark, and very scary setting that the ride reaches its climax. After narrowly escaping velociraptors and those nasty spitting dinosaurs, you come face to face, quite literally, with T-Rex himself. After that, the 85-foot plunge down what was billed as the "longest, fastest, steepest water descent ever built" in pitch blackness will seem like a relief.

Tip: You can speed your way through this ride by asking the attendant to point you toward the single rider line.

This is a great ride to experience at night, especially once you enter the main building. The bright Florida sun tends to give away the approach of the final breathtaking drop; at night it comes as a real surprise.

The best seats in the house. Clearly the first row of the boat is where you thrill seekers want to be; just be warned that you *will* get wet. Of course, you'll probably get wet no matter where you sit, although seats in the center of the craft are a little more protected. The ride attendants are more likely to accommodate a request for a seat that gives you some protection from a drenching than they are to put you in the front row. However, if you come early in the day or late in the evening, when the crowds are thinner, you may be able to pick any seat you want.

Camp Jurassic

Rating: * * * *
Type: Interactive play area
Time: As long as it takes
Our Take: Terrific fun for pre-teens

This 60,000-square-foot interactive kids' play and discovery area is about four times the size of *Fievel's Playland* over at Universal Studios Florida and will appeal to a slightly older age group, although kids of all ages will find plenty to keep them occupied. The place is a minor masterpiece of playground design and is highly recommended for kids who are getting antsy or who just need to burn off some excess energy. Even adults will enjoy sampling its pleasures.

Camp Jurassic transports you to a jungle on the slopes of an ancient active volcano. The roots of banyan trees snake around ancient rock out-croppings and an old abandoned amber mine offers exciting networks of rope ladders and tunnels, as well as subterranean passageways, to explore. There are corkscrew slides, cascading waterfalls, secret hideaways, and a place where kids can do battle with water cannons made up to look like the deadly spitting dinosaurs from the film.

Aside from the water cannons, all the fun here comes from kids burning off energy and exercising their imaginations as they run, climb, and slide their way through this intricate and imaginative maze of a prehistoric envi-ronment. Don't be surprised if your kid gets lost in here for an hour or so, and don't be surprised if you find yourself enjoying it just as much.

Pteranodon Flyers

Rating:	* * * +
Type:	A mild, hanging coaster
Time:	80 seconds
Our Take:	Fun, but not worth a wait
Note:	Universal Express Plus is not available for this ride.

Taking off from the back of *Camp Jurassic* is this "family" ride that glides gently around the camp's tropical perimeter for an enjoyable but all-too-brief soaring experience. The ride vehicle consists of a pair of swing-like seats, one behind the other, that dangle from a metal pteranodon. Pteran-odons, you might remember, were flying dinosaurs with long mean-looking beak-like faces and hooks on their leathery wings. These pteranodons are not at all threatening. In fact, you hardly notice them once you are seated.

Your vehicle glides rather than rides along the overhead track, taking you on a journey that lets you survey *Camp Jurassic* below and the Great Inland Sea in the distance. This ride is a little more "aggressive" than the sky rides you may have encountered at other parks and offers a few mild "thrills" as the flyers bank and curve.

The main problem with this ride is that it accommodates so few riders. Universal has tried to remedy this situation by imposing a 56-inch maxi-mum height requirement; if you are taller than this, you must be accom-panied by a child. This has helped somewhat, but compared to all the other rides in the park, its hourly "throughput" is still laughably low. The result is that the line forms early and lasts a long, long time. You won't be alone if you decide that an hour and a half wait for an 80-second ride is a tad on the absurd side. So if you think this is the kind of thing you'll enjoy, plan on coming first thing in the morning. The wait also tends to be more reasonable shortly before the park closes.

Note: Be aware that some children, especially those with a fear of heights, might find this ride terrifying. And if they do, they won't have Mommy or Daddy to cling to since the two seats are quite separate.

Eating in Jurassic Park

Jurassic Park offers another stunningly beautiful restaurant, Thunder Falls Terrace, where the service is cafeteria style and the knifes and forks are plastic but where the food is a cut above the average. And Burger Digs offers an often-overlooked rear balcony with a great view out over the Great Inland Sea. If (heaven forbid) you have work to do while you're in Orlando, this is a good place to do it; there are even outlets for your laptop. For the rest, there are a number of fast food options and a great outdoor bar that offers a perfect venue for people-watching.

▌ Thunder Falls Terrace

What: Grilled cuisine with flair
Where: On your left as you enter from Toon Lagoon
Price Range: $$

This restaurant takes wonderful advantage of the *Jurassic Park River Adventure*, using it as both backdrop and entertainment. After you've taken your own harrowing journey on the ride, you can repair here, sit in air-conditioned comfort, and gaze through the picture windows at other happily terrified tourists as they emerge from the final 85-foot drop. There is an outdoor seating area that receives the cooling mist from the thundering waterfall next door. The luxurious jungle-lodge atmosphere also contributes to the experience. There are two spacious circular dining areas under soaring conical roofs held aloft by massive log beams and dominated by a large hanging black metal chandelier with amber glass panels and cutouts of dinosaurs.

The food is casual and it's served cafeteria style, but it is very good, with careful attention paid to both quality and presentation. The menu consists of unusually well-prepared backyard barbecue staples such as chicken, ribs, and wraps ($9 to $13). The platters are served with roasted garlic herb potatoes or yellow rice and black beans. The corn on the cob is especially nice. The corn is roasted to perfection, with the peeled-back husks adding a festive touch to the platter. Thunder Falls also dishes up a serviceable soup and two tasty entree-sized salads. The desserts include an appealing key lime cheesecake (about $4). All in all, this is the best "fast food" style restaurant in the park. With a full meal running about $17, it's a real bargain for the quality. In addition to the usual soft drinks, beer and wine are available.

Note: This restaurant may be closed during the park's slower periods or for private events.

The Burger Digs

What: Walk-up indoor fast food counter
Where: On the top level of the *Discovery Center*
Price Range: $

This fast food eatery opened on an adventuresome note by putting alligator meat on the menu, but found few takers. Now you'll have to be content with cheeseburgers, double cheeseburgers, veggie burgers, and grilled chicken sandwiches. All are served with fries and a help-yourself fixin's bar laden with lettuce, tomato, chopped onions, and other burger enhancers. Beer is on tap, and milk shakes and apple pie are for dessert.

You'll find plenty of indoor, air-conditioned seating just a few steps away from the serving windows, in a spacious dining room decorated with murals depicting life in the Jurassic age.

There is also a lovely balcony with a palm-fringed view of the Inland Sea — a great place to sit on a balmy day. Clearly the seating area here was designed with corporate events and private parties in mind. For the casual tourist, it means plenty of room to spread out, even to gain a modicum of privacy and peace on a hectic day.

Pizza Predattoria

What: Walk-up outdoor fast food stand
Where: Near *Jurassic Park River Adventure*
Price Range: $

Personal-sized pizza is the signature dish here. There is also a large meatball sub and a Caesar salad. Sweets, soft drinks, and beer round out the menu choices.

All seating is at nearby umbrella-shaded tables, but you could conceivably take a short stroll to The Burger Digs in the *Discovery Center* and eat your pizza in air-conditioned comfort.

The Watering Hole

What: Outdoor full-service bar
Where: Near the *Discovery Center*
Price Range: $

Rather unusual for a theme park is this walk-up bar specializing in exotic drinks that pack a prehistoric wallop. The main feature is specialty drinks, from margaritas to rum runners to something called Predator Rocks. There's also beer and a full bar for those who prefer a more straightforward drink. Daily happy hour typically runs from 3:00 to 5:00 p.m. Food here includes hot dogs and chips, chicken wings, chili, and nachos.

Shopping in Jurassic Park

Shopping is muted here, but the Dinostore, located on the top level of the *Discovery Center* opposite Burger Digs, is a small shop with a smidge of redeeming educational value. There are dinosaur model kits, books about dinosaurs aimed at the younger set, and dinosaur toys, as well as dinosaur and mineral collectibles. There is also a smattering of Jurassic Park clothing here.

Jurassic Outfitters is the gauntlet you run after splashing down on the *River Adventure* ride. As you might expect, you will find the Jurassic Park logo on every conceivable surface from T-shirts ("I Survived Jurassic Park, the Ride!") to mugs. Of particular interest are some quite nice jungle adventurer hats and Jurassic Park beach towels, which you actually might need. Best of all are the framed photos taken of you and your fellow tourists plunging screaming down the last drop of the ride.

■ TOON LAGOON ■

After the intensity of *Forbidden Journey* and Jurassic Park, the zany, colorful goofiness of Toon Lagoon is a welcome change of pace. Many of the characters you have come to know and love through the Sunday funnies in your hometown newspaper can be spotted here — some appear in blow-ups of their strips, some have been immortalized in giant sculptures, and some will actually be strolling the grounds and happy to pose for photos. A visit here offers a unique opportunity to live out a child's daydream of stepping into the pages of the comic strips and exploring a gaudy fantasy world filled with fun and laughter.

Toon Lagoon's main drag is **Comic Strip Lane,** a short street of shops and restaurants, including those described below. It is an attraction in itself. Nearly 80 comic strip characters call this colorful neighborhood home, including Beetle Bailey (on furlough from Camp Swampy no doubt), Hagar the Horrible, and Krazy Kat. The concept makes for all sorts of serendipitous juxtapositions. Hagar's boat hangs over a waterfall that falls into a big pipe that bubbles up across the way at a dog fountain where all the dogs from the various comic strips hang out.

Turning off Comic Strip Lane is the zany seaside town of **Sweet Haven,** a separate section of Toon Lagoon containing a variety of Popeye-inspired rides and attractions. Water is a recurring theme in Toon Lagoon and you can get very wet here. See *Good Things To Know About...Getting Wet* in the introduction to this chapter for a strategy to follow.

Dudley Do-Right's Ripsaw Falls

Rating: * * * *
Type: Log flume ride
Time: 6 minutes
Our Take: Laughs and screams

In Dudley's hometown of Ripsaw Falls, as you might expect, Nell is once again in the clutches of the dastardly Snidely Whiplash. That's all the excuse you need to take off on a rip-roaring log flume ride that, like so many other attractions in this park, takes the genre to a whole new level.

The build-up takes us through a series of scenes in a "moving melodrama" in which the much-loved characters unfold a typically wacky plot that includes not just Dudley, Nell, and Snidely but Inspector Fenwick and Horse, too, as our five-passenger log-boats rise inexorably to the mountainous heights where Snidely has his hideout. Along the way we pass animated tableaux that advance the tie-her-to-the-railroad-tracks plot. The landscape is dotted with signs that echo the off-the-wall humor of the old cartoons. At one point the boat detours into the abandoned Wontyabe Mine, at another we pass a billboard advertising Whiplash Lager ("made with real logs"). Of course, Dudley triumphs almost in spite of himself. Anticipating victory a bit too soon, he strikes a heroic pose with his foot on a dynamite plunger, precipitating a plunge through the roof of a TNT storage shack as the riders are shot beneath the water surface only to pop back to the surface 100 feet downstream. This is the first log flume to pull off this little bit of wizardry and how they manage it we'll leave you to discover. Another nice touch is that the final drop is curved rather than a straight angle; the result is that, as the angle steepens, you could swear you're hurtling straight down.

Tip: You can speed your way through this ride by asking the attendant to point you toward the single rider line.

This is one ride that just may be as entertaining to watch as to take. If you'd prefer not to take the plunge and actually go on the ride, you can stand and watch others take the steep 60-foot drop into the TNT shack. Or you can use the **Water Blasters** (25 cents) to spray the riders as they pass below you — good, clean, evil fun.

Popeye & Bluto's Bilge-Rat Barges

Rating:	* * * * +
Type:	Raft ride
Time:	About 5 minutes
Our Take:	Super soaking good fun

You may get spritzed a bit on the *Jurassic Park River Adventure* and on *Dudley Do-Right's Ripsaw Falls*, but for a really good soaking, you have to come to Sweet Haven, home to Popeye, Olive Oyl, and the gang. The barges of the name are actually circular, 12-passenger rubber rafts that twirl and dip along a twisting, rapids-strewn watercourse.

Just as Dudley has his Snidely, Popeye has Bluto. Their lifelong enmity and rivalry for the affection of Miss Olive form the basis for the theming on this ride, which involves Olive, Wimpy, Poopdeck Pappy, and all the rest. Water splashes into the sides of the raft in the rapids and pours in from above at crucial junctures. And at least one person in your raft is sure to get hosed by the little devils (actually someone else's kids) manning the water cannons on *Me Ship, The Olive* (see below) before the raft is swept into an octopus grotto where an eight-armed beast holds Popeye in its tentacled grip, preventing him from reaching his lifesaving spinach. Before it's all over, the hapless rafts have been spun into Bluto's fully operational boat wash, which is just like a car wash except it's for boats.

This is the spiffiest raft ride in town and the ride to take at the hottest, stickiest part of the day. Because the free-floating rafts spin and twist as they roar down the rapids, how wet you get is somewhat a matter of luck; you certainly will get damp and you may be drenched. The rafts have plastic covered bins in the center in which you can store things you'd rather not get wet. They do a pretty good job, too. Many people are smart enough to remove and stow their shoes and socks since plenty of water sloshes into the rafts along the way.

Tip: The heavier the raft, the faster the ride. So if you want a little extra oomph in your ride, get in line behind a bunch of weight lifters or opera stars.

Me Ship, The Olive

Rating:	* * *
Type:	Interactive play area
Time:	Unlimited
Our Take:	Nice, but can't beat *Camp Jurassic*

Resist the temptation to come here after the raft ride and throttle the little darlings who were squirting you with the water cannons. Instead, let your littlest kids loose in this three-story interactive play area representing the ship Popeye has named after his one true love. Older kids will find this spot of limited interest.

The ship theme is clever and well executed but makes for cramped spaces. Still there are some good reasons for at least a brief visit. The top level offers some excellent views of *Dragon Challenge*, all of Seuss Landing, and an especially good angle on the *Hulk* coaster. Videographers and photographers will definitely want to take advantage of these **photo ops**. Also on the top level is a tubular slide that will deposit little kids on the middle level where they will find, on the starboard side, four water cannons they can aim at hapless riders on the *Bilge-Rat Barges* ride — and they're free! Also on this level is a "Spinach Spinnet," a cartoon piano that little kids will enjoy banging on. Yet another corkscrew tubular slide takes your tykes to the bottom level, where they can play in Swee' Pea's Playpen. For those who cannot climb the many stairs of *Me Ship, The Olive*, a small elevator is thoughtfully provided.

Toon Lagoon Amphitheater Shows

Rating: * * * to * * * *
Type: Seasonal amphitheater show
Time: About 20 minutes
Our Take: Usually worth watching

This large amphitheater marks the boundary between Toon Lagoon and Marvel Super Hero Island. It hosts an irregular series of short-run live shows and special events (Rosie O'Donnell once taped here, for example). The television show *iVillage Live* broadcast from here before moving to Chicago. It's impossible to anticipate what, if anything, will be on when you visit. Most recently, "Max Hoffman's Agro Circus" stunt shows involving skateboards and BMX bikes have performed. Whatever's on tap will be listed in the 2-Park Map. It may be that these shows will be back or you may encounter something completely different. Or perhaps another television show will recognize the special opportunities this venue offers.

The best seats in the house. During the stunt shows, bikers will periodically zoom out into the audience, fly up a short ramp, and come to a deft stop right in front of the first row of the upper section of seats, making this the prime seating location.

These shows are "seasonal," meaning they run during the summer, at Christmas, and over Spring Break. If something is going on here during your visit, don't miss it.

And all the rest . . .

There are regular **Character Meet and Greet** sessions in Toon Lagoon, either along Comic Strip Lane or in front of the Pandemonium amphitheater. The characters, naturally, are your funny paper favorites like Popeye and Olive Oyl, Beetle Bailey, and Woody Woodpecker. During busier periods, these events may be called out on the 2-Park Map.

Toon Lagoon's Comic Strip Lane offers some terrific **photo ops**. There are cut-outs that put you in the comic strip and many of the palm trees are mounted with comic strip speech balloons. You pose underneath and get a nice shot of you saying things like, "It must be Sunday...We're in color!" or

"Don't have the mushroom pizza before you ride *Ripsaw Falls.*"

Perhaps the best is a trick photo involving Marmaduke, that playful Great Dane. You'll find it on the facade of Blondie's restaurant (see below), and a nearby sign tells you exactly how to set up the shot.

If you turn to the right at *Me Ship, The Olive* and follow the path over the raging rapids of the *Bilge-Rat Barges* ride, you'll find yourself in a delightful snarl of walkways along the Great Inland Sea, another of the park's wonderful get-away-from-it-all spots.

The plaza in front of the Pandemonium amphitheater is the venue for occasional **street shows** that often involve audience participation and appearances by cartoon characters. One recent show featured the Outer Toons, a zany bunch of costumed musicians who lead singalongs and "name that tune" contests featuring songs from television cartoon shows. The area from the plaza to the entrance to Marvel Super Hero Island is sometimes home to a collection of so-called **Games of Skill**.

Eating in Toon Lagoon

Don't look for a gourmet experience in Toon Lagoon, but don't expect to go hungry either. The food is aimed at kids and teens, which is to say it's fast and moderately priced. The eateries are colorful and full of fanciful fun, just like the funnies that inspired them.

▌ Blondie's

What:	Overstuffed sandwich shop
Where:	On the plaza near the entrance to Sweet Haven
Price Range:	$

This one comes with a subtitle, "Home of the Dagwood." It's a sandwich of course, and for those who don't know, it's named after Blondie Bumstead's hapless hubby, who made comic strip history with his colossal, 20-slice, clear-out-the-fridge sandwich creations. The sandwiches here don't quite live up to the gigantic depiction that graces the entrance to the joint, and they sprawl across the plate rather than tower above it as they do on the signage. But you'll likely find them pretty good nonetheless.

Pride of place among the "Side-Splitting Sandwiches," as they are called, goes to The Dagwood, consisting of ham, turkey, roast beef, Swiss and American cheese on several slices of hearty white bread. Other choices are less fully packed subs and "stacked sandwiches" of ham, turkey, tuna, or roast beef, along with Nathan's hotdogs. Indoor seating is limited.

▌ Wimpy's

What: Walk-up burger joint
Where: In Sweet Haven across from *Bilge-Rat Barges*
Price Range: $

Popeye's pal is as closely associated with hamburgers as it's possible to be, so it's good to see him here serving up the apotheosis of the all-American burger. Burger, chili dog, and chicken finger meals are served, with shakes and desserts. Soft drinks are served, and draft beer is available to slake that deeper thirst.

Service is from walk-up but shaded windows in a building that serves as a portside supply shack. All seating is outdoors, only some of it shaded. Perhaps the best spot to grab a table is in the shaded area overlooking the raging rapids of the *Bilge-Rat Barges* ride.

Note: This restaurant is open seasonally.

▌ Comic Strip Cafe

What: Multicultural cafeteria
Where: On Comic Strip Lane
Price Range: $

This large, loud, and boisterous space houses four separate genres of fast food: Fish, Chips & Chicken; Chinese; Burgers & Dogs; and Pizza & Pasta. All of them have about three or four entrees, and you can get any style of food at any open window. The selections are not terribly imaginative and are about what you would expect for their types.

They won't win any awards from the healthy eating crowd either. About the healthiest meal you'll find here is a chicken Caesar salad. Desserts usually include chocolate cake and Jello. Each counter has a separate line and cashier, but all offer the same menu choices.

The room itself is bright and garish in a self-consciously postmodern way. The high ceiling, with its exposed air-conditioning ducts and pipes, is painted a matte black, but the walls are brightly striped and covered with blown-up panels and cutouts from a variety of Sunday funnies comic strips, providing a bit of light reading for those dining alone. There's plenty of table and booth seating indoors and a fair amount of al fresco seating as well.

▌ Cathy's Ice Cream

What: Walk-up stand
Where: On Comic Strip Lane, near the Comic Strip Cafe
Price Range: $

In the comics, Cathy is constantly worrying about her weight. She must have taken leave of her senses, not to mention her scale, when she opened this place in partnership with Ben & Jerry's. The stand takes the form of a huge container brimming with a hot fudge sundae topped not by a cherry but by the disturbingly bikini-ed Cathy herself. Waffle Sundaes are offered, as are milk shakes.

Shopping in Toon Lagoon

The shopping scene in Toon Lagoon is a little chaotic, with merchandise (and even entire shops) changing suddenly. The wares in **Gasoline Alley** seem to change more often than most. Recently, the theme was beach and casual wear with an "Islands" theme, including swim wear, towels, sandals, and flip-flops. (And beware the oil cans stacked at the entrance!)

Tucked away under Betty Boop's piano is the entrance to the **Betty Boop Store**, a shrine to the original boop-oop-a-doop girl. Collectible dolls and figurines are available in a variety of sizes and outfits not to mention price points. There are T-shirts, of course, but the sleepwear is a classier choice, when it's available, which is not always.

The biggest store in Toon Lagoon, **Toon Extra**, is not well marked, but you can enter it through Beetle Bailey's tent, under Flash Gordon's rocket, or through those huge rolled up Sunday funnies that serve as columns for the zany building in which it is housed. This is another Islands of Adventure shop that's worth popping into just to gawk at the decor. What you will find on sale is hard to predict except that it will be a mix of clothing, most of it for kids, plush toys, and miscellaneous souvenirs.

MARVEL SUPER HERO ISLAND

Those from another planet may not know that Marvel is the name of a comic book company that revolutionized the industry way back in the sixties with a series of titles showcasing a bizarre array of super heroes whose psychological quirks were as intriguing as their ingeniously conceived superhuman powers. As might be expected, this cast of characters offers rich inspiration for some of the most intense thrill rides ever created.

After the extensive theming of the other islands, Marvel Super Hero Island can seem a little, well, flat. Some people suspect, erroneously, that Universal was cutting corners or had run out of money when it came to designing this section of the park. Not at all. Marvel Super Hero Island is, in fact, a brilliant evocation in three dimensions of the visual style of the comic books that inspired it. Marvel used strong colors and simple geometric shapes to create a futuristic cityscape with an Art Deco flavor. Against this purposely flat backdrop, they arrayed their extravagantly muscled and lovingly sculpted heroes. Marvel Comics had a profound effect on American visual design, not to mention its effect on contemporary notions of the body beautiful.

But enough art history. What you've come here for are the thrill rides and Marvel Super Hero Island has some of the best examples of the genre you're likely to find in Central Florida.

The Amazing Adventures of Spider-Man

Rating:	* * * * *
Type:	3-D motion simulator ride
Time:	4.5 minutes
Our Take:	The former state-of-the-art in a thrill rides, and still astounding.

Until Harry Potter's arrival, Universal's publicity powerhouse trumpeted this as "the next threshold attraction," the one that takes theme park entertainment to a new level, just as *Back to The Future . . .The Ride* (since closed) and *T2* did when they opened over at Universal Studios Florida.

Visitors step into the offices of the *Daily Bugle* only to discover that the evil villain Dr. Octopus and his Sinister Syndicate have used an antigravity gun to make off with the Statue of Liberty and other famous landmarks as part of a plot to bring New York City to its knees. Since cub reporter Peter Parker and all the rest of the staff are mysteriously absent, crusty editor J. Jonah Jameson drafts his hapless guests into a civilian force with the mission of tracking down the evildoers and getting the scoop on their nefarious doings.

Guests board special 12-passenger vehicles and set off through the streets of the city, where they discover Spidey is already on the case. What ensues is a harrowing high-speed chase enhanced through a variety of heart-stopping special effects.

The vehicles are simulators, much like the ones in *Jimmy Neutron* in Universal Studios Florida. Underneath they have six hydraulically operated stalks that can be used to simulate virtually any kind of motion. But these cars can also move through space, and they do, along tracks that allow for 360 degrees of rotation. The combination of forward motion, rotation, and simulator technology creates startling sensations never before possible.

Further heightening the experience is the environment through which the cars move. This is the world of Marvel comics sprung vividly to life and startlingly real. Intermixed with the solid set elements (that include enormous chunks of a cut up Statue of Liberty) are almost undetectable screens on which three-dimensional films add an extra measure of depth and excitement. Both villains and heroes seem to leap directly at you. At several points, various villains and Spidey himself drop onto the hood of the vehicle with a thud and a jolt. They are insubstantial three-dimensional cartoons, of course, but the effect is amazingly real.

As your ill-fated journey proceeds, it is your bad luck to keep interrupting the evildoers at awkward moments, and they do their utmost to destroy you, with deadly bursts of electricity, walls of flame, and deluges of water. They narrowly miss each time, sending your vehicle spinning and tumbling to its next close encounter with doom.

Finally you are caught in the irresistible force of an antigravity ray that sucks the vehicle ever upward as Spider-Man struggles valiantly to save you. The ride culminates with a 400-foot drop through the cartoon canyons of New York to almost certain death on the streets below. It's quite a ride.

The best seats in the house. Logically, the first of the three rows in the vehicle should be the best, since you don't have the heads of fellow passengers in your field of vision. Still, the other rows, because they are slightly farther from the screens, provide better 3-D effects.

Tip: For a post-ride chuckle, pause to read the newspaper at the ride's exit. Few people do.

Doctor Doom's Fearfall

Rating:	* * * +
Type:	A free-fall ride with oomph
Time:	30 seconds
Our Take:	Gulp!

Near the Bugle building is Doom Alley, a part of town that has been completely taken over by the bad guys of the Sinister Syndicate: Dr. Octopus, The Hobgoblin, and The Lizard. Here the archfiend Doctor Doom has secreted his Fear Sucking Machine, in which he uses innocent, unsuspecting victims (that's you in case you hadn't guessed) to create the Fear Juice with which he hopes to finally vanquish the Fantastic Four.

The payoff is a fiendish twist on the freefall rides that have long been a staple of amusement parks and which were artfully updated in Disney's *Tower of Terror*. But whereas those rides take you up slowly and drop you, *Doctor Doom*, in the true Universal spirit, turns convention in its head.

Sixteen victims, that is, passengers, are strapped into seats in small four-person chambers. Only then do they learn the hideous fate Doctor Doom has in store for them as the chamber fills with smoke and the Doctor's eyes glow a menacing green. Suddenly they are shot upward 150 feet at a force of four G's. There is a heart-flipping moment of weightlessness before the vehicles drop back, bouncing back upward a few times before all-too-quickly returning to terra firma. Most people scream on freefall rides, but this one happens so quickly (less than 30 seconds) and registers such a shock that many riders won't remember to scream until the ride is over.

Tip: You can speed your way through this ride by asking the attendant to point you toward the single rider line.

The Incredible Hulk Coaster

Rating:	* * * * *
Type:	Steel coaster
Time:	1.5 minutes
Our Take:	Aaaargh!

In the scientific complex where Bruce Banner, a.k.a. the Incredible

Hulk, has his laboratories, you can learn all about the nasty effects of over-exposure to gamma radiation. No, it's not more edutainment, it's the warm-up for another knock-your-socks-off roller coaster.

In a high-energy video pre-ride show, you learn that you can help Bruce reverse the unfortunate effects that have so complicated his life. All you have to do is climb into this little chamber which is, in fact, a 32-seat roller coaster. This is no ordinary roller coaster, however, where you have to wait agonizing seconds while the car climbs to the top of the first drop. It seems to get off to a fairly normal start, slowly climbing a steep incline, but thanks to an energizing burst of gamma rays you are shot at one G 150 feet upward, going from a near standstill to 42 miles an hour. From there it's all downhill so to speak as you swing into a zero-G roll and speed toward the surface of the lagoon at 58 miles per hour. This is no water ride though, so you whip into a cobra roll before being lofted upwards once more through the high-est (109 feet) inversion ever built. After that it's under a bridge — on which earthbound (i.e. "sane") people are enjoying your terror — through a total of seven inversions and two subterranean trenches before you come to a rest, hoping desperately that your exertions have, indeed, helped Bruce out of his pickle.

Here's an interesting note for the technically minded: The initial thrust of this ride consumes so much power that, if the needed electricity were drawn directly from Orlando's electric supply, lights across town would dim every time a new coaster was launched. So Universal draws power at a steady rate from the city's power grid and stores it in a huge flywheel hid-den in the greenish building by the Inland Sea labeled "Power Supply." This enables them to get the power they need for that first heart-stopping effect without inconveniencing their neighbors.

Tip: This can be a very discombobulating experience. If you feel a bit weak in the knees at ride's end, look for the Baby Swap area on your right. Here you can sit down in air-conditioned comfort for a few minutes to re-gain your composure before striding out pridefully into the Florida sun.

Note: This ride requires that you stow all your belongings in nearby electronic lockers that are free for a period of time that varies with the queue length, but charge a hefty fee if you overstay your welcome.

Tip: You may be able speed your way through this ride by asking the attendant to point you toward the single rider line, if open.

And on your way out, don't forget to check out the photo of your adven-ture. The high-speed cameras capture each of the eight rows of the coaster as it zooms past, so one of the frames is likely to have a good shot of you.

Storm Force Accelatron

Rating:	* * *
Type:	Spinning cup ride
Time:	1.5 minutes
Our Take:	A standard amusement park ride

Tucked behind the *Hulk* coaster and Cafe 4, under a futuristic purple and blue dome, is this Marvelized version of a fairly standard amusement park ride. A large circular spinning platform contains four smaller circles that spin independently. Each of these small circles holds three cup-like cars that also spin independently. When the whole thing gets up to speed, there are three levels of spin. An added bit of oomph comes from the circular control in each car that allows the riders to control just how fast their car spins.

The cars are designed to hold four adults but with kids aboard the number can increase; apparently the record is eight passengers in a car. The spin control works quite well and with some vigorous turning you can add quite a bit of momentum to your brief spin cycle whirl. Even if you skip the ride, it's worth strolling back here to take a peek at the back end of *Hulk*.

Tip: To get the full effect of the strobe lights that represent Storm's lightning, ride this one at night.

And all the rest ...

Kingpin's Arcade, admittedly, seems less out of place here than its equivalents elsewhere. That's because the world of video games is, after all, a comic book world and some of the machines in here represent the current state of the art in this genre. The games run on tokens, which you can obtain from a vending machine. No refunds are given so you're forced to use them all, which might not be all that much of a challenge since some of the fancier games require six tokens. If you ride *Doctor Doom's Fearfall*, you will exit through this incredibly loud emporium. Look for the hole blasted in the wall that leads to Cafe 4.

Several times a day, according to a schedule listed in the 2-Park Map, there is a **Character Meet and Greet** in the plaza opposite the entrance to the *Spider-Man* ride. Several characters from the X-Men comics — Rogue, Storm, and Wolverine, as well as Spidey — appear to give autographs and pose photogenically with your kids. Unlike the costumed cartoon characters encountered elsewhere, these heroes will actually talk to you.

Eating in Marvel Super Hero Island

In keeping with the style of Marvel Comics, the food choices here are pared down and straightforward. There are several walk-up stands with names like **Chill**, **Frozen Ice**, **Fruit**, and **Cotton Candy** selling exactly what their names suggest for a few bucks. Only slightly more elaborate are two cafeteria-like restaurants.

■ Cafe 4

What:	Italian food cafeteria style
Where:	Straight ahead as you come from Port of Entry
Price Range:	$

That huge gizmo that dominates the center of Cafe 4 and looks like a gigantic prop from a laboratory in a sci-fi movie beams colorful floating images of the Fantastic Four onto the curved ceiling above. The colorful mural behind the gizmo serves as a fitting welcome to this ultramodern cafeteria.

Judging by the menu, the Fantastic Four must be Italian food fans. Pizza is sold by the slice or whole pie. The BBQ chicken pizza is especially tasty. You'll also find standard pasta dishes and subs. A spaghetti meal is offered for kids 11 and under. Breadsticks with marinara dipping sauce and Caesar salads round out the Italian theme. Desserts and draft beer are served here along with the usual array of soft drinks.

There's plenty of indoor seating but it can get loud when it's filled with noisy kids. There's also a fair amount of outdoor seating that can also get loud because of the screams from *Incredible Hulk* riders. A hole torn in the wall leads to the video game arcade (see above).

■ Captain America Diner

What:	All-American diner fare
Where:	Near *Spider-Man*
Price Range:	$

The food here is perfectly themed: All-American Burgers and Super Hero Sides. The burgers are actually pretty good, and chicken fingers, chicken salad, and sandwiches are also served. Any diner worth its salt should serve milk shakes and this one does, chocolate and vanilla.

The decor is techno-modern, with steel seats and metal benches in the booths and huge mural-like depictions of characters from the Captain America comics looming overhead. There are two circular dining areas with tall walls of windows looking out to the Great Inland Sea. A small outdoor seating area is right on the Sea and makes a great place to eat, if you don't mind the occasional freeloading bird. These seats not only look out to the Lost Continent, but also offer one of the best vantage points for watching riders on *Hulk*.

Shopping in Marvel Super Hero Island

The shops here tend to mix and match their wares and styles come and go, so take the following notes with a grain of salt.

The **Comics Shop** is your chance to fill in that unfortunate gap in your literary education by immersing yourself in the Marvel universe. Colorful wall displays feature the last two or three issues of virtually every title in the Marvel comic line. You can also get large format paperback collections and novelizations based on popular characters. For collectors without the big bucks needed to acquire the real thing, there are hardbound, full-color volumes containing ten issues of The Avengers, X-Men, Spider-Man, and other popular titles. Collectible — and high-priced — Marvel figurines are also available. T-shirts, videos, model kits, and the standard Marvel souvenirs round out the offerings here.

The vest-pocket **Oakley** shop sells high-end sunglasses and watches, most of them bearing the ultra-hip Oakley brand for $75 to $400. (There's a price to be paid for being on the cutting edge of fashion.) They also offer shoes and backpacks, just in case you have any money left. It's a virtual carbon copy of the Oakley shop in San Francisco/Amity over at Universal Studios Florida.

You can't miss the Spider-Man Shop unless you're foolish enough to skip the Spider-Man ride. (If you're entering from the street, look for the "5 & Dime" sign.) T-shirts form the bulk of the merchandise on display. Sometimes you will find other clothing items like flashy sports jerseys and sweats (in season). Those who really identify with Spidey can pick up Spider-Man action figures, figurines, toys, glasses, mugs, key rings, towels, and costumes.

Across the street, the **Marvel Alterniverse Store** offers pretty much the same range of merchandise as the Spider-Man Shop except it's not limited to a single character. In other words, this is Marvel T-shirt central, and if you're into this sort of thing, the assortment is fabulous. For the well-to-do kid, there are figurines, signed posters, and even animation cels from Marvel cartoons costing several hundred dollars. More affordable are videos, mugs in the shape of the heads of various Marvel characters, and models and action figures for younger kids.

CHAPTER FOUR:

(ITYWALK

O rlando's nightlife epicenter has shifted several times over the decades. In the 1970s and 80s, downtown's historic Church Street Station was world-famous for its entertainment (and is now attempting a comeback). In the 1990s, Disney's Pleasure Island (currently defunct and under redevelopment) cornered the after-hours adult market. But today, the preferred place for post-attraction partying is at Universal Orlando. CityWalk is a happening enclave of heavily themed restaurants, nightclubs, shops, and movie theaters that rocks long after the nearby theme parks have closed up for the night.

Orientation

The layout and setting of CityWalk is ingenious. It is a 30-acre lozenge-shaped area plopped right down between Universal Studios Florida and Islands of Adventure. It is impossible to get from your car to either of the parks, or from one park to the other, without passing through CityWalk. On top of that, a river runs through it — or rather a man-made waterway that separates most of CityWalk from the theme parks and links CityWalk to the Hard Rock and Portofino Bay Hotels, and the Royal Pacific Resort.

Most of the buildings in CityWalk are arrayed along the perimeter closest to the parking structures, facing in toward the waterway. To mask the backs of the buildings and their service areas, the park's designers created an immense steel latticework that curves up and over CityWalk. The idea was that climbing vines and other plants would cover it in a camouflaging green cocoon. So far it hasn't worked. Mostly what you see is the latticework.

There are three major streets: a straight avenue that leads from the parking structures, a curving boulevard that leads from Universal Studios

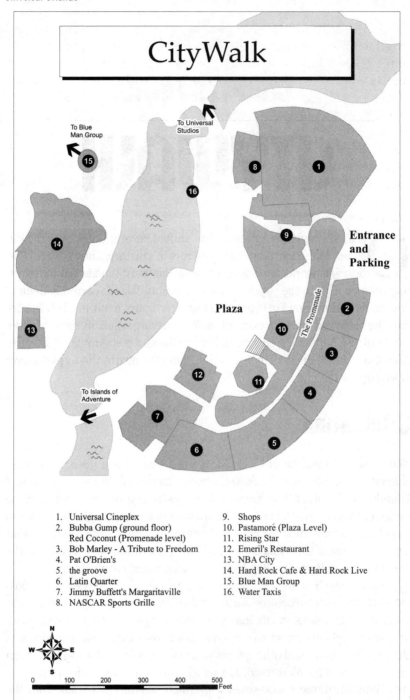

CityWalk

To Blue Man Group

To Universal Studios

Entrance and Parking

Plaza

The Promenade

To Islands of Adventure

1. Universal Cineplex
2. Bubba Gump (ground floor)
   Red Coconut (Promenade level)
3. Bob Marley - A Tribute to Freedom
4. Pat O'Brien's
5. the groove
6. Latin Quarter
7. Jimmy Buffett's Margaritaville
8. NASCAR Sports Grille
9. Shops
10. Pastamoré (Plaza Level)
11. Rising Star
12. Emeril's Restaurant
13. NBA City
14. Hard Rock Cafe & Hard Rock Live
15. Blue Man Group
16. Water Taxis

0 100 200 300 400 500 Feet

to Islands of Adventure near the waterway, and the Promenade that runs past the major nightclubs. Smaller streets wind between CityWalk's few freestanding buildings; one of these is a zigzag stairway that descends from the upper exit of the Cineplex to the waterway. It used to be called Lombard Street and that's how it will be referred to in this Chapter because "Zigzag Stairway with No Name" is awkward. Along the waterway runs an esplanade in the middle of which is an outdoor performance space for special concerts and other events. Also along this esplanade is a dock where you can pick up an elegant complimentary motor launch for the short trip to the resort hotels.

Smack dab in the middle of CityWalk is a large open space called simply the Plaza. On one side, a series of grass and stone platforms descends toward the water, forming a seating area for the performance space at water's edge. On the other, a stage sits over a sloping, waterfall-like fountain. Here you are likely to see a band entertaining the passing crowd with high-decible cover tunes. From time to time you may see other off-the-wall entertainers — jugglers, stilt-walkers, and the like — roaming the grounds spreading smiles and good cheer.

Also in the Plaza is a street-level "fountain" consisting of several rows of hidden water jets that send up columns of water of various heights, at various times, in various patterns. It is seldom without a crowd of young kids and adults old enough to know better dodging and weaving through its liquid columns, getting thoroughly drenched.

With one exception, the nightclubs in CityWalk are located along the Promenade, which rises gradually from Plaza level, curving behind the Plaza, to the upper exit from the Cineplex. This clever arrangement makes the nightclub area a separate and easily policed enclave within an enclave. The exception is Hard Rock Live (a concert hall more than a nightclub), which is connected to the Hard Rock Cafe and lies across the waterway along a short walk that connects Universal Studios Florida and Islands of Adventure.

Getting Information

There are a number of ways to get information about what's going on at CityWalk prior to your visit. On the Internet, you can get information on upcoming events by visiting www.citywalkorlando.com. CityWalk advertises prominently in the *Orlando Sentinel*'s Friday Calendar section and the free *Orlando Weekly*, which also carry listings of many CityWalk entertainment events. The main CityWalk number for "reservations and additional information" is (407) 224-3663. You can also dial (407) 363-8000 and follow the prompts through an extensive inventory of recorded announcements about CityWalk's various restaurants and clubs.

Arriving at CityWalk

You arrive at CityWalk just as you would arrive for a visit to the theme parks. You park in the same parking structures and pay the same parking fee. Of course, you also have the option of valet parking, if you wish (see *Chapter One*).

If you arrive between 6:00 p.m. and 10:00 p.m., parking will be $3. Parking after 10:00 p.m. is **free**. If you are arriving just for lunch and plan to stay for less than two hours, valet parking is free with restaurant validation (see below).

You enter CityWalk itself down a long broad avenue that passes by the Cineplex on your right (see map, above). That bridge you pass under is the Promenade and it leads from the upper exit of the Cineplex past CityWalk's string of nightclubs. An escalator to the bridge is available if you can't wait.

Note: If you are arriving by motor launch from one of the resort hotels, you will disembark at a dock just below the NASCAR Sports Grille.

Also by the bridge and the escalator is a kiosk called **Dining Reservations and CityWalk Information**. Here you can peruse menus of the various CityWalk restaurants, but despite the name you can't really make reservations for CityWalk restaurants, except for Emeril's (see below). You can, however, make priority seating requests (a process described below) and get pretty decent advice on how to plan your evening. Pick up here a brochure called **Times & Info**, which is published monthly. It contains a colorful if hard-to-read map of the enclave and an extremely helpful list of events at the various clubs. You can also pick up maps and show schedules for the two theme parks here, although they sometimes run out.

Just past the bridge, on your left, you will see the **Guest Services** window; come here with questions and problems. A short walk will bring you to the Plaza, CityWalk's broad open center. From here you proceed straight ahead to Islands of Adventure, turn right to head to Universal Studios Florida, or turn left to make your way to the Promenade and the nightclubs.

The Price of Admission

Officially, there is no admission to CityWalk, but that's only partially true. First, if you are coming to Universal Orlando just to visit CityWalk, there's the parking fee to consider — unless, of course, you arrive after 10:00 p.m., which may be the perfect time to begin a visit to what is primarily a nighttime attraction. More importantly, CityWalk's biggest draws, the nightclubs, all levy a $7 cover charge for the live evening entertainment starting at 9:00 p.m. Hard Rock Cafe never charges a cover, even when there's entertainment (which is rarely), and Hard Rock Live is not really a nightclub, so cover charges don't apply there. The Cineplex also charges admission.

If you are coming simply to enjoy the pleasures of CityWalk, you have a choice of paying each cover or admission charge individually or purchasing a one-day **CityWalk Party Pass**, which is sort of an "open sesame" to all the entertainment venues except Hard Rock Live, which always charges its own, separate admission. The Party Pass costs $12.77; annual passholders receive a 20% discount. If you have purchased a FlexTicket or any multi-day pass to the theme parks (a very likely scenario), then you already have seven consecutive days of access to CityWalk's clubs, starting on the day you first use your ticket or pass. Be aware that the Party Pass will not be honored at clubs with special events and some clubs will occasionally levy an additional cover charge on Party Pass holders.

To purchase your Party Pass, turn left at the Plaza and look for the box office windows outside the groove discotheque. If these windows are closed, check with the Guest Services window between the Endangered Species store and the Pastamoré Market Cafe.

CityWalk also offers a **Meal and Movie Deal** ($21.95 including tax and gratuity), which combines a meal at your choice of CityWalk restaurants (except Emeril's) and a film at the Cineplex (upgrade to 3D or IMAX for an extra $3); a **Meal and Party Deal** ($21 including tax and gratuity) combines a meal with club admission. The selection of entrees offered is somewhat limited, with a half-dozen options at each restaurant. Standbys like Hard Rock cheeseburgers and Pastamoré lasagna are on the menu, but so are more exciting choices like Bob Marley's curry chicken, Latin Quarter's arroz con pollo, and Pat O'Brien's jambalaya.

A slightly better deal is the **Party Pass with a Movie** ($15.98 including tax), which combines the standard Party Pass with a movie at the Cineplex. With this deal the incremental cost of a flick is about $3.21; or from another perspective, you're paying for the film, and getting into the clubs for $5.98.

What's The Best Price?

If you purchased a multi-day theme park pass, then price is not a consideration: 14 consecutive days of CityWalk club access is included. Go. Boogie. Enjoy. Otherwise, you may want to spend a few moments considering your options. If you plan on visiting most, if not all, of the clubs on a single night, the Party Pass is a fabulous deal. Of course, it's nearly impossible to visit all the clubs in one night, so you'll miss a lot. But even if you only visit two, the Party Pass pays for itself.

However, be aware that it is possible to visit two clubs and pay only one cover charge. It works like this: The cover charge clicks in at 9:00 p.m., but they don't go around from table to table to collect the cover from those already in the club. So you could arrive at, say, Marley's half an hour before the cover takes effect, grab a good seat and catch the first show. Then you could move on to, say, Rising Star, paying the $7 cover there. If you call it a night then, you've only spent $7 in cover charges and saved a little money — $5.77, to be exact.

Since the additional cost of a Party Pass is so small, why not go for it? That way you can satisfy your morbid curiosity about clubs you otherwise wouldn't try. And who knows? You might discover a place you really love.

Good Things To Know About . . .

■ Discounts

Your Universal Orlando Annual Pass is good for a 20% discount for up to four people on the CityWalk Party Pass. At some times of the year (which seem to vary), your Annual Pass is good for a complimentary Party Pass from Sunday to Thursday. Your Preferred Annual Pass will also get you a 10% discount on food and beverages (excluding alcohol) at many restaurants and clubs, and 2-for-1 beer at the groove; Premier passholders get an additional 5% (except at Bubba Gump) plus 2-for-1 well liquor at the groove and Rising Star. Members of the American Automobile Association (AAA) are eligible for discounts at some restaurants (indicated in the Times & Info brochure) and shops.

However, which card gets what discount where is subject to constant change, so the best policy for the traveling tightwad is to ask about discounts every time you have to pay for something.

Drinking

The legal drinking age in Florida is 21 and the law is strictly enforced in City-Walk. The official policy is to "card" (i.e. ask for identification) anyone who appears under 30. So if you fall into this category make sure to bring along a photo ID such as a driver's license or passport to prove your age. Once you've passed muster, your server will attach a plastic bracelet to your wrist, so you don't have to produce ID for the rest of the evening.

Alcoholic beverages are sold quite openly on the streets of CityWalk and from walk-up stands at the various clubs along the Promenade. To prevent those over 21 from purchasing drinks for underage friends, a standard policy is to sell one drink per person. Just to make sure, CityWalk maintains a very visible security presence (see below).

First Aid

And speaking of drinking, if you fall down and injure yourself, or have another health problem, there is a first aid station located near Guest Services. Just follow the passage to the restrooms and look for the door at the end of the passage.

Happy Hour

Some restaurants and clubs in CityWalk have a generous happy hour that runs from 3:00 to 7:00 p.m. when draft beers are $2 and well drinks $3. Occasionally, some places will have a happy hour that runs all day. The bar in Cigarz, however, does not offer a happy hour.

Money

There is an ATM on your left as you enter CityWalk, near the Guest Services window. There are others just outside the upper exit from the Cineplex, near Cigarz, and near the groove disco.

Private Parties

Most of CityWalk's restaurants have facilities for private parties. The central number for information is (407) 224-CITY (2489) for groups of more than 20 and (407) 224-FOOD (3663) for smaller groups.

Reservations

Of the restaurants and nightclubs, only Emeril's officially accepts (indeed, demands) reservations, which can be made up to six months in advance by calling (407) 224-2424 or faxing (407) 224-2525. Most others officially operate on a first-come, first-served basis. You may have to stand on line for admittance, but some restaurants take your name and give you a silent pager (it vibrates) to alert you when your table is ready.

However, there is a way around this no-reservations policy. If you dial (407) 224-3663, between 8:00 a.m. and 4:00 p.m. on the day you wish to dine, you will reach the "Priority Seating Request Line." You can also make a request at the information kiosk you see when you enter CityWalk. Priority seating is available at all restaurants except Emeril's.

Note: If you are a guest at a Universal Orlando resort hotel, you can flash your room key card at the restaurant for priority seating.

Priority seating is subtly different from a reservation. A reservation, in theory, guarantees you a seat at the specified hour. Priority seating carries no such guarantee. It means that the restaurant will give you the first table that will accommodate your party that becomes available at or after the time you requested. That can mean immediate seating or a long wait; still, a priority seating request should make the wait shorter than it would be without it.

Restrooms

Most restrooms are inside the restaurants and nightclubs. You'll find "public" restrooms tucked away down corridors next to Guest Services, near NASCAR Sports Grille, and near The Latin Quarter on the Promenade.

Security

CityWalk's security is so pervasive and so visible that some people might wonder if there's something to be worried about. In addition to the in-house security staff with their white shirts emblazoned with the word "SECURITY," you will see armed members of the Orlando police force. What you won't see are the undercover security personnel who mingle with the crowds.

The primary mission of all these security elements is to prevent any abuse of state liquor laws. For example, while you can stroll around City-Walk with your beer or cocktail, you are not allowed to carry it back to your car or into the parks.

Valet Parking and Validation

Most restaurants will validate your valet parking ticket during lunch hour (11:00 a.m. to 2:00 p.m. Monday through Friday only). A two-hour stay is free. Emeril's validates anytime including Saturdays and dinner. The Cineplex does not validate parking.

The Talk of the Town

Just as the theme parks have their five-star attractions, there are some very special things in CityWalk. We have not attempted a star rating system for CityWalk but instead offer this highly subjective list of personal favorites in a number of categories.

Best food. Emeril's has to be the choice here. Best wine list, too. There's really no serious competition.

Best bar. The funky bar at the back of Cigarz, a cigar shop near the upper exit of the Cineplex, is hip and hidden. The bar at Hard Rock Cafe with its spinning Caddy takes second prize.

Best food value. When you factor in what you pay for what you get, NBA City comes out on top, with Bubba Gump a close second.

Best place to take the kids. Hard Rock Cafe is the best, but NBA City, NASCAR Sports Grille, and Margaritaville all have kid-friendly aspects.

Friendliest service. Bubba Gump.

Best burgers. The Hard Rock Cafe. Have yours with one of their rich chocolate milk shakes.

Best dessert. Emeril's elaborate creations take the cake in this category.

Best for the midnight munchies. Finding food after midnight is not always possible, but if Pat O'Brien's is serving late, that's the clear winner. Otherwise, check out the "grazing" menu at Jimmy Buffett's.

Most romantic. If you're idea of "romantic" is letting your date know you're dropping a bundle on the meal, then Emeril's is the place for you. Otherwise, there's nothing at CityWalk that meets the "dinner by candlelight" definition of romantic. For free romance, take a moonlight cruise to the resort hotels on a shuttle boat.

Most fun. Jimmy Buffett's Margaritaville, with its wild and wacky decor and exploding volcano, wins the prize here.

Best decor. The Hard Rock Cafe. Never has the teenage wasteland looked so elegant.

Coolest. The hip and witty Red Coconut Club is one of the best clubs in Orlando. At the opposite end of the style spectrum, the funky cigar shed bar at Cigarz offers its own brand of hipness.

185

AMC Universal Cineplex

This is the mall multiplex writ large and it's hard to miss because it's the first thing you see on your right as you arrive from the parking lots. Given its 4,800 seats in 20 theaters on two stories, it's unlikely you have anything quite like it at home.

The soaring lobby is decorated with giant black and white banners depicting cinema heartthrobs, and escalators whisk you past them to the nine theaters upstairs. The theaters range in size from an intimate 150 seats to nearly 600. Unfortunately, 20 theaters does not mean 20 films. Expect the usual assortment of first-run features with the very latest releases playing in multiple theaters and midnight screenings of cult favorites. If you live in or near any moderately sized city in the United States, chances are all the films playing at the Cineplex are playing back home; it's just that here they're all under one roof. Of course, all the theaters here have stadium seating with plush high-backed seats that rock gently, and the screens are about twice the size of those you are probably used to. The Cineplex shows the new "RealD" digital 3-D films, and you can keep the glasses. Every theater is also equipped with Sony Dynamic Digital Sound (SDDS), touted as "the most advanced digital cinema sound system in the marketplace today." So all in all, catching a movie here is a viable option for a rainy Florida afternoon.

There is also an IMAX screen in the Universal Cineplex. If you're wondering how they removed the roof to install one of those massive screens you remember from the science museum, don't worry: they didn't. This is the new all-digital version of IMAX, dubbed by some "LieMAX." An existing theater (in this case screen 17, already the Cineplex's largest) was retrofitted with dual 2K projectors and a beefier sound system. The original screen was replaced by one marginally larger and closer to the audience, and the first couple rows of seats were removed (though not enough to make sitting in front on the sides anything but nauseating). This "patented geometry" is supposed to create the illusion of a much larger picture, but in our opinion the modest improvement isn't worth the premium price. A possible exception is for IMAX 3D, which is more impressive than its RealD competition. Even then, we'd recommend driving down Universal Boulevard to Pointe Orlando's Regal Cinema, which has a "real" giant-screen IMAX.

Admission (including tax) for adults is $10 for evening shows; bargain matinees (all shows that start before 3:55 p.m.) are $8. Children 2 to 12 pay $7. "A.M. Cinema" (shows that start before noon on weekends and holidays) are $5. Seniors (60+) pay $9 and student tickets are sometimes offered. Add an additional $4 per ticket for RealD 3D, $5 for IMAX, and

$6 for IMAX 3D. Annual Pass holders save $2 off the admission price (no further discounts).

In addition to the regular box office windows, there are vending machines to your right that allow you to skip the line and purchase tickets, at no extra charge, using your credit card. More detailed information can be obtained from a human being by calling (407) 354-3374. Or purchase tickets in advance online at www.fandango.com. Fandango charges a "convenience fee" of "up to" $2; tickets can be printed out at home or picked up at the box office.

Don't worry about going hungry while you watch. There is the usual array of soft drinks, popcorn, and candy, all at inflated prices. More interesting are the mini-pizzas, nachos, and ice cream sundaes. There's even a coffee bar if you crave a latte and a full liquor bar serving up exotic cocktails, beer, and wine coolers.

Anyone who has suffered through a serious drama with a kid kicking the back of their the seat will appreciate AMC's "Distraction-Free Entertainment" policy. To quote: "In order to provide the most enjoyable experience for adults attending R-rated features in the evenings, no children younger than 6 will be admitted to these features after 6 p.m." Bravo, we say!

A major disappointment, however, is the lack of a "revival house" — a theater dedicated to showing classic films. Since Universal Studios produced films by Mae West, W.C. Fields, and the Marx Brothers, among many other greats, this would be a logical addition. It would also be a terrific way for Universal to help educate the next generation of filmmakers who have precious few opportunities to see the great films of the past. On the other hand, the Cineplex has regular midnight performances of cult classics like *The Rocky Horror Picture Show*, complete with a live cast of bizarro fans in costume acting out on stage, so maybe film buffs won't be too disappointed (visit www.richweirdoes.com for midnight movie information).

Tip: You may want to exit on the upper level, even if you are seeing a film on the Cineplex's bottom level. From there you can either descend the narrow zigzag street lined with shops, or stroll along the sloping Promenade, home to CityWalk's row of restaurants and nightclubs.

RESTAURANTS AT CITYWALK

We make a distinction between CityWalk restaurants and CityWalk night-clubs, although some don't. The difference is somewhat hazy in practice, since some restaurants offer terrific entertainment (usually at night, usually with a cover charge) and some nightclubs serve excellent food. The main distinction seems to be that "restaurants" open early in the day and serve full meals, while "nightclubs" open in the late afternoon or early evening and serve only a limited food menu. Among the restaurants, Jimmy Buffett's Margaritaville turns into a nightclub, with cover charges, in the evenings. NASCAR Sports Grille and Latin Quarter offer the occasional entertainer in their al fresco dining areas, and NBA City screens great moments in basket-ball history all day. All the others are strictly dining establishments. All restaurants (except Emeril's) serve the same menu at the same prices all day.

Hard Rock Cafe

What:	American casual cuisine
Where:	Across the waterway
Price Range:	$$ - $$$
Hours:	11:00 a.m. to midnight (kitchen closes at midnight)
Reservations:	None
Web:	www.hardrockcafe.com

The immense structure across the water, with the peculiar hodgepodge architecture, the Caddy sticking out of the facade, and the huge electric signs, is the world's largest and busiest Hard Rock Cafe. Those who have visited other Hard Rocks will know what to expect — just expect more of it. For the uninitiated, the Hard Rock Cafe is a celebration of rock and roll his-tory and lifestyle that has become an international marketing and merchan-dising phenomenon. From its auspicious beginnings in London's Mayfair section, Hard Rock has grown to a mega-chain, with restaurants in virtually any city that has pretensions to world-class status.

The Hard Rock's primary claim to fame is its extensive and ever-grow-ing collection of rock memorabilia that is lovingly and lavishly displayed.

As befits the largest Hard Rock in the world, the Orlando outpost has some spectacular mementos. After your meal, take the time to wander about and drink it all in. The staff won't mind; they're used to it. If you're lucky, they will be running free tours of the memorabilia collection.

There is dark paneling and deep carpeting on the floors and winding wooden staircases. There are rich gold frames on the photos, album covers, gold records, and other memorabilia that fill every inch of wall space. "Rock and roll is here to stay," they like to say. "We've got it screwed to the walls!" Upstairs, take note of the two circular rooms, one at each end, dedicated to the Beatles and the King. There's even an elegant wood-paneled library.

At the heart of the restaurant, downstairs, is a circular bar open to the second level. A magnificent 1961 pink Cadillac convertible spins lazily over the bar and above that is a splendid ceiling mural straight out of some domed chapel at the Vatican. Except that here the saints being serenaded by the angels are all dead rock stars, most of whom died from drug overdoses. To one side is a trio of towering stained glass windows paying homage to Chuck Berry, Elvis Presley, and Jerry Lee Lewis. All in all, this expansive Hard Rock has the look and feel of a very posh and very exclusive men's club — which is perhaps what rock and roll is, after all.

Tip: If your party is small, the bar is an excellent place to eat. The bar offers the full menu and quicker seating when the place is crowded. A seat here gives you an excellent vantage point from which to soak up the ambiance. If the downstairs bar is full, there is another upstairs.

The Hard Rock Cafe is also justly famous for its American roadhouse cuisine, which gives a nod to the black and southern roots of rock. Burgers, barbecue, and steak are the keynotes, with sweet and homey touches like milk shakes, root beer floats, and outrageous sundaes. It's no wonder the place was an instant hit when it opened in the midst of London's culinary desert. The menu also reminds us that, in its heyday, rock's superstars were scarcely more than kids. This is teenybopper comfort food prepared by expert cooks for people who can afford the best.

Probably the heart of the menu is the selection of barbecue dishes ($12 to $24), with the chicken and ribs combo a popular favorite. For those who prefer their barbecue Carolina-style, there's a pulled-pork pig sandwich. A big step up in sophistication are steaks like the succulent New York Strip.

Of course, if you're still a teenager at heart, you'll order a burger ($10 to $15). The best is the Hickory BBQ Bacon Cheeseburger, but there's also a Veggie Burger to keep Sir Paul happy. If you want to return to your pre-cholesterol-crisis youth, you'll have a milk shake or a root beer float with your burger. The fries that go with them are very good, too.

Tip: Root beer floats aren't on the menu, but they'll whip one up if you ask nicely.

Lighter appetites can be satisfied with one of the appetizers ($7 to $18) or a salad ($10 to $12), while bigger appetites can order a small Caesar salad to go with their entree. But save room for dessert ($6 to $8) because the HRC Hot Fudge Brownie lives up to its fabled reputation.

Your meal comes complete with a soundtrack, of course, and the excellent choice of songs leans heavily to the glory days of rock in the late sixties and early seventies. Television monitors, dotted around the restaurant and gold-framed like the rest of the memorabilia, identify the album from which the current track is taken. The volume has been turned up (this is rock and roll, after all) but not so high as to make conversation impossible.

No self-respecting Hard Rock Cafe would be without a shop hawking Hard Rock merchandise, and this one has two. They are labeled simply **Hard Rock Store** in big bold letters. Believe it or not, the shops sometimes have lines just like the restaurant and they are handled the same way, with a roped-off queue filled with people who can't wait to add another Hard Rock shot glass to their growing collection.

NBA City

What:	American casual cuisine
Where:	Across the waterway
Price Range:	$$ - $$$
Hours:	Sunday through Thursday 11:00 a.m. to 11:00 p.m.; Friday and Saturday to 11:30 p.m. During busy times they will stay open later.
Reservations:	(407) 363-5919
Web:	www.nbacity.com

This modern mélange of weathered brick, steel, glass, and concrete is almost dwarfed by the statue of a dribbling basketball player that graces its entrance. Both the building and its interior evoke the ambiance and mystique of a classic 1940s-era basketball arena, and devotees of the game will find much to enjoy here.

The two-level dining area, dubbed the CityWalk Cage, seems intimate but it holds nearly 375 people at capacity. The floor is that of a highly polished basketball court filled with tables. In fact, this is a regulation half court that can be cleared of tables and booths so that visiting NBA stars can hold clinics with eager youngsters, while fans watch from the upper level. Two massive projection screens flank the hoop and multiple monitors dot the walls. A constant stream of taped highlights from championship seasons past plays during your meal, with the volume thoughtfully turned up for the hard of hearing. There is the occasional nod toward women's professional basketball, but the emphasis is plainly on the guys.

This is hardly the place for a quiet business discussion or a romantic tête-à-tête. But if your idea of a good time is watching your hoop heroes' finest moments while you drop food into your lap, you'll love it here.

If you'd like some relief from the general din, try the **Skybox Lounge**, a bar and lounge on the second level, to the front of the building. Its decor is that of a posh sports club with cushy sofas and banquettes. If you wish, they will serve your meal here. The Skybox Lounge also offers an extensive menu of pricey specialty drinks. The drinks, as well as a modest wine list ($25 to $55), are available in the main restaurant. There is another quiet refuge on the second level, a glassed-in wedge of a dining area that is sometimes set aside for VIPs and private parties, but you can ask for it and see.

The food is good enough to deserve a little attention of its own. The cuisine, which might be described as upscale sports bar, is very good and the portions seem to have been designed to fill up those eight-foot-tall basketball behemoths. Eating a starter and an entree may well force you to skip the scrumptious desserts. Many people will find a starter plenty big enough for a satisfying meal.

Appetizers ($9 to $16) include such standards as chicken wings, flatbreads, and quesadillas. The Parmesan Chicken Tenders could make a full meal, with a biting mustard sauce worthy of the name. For the lighter appetite, entree salads ($12 to $15) are offered, with side salads ($5) also available.

The main entrees ($16 to $29) lean heavily to hearty meat and fish dishes like pork chops, steak, and salmon. Pastas ($14 to $15) tend to feature chicken and fish, with some daily specials priced slightly higher. Sandwich offerings ($9 to $11) include a Philly Cheesesteak and a Caribbean-spiced grilled mahi mahi. Ten-inch personal pizzas ($11 to $13) round out the menu. A "Rookie Menu" for kids features a small choice of entrees and a drink for $7 to $9.

Among the desserts ($6 to $8), the star is an NBA City original, the Cinnamon Berries. Exquisitely ripe strawberries are dipped in batter, flash fried, coated in cinnamon sugar, and elegantly displayed in a circle on a bed of vanilla cream filigreed with strawberry sauce; a dollop of vanilla ice cream in a cinnamon tortilla cup topped with another fresh strawberry forms the centerpiece. It may sound a little weird but it's delicious.

Tip: The food and drink are only part of the fun here. In fact, you don't have to have a meal to enjoy NBA City. The entrance is flanked by a display of bronze basketballs bearing the handprints of basketball greats. If you've ever wondered why you're not in the NBA, losing your own hand in these massive prints will give you a hint. Inside, before you enter the dining room, you'll find the **NBA City Playground,** a place where you can test your free-throw skills and, if you're good enough, get some fleeting fame on the electronic scoreboard.

There is also a shop filled with NBA-branded clothing, personalized jerseys, and novelty items. This area stays open for about an hour after the restaurant stops serving.

Jimmy Buffett's Margaritaville

What:	Casual food with an island flair
Where:	Near the bridge to Islands of Adventure
Price Range:	$$ - $$$
Cover:	$7 after 10:00 p.m.
Hours:	11:00 a.m. to 2:00 a.m. (full menu until 11:00 p.m., snacks until 1:00 a.m.)
Reservations:	Priority seating only; (407) 224-2155
Web:	www.margaritavilleorlando.com

After crossing the bridge from Islands of Adventure and the NBA Restaurant, this is the first place you encounter in the main section of CityWalk, and a welcoming joint it is. Owned by singing star Jimmy Buffett and reflecting the easygoing themes of his popular songs, Margaritaville is a hymn to the laid-back life of the Parrot Head.

Probably the first thing you'll notice is the Hemisphere Dancer, the actual Grumman Albatross Jimmy immortalized in his book *A Pirate Looks At Fifty*. Today it serves as an over-the-top prop for **Lone Palm Airport,** a walk-up bar with a kids' play area and outdoor seating (see *Fast Food at CityWalk*, below).

After a fortifying drink, you'll be ready to step inside. The various sections of the bar-restaurant are decorated to reflect Jimmy's many interests and the songs he wrote about them. The **Volcano Bar** answers the question, "Where you gonna go when the volcano blows?" Every 45 minutes or so the volcano atop the bar rumbles ominously to life and spews out bubbling margarita mix that cascades down the slopes into a huge blender on the bar.

In the restaurant section, the booths are styled to evoke the back end of a fishing boat. Look up and you'll see a model of the Hemisphere Dancer. Huge whales and hammerheads "swimming" overhead decorate another bar section. Outside, facing Islands of Adventure, is the **Porch of Indecision**, a verandah seating area that frequently features its own entertainment. Buffett fans will enjoy spotting the insider references scattered through the decor while others will be having too much fun to care.

The "Floribbean" cuisine draws its inspiration from all aspects of Buffett's life story, from his Gulf Shore roots to his Caribbean island-hopping. The food also reflects the atmosphere of the ultra-casual off-the-beaten-track island bars where Buffett used to perform, chow down, and waste away.

There's a heavy emphasis on fresh seafood and the corn and crab chowder (under $5) is quite good. Those who are serious about their food will probably find their best choice the ever-changing Catch of the Day, prepared to order. The rest of the menu runs heavily to salads, sandwiches, and junk food (in the best possible sense of the term). There are nachos, conch fritters (super!), and fried calamari, and the servings are generous to a fault. Prices are moderate; only a couple of choices are over $20. A separate kids' menu features meals for $7.

Perhaps the spicy Louisiana- and Jamaican-inspired dishes like Jambalaya and Bayou Shrimp Pasta fare best. The Cheeseburger in Paradise ($11), alas, is merely a large but otherwise undistinguished example of the genre. Far better are sandwiches like the Pulled Pork, about $11. Better still is the King Crab and Shrimp Salad ($15), which is served as an entree in a huge shell-shaped bowl. There's good news on the desserts ($4 to $6). The Key Lime Pie is a winner and the Chocolate Banana Bread Pudding is to die for.

Beer drinkers will appreciate the wide selection of premium bottled brews (about $5). For those who like their drinks on the sweet side, the specialty drinks run about $7 and are available in non-alcoholic versions for less.

A restaurant by day, Margaritaville transforms itself after the dinner crowd thins out into a cross between a nightclub and a full-fledged performance space showcasing bands and live performers that reflect in one way or another that certain indescribable Jimmy Buffett style. The house bands here are very good, alternating between Buffett standards and a mix of calypso, easy-going rock, and country-western. Every great once in a while, Buffett himself drops by. When that happens, Margaritaville becomes the hottest spot in all of Florida.

Jimmy Buffett has been very savvy in marketing himself, so it's no surprise that there's a very well stocked gift shop, the **Margaritaville Smuggler's Hold**, attached to the restaurant with a second entrance from the

Plaza. Here Parrot Heads can fill in the gaps in their Buffett CD collection or buy one of his books (he's a pretty good writer it turns out). In addition, there are plenty of T-shirts, gaudy Hawaiian shirts, and miscellaneous accessories that the well-dressed beach bum simply can't afford to be without.

Latin Quarter

What:	Nuevo Latino cuisine
Where:	Next to Jimmy Buffett's
Price Range:	$$$
Cover:	$7 after 9:00 p.m.
Hours:	Daily 4:00 p.m. to 10:00 p.m. for food; club stays open until 2:00 a.m. Thursday to Saturday
Reservations:	None

This restaurant and part-time nightclub salutes one of the newer ethnic groups to get stirred into the cultural menudo that is the United States — the natives of the 21 Spanish-speaking nations that lie south of the border. It does this most notably through its pan-South-American cuisine. If you're thinking of Tex-Mex cliches with their heavy leaden sauces, think again. The cooking style here draws its inspiration from traditional recipes but reinterprets them in very modern fashion.

The large, two-level space with its arching blue walls creates the illusion of a sultry tropical night in the ruins of an ancient city. The first-floor stage is flanked by two massive Aztec gods and backed by what surely must be the Andes. Upstairs, a balcony seating area looks down on the spacious dance floor in front of the stage.

The food here is hearty but unexceptional. The kitchen makes a stab at so-called Nuevo Latino cuisine, with its elaborate presentations, but falls far short of the standards set by the best restaurants in this genre. Among the appetizers ($8 to $14), the cheese-stuffed, bacon-wrapped grilled shrimp is a real winner. Salads ($4 to $14) are delicious and make an excellent choice if you'd like a light meal. Try the chicken breast or the grilled Chilean salmon over greens.

The entrees ($10 to $29) were designed with the he-man meat-lover in mind. The Churrasco Skirt Steak takes the humble skirt steak, rolls it up into a tower and serves it over a bed of garbanzos, ham, and chorizo. Among the seafood entrees the more interesting choices include the Caribbean crusted mahi mahi and the red snapper topped with chorizo sausage. They also do a daily special with Chilean sea bass that is worth considering. There is a separate menu section highlighting a variety of fajitas ($15 to $16).

The desserts ($6) include a caramelized banana custard and mango cheesecake. To ease the strain on the family pocketbook, a kids' menu featuring $6 meals is offered.

Drinkers have their choice of a lengthy menu of specialty drinks that salute various Latin American countries ($7 to $10). Mixed drink enthusiasts could do worse than set a goal to sample them all. For the less adventuresome, beer is also served and it makes an excellent accompaniment to most of the dishes. A small wine list is offered ($24 to $48).

In the evening, on Thursday (Ladies' Night) through Saturday, Latin Quarter features low-key, live entertainment. Typically it will be an excellent flamenco guitarist, playing on the outdoor patio when the weather cooperates or indoors when it doesn't. At 10:30 p.m., Latin Quarter turns up the heat with a Latin D.J.

Emeril's Restaurant Orlando

What:	Gourmet dining
Where:	On the Plaza
Price Range:	$$$$+
Hours:	Lunch 11:30 a.m. to 2:00 p.m.; dinner 5:15 p.m. to 10:00 p.m. Sunday through Thursday; to 11:00 p.m. Friday and Saturday
Reservations:	Mandatory. Call (407) 224-2424; fax (407) 224-2525
Web:	www.emerils.com

Emeril Lagasse, the popular TV chef and cookbook author, brings his upscale New Orleans cuisine to Orlando in this lavish eatery decorated (if that's the word) with over 10,000 bottles of wine in climate-controlled glass-walled wine cases. This is an extremely handsome restaurant that evokes and improves upon Emeril's converted warehouse premises in the Big Easy. The main dining room soars to a curved wooden roof and the lavish use of glass on the walls facing the Plaza makes this a bright and sunny spot for lunch. The exposed steel support beams contrast with the stone walls and rich wood accents, while stark curved metal chandeliers arch gracefully overhead. It's a hip, modern look that matches the food and the clientele.

The cuisine is Creole-based, but the execution is sophisticated and the presentation elaborate. Many dishes follow a standard Emeril architectural template: A layer of hash, relish, or puree is topped by the main ingredient, which in turn is topped by an antic garnish of potatoes, onions, or some other vegetable sliced in thin strips and flash fried; the plate is then decorated with a few swirls or dots of various sauces, sprinkled with spices and greenery, and delivered to the table with a flourish. Many dishes are based on home-style comfort foods like barbecue, fried fish, or gumbos, and there's an unmistakable spiciness to much of it. The result is a cuisine that is fun and festive with only the occasional tendency toward self-conscious seriousness, making Emeril's a great choice for a celebratory blowout.

Despite its noisy, bistro-like atmosphere, this is a first-class restaurant where dining is theater and a full meal can last two and a half hours, with the per-person cost, with drinks and wine, easily rising to over $100. In the European fashion, Emeril's closes after lunch to allow the kitchen a chance to catch its breath and ready itself for a different and more extensive dinner menu.

Appetizers ($8 to $15 at lunch and dinner) include Panko-crusted fried green tomatoes and fried calamari along with the occasional more exotic creation. Soups and salads ($6 to $13) enjoy their own section on the menu and typically include a sturdy gumbo, savory oyster stew, and some artfully presented and deceptively simple green salads.

Entrees are in the $14 to $24 range at lunch, $26 to $45 at dinner. They include the odd-sounding but delicious andouille-crusted Texas redfish at dinner (a pecan-crusted version is offered at lunch). A four-course "degustation" menu with optional wine pairing, and a five- or six-course "tasting menu" served at a Chef's Table is also sometimes offered. At lunch, look for a moderately priced three-course prix fixe offering.

Desserts ($8 to $12) are equally elaborate, although it says something about the chef that his signature dessert is a homey banana cream pie served with chocolate shavings on a latticework of caramel sauce.

Dining here is a special experience. Emeril's is not the kind of place where you will feel comfortable in full tourist regalia, even though the management officially draws the line only at tank tops and flip-flops. Stop back at your hotel to change and freshen up.

Tip: If you are dining alone or there are just two of you, you might want to try the "Food Bar," a short counter with stools that looks into the kitchen. The primo dining location is the L-shaped dining area by the windows; VIPs are seated here, so reserve well in advance if it's your preference.

Emeril's, by the way, is strictly a restaurant; there is no entertainment. For most people, the tongue-tingling food will be entertainment enough.

Special note on reservations: Again, do remember that reservations are mandatory. Emeril's accepts reservations six months in advance and often books up completely several weeks in advance. So if you are planning on visiting at a busy time or are planning a special-occasion meal here, you will be well advised to book as early as possible. A day or two before your visit, the restaurant will call you to remind you of your reservation. By the way, the concierges at the resort hotels have no special pull with Emeril's.

During February and March, the height of the convention trade, reservations are extremely hard to come by; you'll have better luck in the hot summer months. So how do you get seats at the last minute? Most often you don't, but your best shot is to call at 3:15 p.m. on the day you want to dine. If all else fails (and this may, too), show up early and ask for a seat at the main bar, where people are seated on a first come-first served basis and can order from the full menu. Generally, it's easier, but by no means a slam-dunk, to come by a table on short notice at lunch.

Pastamoré

What:	Home-style Italian
Where:	On the Plaza
Price Range:	$$ - $$$
Hours:	5:00 p.m. to 11:00 p.m.
Reservations:	None

This cheerful and noisy Italian eatery blends contemporary decor with the homey touch of that old neighborhood Italian restaurant you loved as a kid. The decor is trendy postmodern with terra cotta walls and blue banquettes. Decorative accents are provided by Roman stone heads and words like "cucina," "pizza," and "antipasto" spelled out in cursive red neon. The menu features the kind of comfortable Italian dishes that won't have you reaching for your Italian-English dictionary.

Appetizers and salads ($4 to $10) include fried calamari, portobello mushroom ravioli, and Italian wedding soup. Pasta dishes ($13 to $18) range from straightforward lasagna and spaghetti to lobster ravioli and shrimp pasta with a spicy red pepper sauce. They also serve up some very tasty personal pizzas ($8 to $9) from a wood-fired pizza oven.

Meat and poultry dishes ($14 to $29) include such Italian staples as veal parmigiana or osso buco, and chicken marsala or piccata. Among the seafood entrees ($18 to $20) the Seafood Fra Diavolo is a standout. Vegetable side dishes ($3 to $5), include a wonderful broccoli with roasted garlic and lemon.

The wine list features Sangiovese reds for $23 to $110; half bottles of California wines are considerably less. Desserts ($3 to $5) are of the standard Italian variety and for $12 you can pig out on your choice of three of them.

Because everything is a la carte, the bill can add up quickly. A 15% gratuity is added to the bill for parties of six or more. Pastamoré has an attached deli and espresso bar that opens early; see the *Fast Food* section, below.

NASCAR Sports Grille

What:	All-American cooking
Where:	Near the bridge to Universal Studios Florida
Price Range:	$$ - $$$
Hours:	11:00 a.m. to 10:00 p.m.
Reservations:	(407) 224-RACE for priority seating
Web:	www.nascarsportsgrille.com

Just by the bridge that leads to Universal Studios, the large building that houses the NASCAR Sports Grille is an ode to speed. It swoops and leans and looks for all the world as if it's doing 120. In front of the main entrance (a two-story-tall evocation of the Nextel Cup trophy) sits a row of winning cars from NASCAR races.

NASCAR, in case you don't know, stands for National Association of Stock Car Automobile Racing, the organization that sets the rules for stock car racing and owns the tracks on which hard-driving, all-American folk heroes are created. Stock car racing is a distinctly American sport, with roots in the rural and blue-collar south. But if you were expecting a restaurant in which a grease-smeared good ole boy might feel at home, think again.

NASCAR Sports Grille is more upscale sports bar than down-home beanery. The decor is chic and sleek, with brown-on-brown booths, banquettes, and marble-topped bars. The design references to racing are mostly muted and discreet, although upstairs two race cars hang from the ceiling and periodically roar to life as their wheels spin furiously.

In true sports bar fashion the place is alive with television screens, small ones in the booths, plasma screens on many columns and a 37-foot "media wall" on the main level. They are just as likely to be tuned to baseball or football as racing, although on race days, the majority are given over to NASCAR.

There is seating on two levels. Downstairs, an entire wall can be opened up to the verandah on nice days creating a wonderfully spacious ambience. Upstairs, there is a narrow balcony that is a great place to dine on a balmy evening. Also upstairs is a small racing-themed arcade where you can let those antsy kids loose while mom and dad eat.

Tip: If you want to eat upstairs, let the hostess at the main entrance know. She will pass you on to the upstairs hostess.

The food follows the sports bar model, with an accent on steaks, ribs, and burgers and with seemingly no desire to dazzle. Appetizers ($7 to $17) include coconut shrimp, fried onion rings with a dipping sauce (excellent!) and nachos. There is also chili and a variety of salads.

Steaks ($17 to $25) range from a top sirloin to filet mignon. More affordable (and often better) are the chicken and ribs dishes ($12 to $23), including BBQ ribs and grilled pork chops. Seafood and pasta ($12 to $17) includes mahi mahi and "points leader" shrimp alfredo pasta. Burgers and other sandwiches ($10 to $12) are probably the most reasonable choices on the menu. The desserts, alas, are merely serviceable.

During **"Thursday Madness"** (7 p.m. to close) you can enjoy food and drink discounts while playing free video games in the Speed Zone Arcade. A small **NASCAR shop** with a separate entrance is filled with some nice logo-ed clothing and other NASCAR souvenirs.

Bubba Gump Shrimp Co.

What:	Seafood with a Southern flair
Where:	At the entrance to CityWalk
Price Range:	$$ - $$$
Hours:	11:00 a.m. to midnight
Reservations:	None
Web:	www.bubbagump.com

The infectious charm of the hit Tom Hanks film, *Forrest Gump,* suffuses the rambling, ramshackle bayou shrimp shack that greets you as you arrive at CityWalk. The wooden walls are covered with license plates, photographs from the film, little signs with pithy sayings, and flat-screen TVs that show the film over and over, without sound but with subtitles should you want to follow along. The place seems deceptively small from the outside, but it seats 500 in a series of dining rooms and two bars. Cajun music and 50s rock plays constantly and everyone seems to be in a great mood.

The servers are every bit as peppy as the soundtrack, smothering you with attention and good cheer. A signaling system at each table uses license plates to flag down passing servers should you need anything and before your meal is through it may seem like everyone in the place has stopped by to see how you're doing or challenge you to a *Forrest Gump* trivia test.

Shrimp is the order of the day here. It's everywhere on the menu and the cooks obviously know their way around this tasty little crustacean. Everything sampled here is very good indeed, but if you need guidance, the menu helpfully calls out "Bubba's All Time Best" choices with a little Bubba Gump shrimp logo. Appetizers ($5 to $14) feature breaded popcorn shrimp and the marginally more healthy Cajun shrimp, which is sauteed in butter and served with Gump's signature garlic bread for sopping up the sauce. Neither is too spicy. The Hush Pups, which are a good sight better than any hush puppies we've ever tasted, also deserve special mention.

The entrees ($16 to $20) showcase shrimp in a dazzling variety of guises, including fried, boiled in broth, stuffed, sauced, and in a spicy New Orleans style preparation over rice. A separate list features "Forrest's Favorites," such as Bourbon Street Mahi Mahi, a Salmon (or Mahi Mahi) Veggie Skillet, and non-shrimp dishes like fried chicken and baby back ribs.

Salads and sandwiches ($8 to $12) include a Dixie Fishwich, a Shrimp Po'Boy, and a Tossed Chicken Cobb. Desserts ($5 to $10) include "That Chocolate Thing" and an architecturally striking strawberry shortcake.

There is, of course, a **gift shop** offering Gump T-shirts and souvenir glasses, but perhaps the best choice here is a container of Bubba Gump shrimp boil and the restaurant's own cookbook that will let you take the taste of Bubba Gump's home with you.

Fast Food at CityWalk

There are a few less elaborate, less costly dining choices in CityWalk for those looking for morning coffee, a quick bite, or a budget-saving alternative to a full-course, full-price blowout meal. There are also a few al fresco spots to grab a quick drink!

▋ Pastamoré Marketplace Cafe

What:	Italian snacks, sweets, and wine
Where:	Between the Cineplex and the Plaza
Price Range:	$

This annex to the Pastamoré restaurant opens bright and early (at 8:00 a.m.) to serve strong coffee and strength-building pastries to the crowds arriving for a busy day at the theme parks. They also have "breakfast pizzas" that are worth a try. At lunch, the emphasis turns to Italian-style panini, pizza, pasta, and antipasto salads. Finally, late in the day, you can stop by again for dessert or a glass of wine. Indoor seating is limited and the few outdoor tables let you survey the passing scene.

Cinnabon

What:	Cinnamon buns and ice cream
Where:	Between the Cineplex and the Plaza
Price Range:	$

Across the street from the Pastamoré Marketplace Cafe is this branch of the nationwide chain famous for its oversized, gooey and delicious cinnamon buns at moderate prices. Ice cream and a small selection of desserts are also available. Seating is very limited and all outdoors. This place opens early to snag the breakfast crowd.

TCBY

What:	Frozen yogurt
Where:	Between the Cineplex and the Plaza
Price Range:	$

This outpost of the popular frozen yogurt chain serves up the usual variety of cold and creamy treats.

Starbucks

What:	Coffee, latte, and light snacks
Where:	On the Promenade near the escalator
Price Range:	$

The best thing about this airy coffee shop is the view over the plaza and the crowds below. Otherwise, it's pretty much like every other Starbucks you've ever been in, which is presumably the point. If you like the jolt of Starbucks, note that this one opens at 8:30 a.m. and stays open late. No wireless Internet access, though.

Fusion Bistro Sushi & Sake Bar

What:	Walk-up Japanese food
Where:	Near Cigarz
Price Range:	$-$$

This small, sleek outlet outside the Cineplex's second-story exit, serves serviceable, if not exquisite, sushi and sashimi. The stainless-steel bar isn't actually that inviting to sit at, but you can watch the chef inside through the window or on the closed-circuit TVs.

Appetizers ($3 to $5) include miso and edamame, and rolls ($5 to $12) range from simple California to Dancing Eel and Red Dragon (spicy tuna with jalapeño). Bento boxes ($12 to $16) include sushi, soup, salad, and a cookie; they are a slightly better value than buying a la carte. For dessert, try an oddly addictive Mochi rice cake ($4 for 3 pieces). Beverages include

Japanese beer ($4 to $5) and hot or chilled sake ($5 to $15).

The sushi here is a cut above your local supermarket and should give a satisfactory fix to vacationers in wasabi withdrawal. Just don't look for "expert" items like mackerel, yellowtail, or soft-shell crab on the menu; you'll have to go to Loews Royal Pacific for that (see the Orchid Bar in the next chapter).

▌ Whopper Bar/ Panda Express/ Moe's Southwest Grill

What:	Walk-up indoor burgers, Chinese, and Mexican
Where:	Opposite Cigarz
Price Range:	$

Three familiar franchises fill this mall-style food court, strategically located near the upper exit of the Cineplex. Burger King's outlet is the first in a spin-off chain centered on their signature sandwich. For a little more than your local drive-thru ($6 to $8 with small drink and fries) you can get a Whopper covered in gourmet toppings like guacamole, peppercorn bacon, and "angry onions." Panda Express serves passable stir-fry combo plates for $7 to $8, and Moe's tacos and burritos ($3 to $7) come with a free fresh salsa bar. A narrow balcony offers limited seating with a view of the plaza.

Tip: This is one of the only places on Universal property where you can comparison shop for soda — Panda's is the cheapest.

▌ Big Kahuna Pizza

What:	Walk-up pizza window
Where:	On the Promenade across from Starbucks
Price Range:	$ - $$

Nicely framed by gaudy pizza-themed surfboards, this simple stand serves up cheese or pepperoni pizzas, whole ($14 to $16) or by the slice ($3 and $4). Chicken wings are $6. You can wash it all down with draft beer ($5 to $6) or a soft drink.

▌ Fat Tuesday

What:	Walk-up daiquiri window
Where:	On the Promenade near the groove
Price Range:	$

Did you know that Louisiana allows drive-through alcohol sales? New Orleans staple Fat Tuesday has set up shop next to its hometown neighbor Pat O's to offer the next best thing: a stumble-through daiquiri bar. A chorus-line of slushy machines spin merrily and dispense frozen concoctions ($7, $10 in a souvenir cup with $6 refills) in flavors ranging from strawberry and mango to the aptly-named "Cat 5 Hurricane" and "190 Octane." $1 Jello shots and "tooters" are available for those who really want to get their party on, along with beer and soda.

Latin Express

What:	Walk-up snacks
Where:	On the Promenade near the Latin Quarter
Price Range:	$

Most of the nightclubs along the Promenade have walk-up windows dispensing specialty alcoholic drinks, but the Latin Quarter also serves up some tasty and inexpensive munchies for about $5 to $7. Choices include Cuban sandwiches, empañadas, and ropa vieja. Latin Express has irregular hours, but is generally open Wednesday through Sunday evenings.

Galaxy

What:	Walk-up bar
Where:	Near the Latin Quarter
Price Range:	$

No fast food, just fast booze. This walk-up full-service bar has a small seating area in the plaza framed by the groove, the Latin Quarter, and Emeril's. A nice place to sit and people watch.

Lone Palm Airport

What:	Walk-up bar with snacks
Where:	Opposite Margaritaville
Price Range:	$

Just outside Margaritaville stands a palapa-shaded bar that uses Jimmy Buffett's Hemisphere Dancer plane as the perfect backdrop. Makeshift tables are scattered about, surfboards lean against palm trees, and a sandy area is filled with kids' digging toys. It all evokes the kind of beachside dives Jimmy sings about so eloquently. Sit at the bar and watch Buffett music videos while munching on snack food and sipping (what else?) margaritas.

Every weekday, a 3:00 to 5:00 p.m. Happy Hour offers discounted appetizers and drinks.

ENTERTAINMENT AT CITYWALK

There are two theatrical entertainment venues at CityWalk, both located conveniently on either side of Hard Rock Cafe. One hosts a resident attraction while the other welcomes touring artists.

Blue Man Group

What: Avant garde theater performance

Where: Across the waterway next to Hard Rock Cafe

Tickets: Adults $78.81 to $89.46 at box office, $68.16 to $78.81 online; children 9 and under $25. 10% annual passholder discount

Hours: Varies widely. Call (888) 340-5476 or (407) 224-3200

Web: www.blueman.com or www.universalorlando.com

Back in the 80s, three "performance artists" created Blue Man Group in New York's seedy East Village. They were weird, hip, edgy, incomprehensible. They were the most avant of the avant garde. Today they are family entertainment. Such is cultural progress.

Now an international phenomenon, the Orlando edition of the troupe holds forth in an industrial-looking thousand-seat theater at the end of a long, winding pathway next to the Hard Rock Cafe.

And just what awaits at the end of that path? Well, perhaps the greatest compliment that can be paid Blue Man Group is that it is pretty much indescribable. Three very bald, very blue, very silent guys in black pajamas (could they be space aliens?) appear on a stage that seems to be part of a strange factory and do a series of odd things, some of which take real skill, some of which are very funny, and some of which are just plain wacky. They are at once consummate masters of ceremony and befuddled innocents who seem constantly surprised by the presence of the audience.

Some of the best segments involve the trio's considerable skill as percussionists (a four-man, day-glo combo assists from overhead). And who could have guessed how much entertainment value there was in pouring colored liquids onto drum heads? There's plenty of audience interaction and the show wraps up with a chaotic finale that involves everyone and sends the crowd out in a festive mood.

So what's it all about? Some see a critique of modern society, others detect commentary on the pretensions of modern art. Perhaps the best advice is to check your brain at the door and let the fun of the evening take over; the more you try to analyze, the less you'll enjoy the experience. They do not recommend the show for children under three; that could be stretched to five or six.

There is a tendency to compare this show to *La Nouba*, the Cirque du Soleil show over at Downtown Disney. This is unfair. *La Nouba* is a multi-million-dollar extravaganza with a large cast. *Blue Man* is, essentially, a three-man show that has grown over the years but that still sticks close to its Off Broadway origins. It's really an apples and oranges comparison.

Tip: The show lasts one hour and forty-five minutes, there is no intermission, and beer vendors work the crowd beforehand. You have been warned! (At least there's appropriate music in the restroom.)

The best seats in the house. All things being equal, the closer and more centrally located your seat, the better. The first four rows are designated as the "poncho zone" and those seated there are issued cheap plastic cover ups, just in case. But it's a far cry from a "splash zone" at SeaWorld and more marketing than anything else. Besides, the ponchos are a bit uncomfortable. Unless you're a die-hard fan, sitting a few rows farther back won't decrease your enjoyment one little bit. Zone 1, center is just about ideal. The "cheap seats" (Zones 3 and 4) are on a steeper incline and offer good sight lines of the whole stage.

Tickets can be ordered over the phone by calling (888) 340-5476 or (407) 224-3200 from 9:00 a.m. to 7:00 p.m. daily; you can also order online at the two web sites above (follow the prompts). There is a box office at the theater as well. You may also see offers combining a Blue Man ticket with theme park admission and a CityWalk Party Pass (typically saving around $15). College students with a valid school ID or ISIC card can get "rush" tickets at the box office on the day of the show for $30 each (limit two per ID).

The show schedule is somewhat erratic. Typically there are two shows a day at 6:00 and 9:00 p.m. But some days there is just one show at 8:00 p.m., or three shows at 3:00, 6:00, and 9:00 p.m. Some days there are none. Call or check the web sites for show times during your visit.

Hard Rock Live

What:	Rock performance space
Where:	Across the waterway next to Hard Rock Cafe
Tickets:	$10 and up, depending on the act
Hours:	Most shows start at 8:00 p.m. Box office open 10:00 a.m. to 9:00 p.m. daily.
Web:	www.hardrocklive.com

The Orlando Hard Rock Cafe may be the world's largest, but what really makes it special is its next door neighbor, Hard Rock Live, the chain's first live performance venue. Underneath that retro take on Rome's ancient Coliseum is a cutting-edge rock performance space loaded to the gills with sound, light, and video technology, including two video walls flanking the stage. In its standard configuration the joint holds 1,800. If they pull out the seats and turn the first floor into a mosh pit they can pack in 2,500, which still makes it "intimate" by rock standards. At the other end of the spectrum, they can use flywalls and props to shrink the performance space to the size of a truly intimate club.

The large stage (60 feet wide and 40 feet deep) offers bands plenty of room in which to rock and the computerized lighting system, strobes, and fog machines create the kind of dazzling effects that rock fans used to have to roll up and bring with them. Most important for the true aficionado, the sound system answers the burning question, "What does it sound like at ground zero of a nuclear explosion?" In other words, the place totally rocks.

Given the limited capacity, it's unlikely that the real giants of rock will be able to play here (at least not too often), but Elton John has fluttered like a candle in the wind here and hemi-demi-semi-stars both rising and falling are booked here with some regularity, including thus far the likes of Weird Al Yankovic, the Pet Shop Boys, Indigo Girls, and Elvis — Costello, that is.

If the music isn't blowing you away, you can repair to one of six bars and, depending on the show, you may be able to get something to nosh on from the Hard Rock Cafe kitchen, like hot dogs, wood-oven pizzas, or nachos.

Ticket prices are moderate, with most acts checking in at between $25 and $35 with the occasional show rising to $75 or so. Every once in a while you can catch an evening of rocker wannabes for as little as $10. Tickets can be purchased at the box office or, for an additional fee, from TicketMaster at (407) 839-3900. Tickets for some events can also be purchased online at www.hardrocklive.com. Most shows begin at 8:00 p.m., with the box office opening at 10:00 a.m. Information about upcoming events is available by calling (407) 351-5483 or online at the address just given.

NIGHTCLUBS AT CITYWALK

As mentioned earlier, nightclubs at CityWalk are those entertainment venues that open only in the evening and serve either no food at all or a limited food menu. Fortunately, the food served in the clubs is very good indeed. A brief rundown on the clubs, but very little additional information, can be found online at www.citywalkorlando.com.

Note: All clubs have a **$7 cover charge** that clicks in at 9:00 p.m. See *The Price of Admission* and *What's The Best Price?* at the beginning of this chapter for advice on how to avoid or, at least, minimize these cover charges.

Red Coconut Club

What:	Hip, retro dance club
Where:	On the Promenade
Hours:	4:00 p.m. to 2:00 a.m.

It's the Rat Pack meets the Jetsons in this witty evocation of 50s-era Las Vegas-style futuristic chic. Step inside and it's as if you are entering the living room of Frank Sinatra's Palm Springs getaway. Continue on and you step onto the palm-fringed outdoor patio, where the swimming pool serves as the dance floor and many-pointed stars hover in the dark blue night sky above. But this isn't a nostalgia trip. The club has a hip, ironic edge that's very twenty-first century. The tone is captured perfectly by Paul Anka, in his best Sinatra mode, crooning "Smells Like Teen Spirit" just like Old Blue Eyes himself might have put it across at the Copacabana. If Kurt Cobain ever heard it, he'd kill himself all over again.

The club has a surprisingly large capacity, yet it manages to seem quite intimate. The upstairs balcony offers a great perspective on the dance floor and bandstand below. It is usually open only on weekends, but it is available for private rental throughout the week. There's live music, too, of course, with a hip combo holding forth from a raised platform behind the patio bar.

The band tailors its repertoire to suit the crowd, moving easily from laid-back sophistication to more upbeat and harder edged selections. Late at night, a D.J. takes over to keep the crowd rocking until closing.

Martinis and Cosmopolitans ($10) are the featured drinks here, but you can also get mojitos and tropical specialties like Mai-Tais and Zombies ($9) as well as Red Coconut Clubs ($8), which are chilled shots mixed with Red Bull. There's wine, too, most of it Californian, but with a smattering of Australian and New Zealand imports. When it comes to champagne, the Club doesn't mess with success and offers a generous selection of French classics.

There is a brief and evolving menu of appetizer-sized nibbles ($7) including mini beef filets, coconut fried shrimp, sesame chicken skewers, and vegetable spring rolls with a honey soy dipping sauce. All the ones we've tried have been excellent.

Thursday is "**Ladies Night**," with complimentary admission and drink specials for females. Sunday's "**In-Crowd**" offers the same for hospitality workers.

What sets the Red Coconut apart from all other theme-park clubs is its bottle service. Order up a full bottle of premium liquor, wine, or champagne for your party ($120 to $420) and your table instantly becomes its own private club, complete with a red velvet rope limiting access to you and your guests. The bottle is delivered on a silver tray with your choice of two mixers. Pour it yourself or have your server do the honors. What a great way to impress your friends or business associates! And when you consider what it would cost to order drinks a la carte, it can be surprisingly cost-effective.

Bob Marley — A Tribute To Freedom

What:	Reggae club
Where:	On the Promenade
Hours:	4:00 p.m. to 2:00 a.m.; kitchen closes at 10:00 p.m.
Web:	www.bobmarley.com

Reggae fans will appreciate this salute to Bob Marley, the Jamaican-born king of reggae, where the infectious backbeat of Marley's lilting music mingles with the spicy accents of island cooking. Created under the watchful eye of Marley's widow, Rita, who has contributed Marley memorabilia for the project, this venue is as much a celebration of Marley's vision of universal brotherhood as it is a restaurant or performance venue.

When Marley first hit the U.S. scene, he was regarded as something of a dope-smoking revolutionary barbarian. Like many black artists, he suffered the indignity of having his songs "covered" by white artists (like Barbara Streisand!). But music hath charms to soothe the conservative as well as the savage breast and Marley's infectiously charming music gradually became domesticated, despite his occasionally radical-sounding lyrics. Today, his lilting "One Heart" is the unofficial national anthem of Jamaica, made universally familiar through the magic of television commercials.

Marley was a member of the Rastafarians, a religious sect with roots in 1920s Harlem, that believes in the divinity of the late Emperor Haile Selassie and the coming of a new era in which the African diaspora will return in glory to the Ethiopian motherland. "Rastas" shun alcohol, adhere to a vegetarian diet, and smoke copious quantities of ganja, or marijuana, which is seen as a gift from God and something of a sacrament. The nightclub that bears his name violates all those principles; there's plenty of booze, meat on the menu, and no ganja.

One thing close to Marley's heart that does get full expression here is the theme of universal brotherhood. It is preached by the M.C. and practiced by the patrons, making Bob Marley's perhaps the most multicultural entertainment venue in Orlando, a place that turns up the volume and lives out the words of Marley's most famous song: "One love. One heart. Let's get together and feel all right."

The exterior is an exact replica of 56 Hope Road, Marley's Kingston, Jamaica home. Inside you will find two L-shaped levels, each with its own bar, opening onto a spacious palm-fringed courtyard with a gazebo-like bandstand in the corner. Because both levels are open to the courtyard, Marley's is not air-conditioned but fans do a good job of keeping a breeze going.

The predominant color scheme is yellow, red and green, the national colors of Ethiopia; the lion statues evoke Haile Selassie's title of Lion of Judah, a motif that is repeated in the mural on the bandstand. The walls are covered in Marley memorabilia and the sound system pumps out a steady stream of Marley hits.

The nighttime entertainment, which kicks off at about 8:00 p.m., typically consists of a house band of skilled reggae musicians performing a mix of Marley hits, other reggae classics, and the occasional pop standard adapted to the reggae beat. The music of the house bands is good, but not so good that it makes you forget how much better Bob Marley and the Wailers were. Still, their main job is to get people out onto the dance floor, and they accomplish that task easily. After a few drinks and once you are gyrating with the crowds, you'll find no reason to quibble.

The "Rastafarian Tings" ($3 to $6) are non-alcoholic. However, the "Island Favorites," "Frozen Tings," and "Extreme Measures" ($8 to $9), fueled with island rum and other potent potables, are designed to help get you past your inhibitions and onto the dance floor. Of course, Red Stripe, Jamaica's favorite beer, is also available.

The food is designed more as ballast for the drinks than anything else, but it is quite good and a nice introduction to Jamaican fare for the uninitiated. The portions are about appetizer size, so you could well sample several in the course of a long evening.

Stir It Up is a cheese fondue laced with Red Stripe and served with vegetables for dipping; Jammin' is an island version of chips and salsa. The "Catch a Fire" chicken sandwich ($10) is marinated in "jerk" seasoning (a sort of all-purpose Jamaican marinade), grilled, and served with a creamy cucumber dipping sauce.

There are also both meat and vegetarian versions of Jamaican patties ($9 or $10), filled flaky pastries. More substantial fish entrees ($12 to $17) include grilled mahi mahi and pan-seared corvina. Several dishes are served with yucca fries, which look deceptively like French-fried potatoes but have a taste and texture all their own. Desserts ($5 to $7) are worth sampling, with the Is This Love mango cheesecake especially good. Fresh fruit on a skewer is also available.

A small shop counter in a downstairs corner hawks Marley T-shirts and polos as well as Marley CDs. This is probably as close as you'll get to finding the complete Marley discography in one place, a perfect chance to fill in the gaps in your collection. There is a small selection of books on reggae and Marley for those who would like to learn more.

"Legendary" Thursdays feature half-price appetizers and drink specials from 9:00 p.m. to close, and Sundays are "Ladies' Night."

Bob Marley's is a popular joint and on weekends can spawn long lines of people waiting for one of the 400 spaces inside to open up. Even early in the week, space can be hard to come by for those who don't arrive early. If you want to be in the thick of it, you'll definitely want to be downstairs. If you're not the dancing type, a row of stools along the railing of the upstairs balcony offers excellent sightlines to the stage. For a change of scenery, you can take your drink onto a second floor balcony that looks out over the Promenade.

Anyone looking for a fun evening of dancing and drinking and infectious music to go along with it will find little to complain about here. True Marley devotees will find everything they are looking for.

Everything but the ganja.

Pat O'Brien's

What:	The original dueling pianos, plus New Orleans cuisine
Where:	On the Promenade
Hours:	4:00 p.m. to 2:00 a.m.
Web:	www.patobriens.com

Step into Pat O'Brien's and you'll believe that you've been magically transported to the Big Easy. At least you will if you've ever visited the original Pat O'Brien's in New Orleans' French Quarter, because CityWalk's version is virtually a photographic reproduction. This is the first attempt to transplant the O'Brien's experience and word is that when O'Brien's owner visited CityWalk he marveled that Universal's design wizards had captured the place "right down to the cracks in the walls."

There are three main rooms at Pat O'Brien's. The Piano Bar houses the famed copper-clad twin baby grand pianos that are an O'Brien's trademark. This is strictly a bar, its brick walls and wooden beams hung with dozens of gaudy German beer steins that let you know this is a place for serious drinkers. Here a steady stream of superbly talented pianists keeps the ivories tickled almost constantly as patrons sing along, pound on the tables, and shout requests. In fact, Pat O'Brien's is credited with inventing the "dueling pianos" format that has been copied so often. The word seems to have gotten around that this is a great place to bring a bunch of old friends (or new acquaintances from the latest convention to blow through town) to drink and blow off some steam.

O'Brien's draws a somewhat older crowd than Marley's or Buffett's. If you're old enough to remember when popular music meant songs with lyrics you could actually understand, you'll probably have a good time here, especially if you can carry a tune and aren't shy about singing along.

Across from the Piano Bar is a smaller version, called the **Local's Bar**, minus the pianos but with a jukebox and large-screen projection TV that always seems to be tuned to some sporting event. Out back is a delightful open-air patio dining area. Here, at night, the ambiance is highlighted by yet another O'Brien's trademark — flaming fountains.

Upstairs is given over to private party rooms, but you can mount the stairs and find your way to a narrow balcony overlooking the Promenade. It's a great place to sip a drink and survey the passing scene.

And speaking of drinks, Pat O'Brien's (for those who don't know) is the home of the Hurricane ($10), a lethal and lovely concoction of rum and lord knows what all else that has made the place famous worldwide. In fact, the original New Orleans location pulls in more money than any other bar its size in the world.

Pat O'Brien's hasn't skimped on the food side of the equation. Devotees of New Orleans' spicy Creole- and French-influenced cuisine won't be disappointed even though the presentation and service are decidedly casual. Your meal arrives in little fake skillets lined with shamrock-dotted wax paper. Plates and utensils are black plastic. But the offhand presentation belies the sophistication of the cuisine. Prices are moderate, too, with nothing on the menu over $17 and many choices under $10.

The Jambalaya is a spicy medley of shrimp, chicken, andouille sausage, and rice flecked with vegetables. The blackened Louisiana redfish is a signature New Orleans dish and done well here. Perhaps best of all is the Cancun Shrimp, with its coconut-tinged frying batter and sweet, fresh fruit salsa. It's served over Pat O'Brien's signature French fries, dusted with paprika and ever-so-lightly spiced with cayenne before being fried to the perfect texture, and at $10 it's a real bargain. The Shrimp Gumbo appetizer comes in a small portion just right for the lighter appetite.

The Po' Boy sandwich is another Big Easy signature dish. It's a Creole take on the heroes and hoagies from up north. Pat O'Brien's version is a heaping portion of popcorn shrimp, fried oysters, or fried crawfish served on an open-faced baguette with a rich Cajun mayonnaise on the side. Eating it as a sandwich is a bit of a challenge, but worth it as the bread, veggies, seafood, and rich Cajun sauce play off each other very nicely indeed. It's served with those magnificent spicy French fries.

The Crawfish Nachos sounds better than it tastes. The delicate flavor of crawfish etouffé (very nice on its own) doesn't stand up well against the tortilla chips, melted cheese, and sour cream. For dessert ($4 to $6) choose from the Strawberry Hurricane Cheesecake or Pat O's Bread Pudding, redolent of nutmeg and cinnamon and served with a whisky sauce that packs a 100 proof wallop. There is also a kids menu, featuring simple meals for about $5.

"2 For Tuesdays" specials include half-price appetizers and 2-for-1 drinks, including Hurricanes (souvenir glass not included).

Out front, facing the Promenade, you'll find a small gift shop offering Pat O'Brien's souvenir glassware and other gewgaws.

the groove

What:	High-tech, high-gloss disco
Where:	On the Promenade
Hours:	9:00 p.m. to 2:00 a.m

the groove (the lower case is intentional) is CityWalk's dance club and it sets out to compete head to head with the legendary nightspots that have caught the public imagination in urban centers like New York, Chicago, and Los Angeles. It is also the only venue that does not come with a recognizable brand name. No Jimmy Buffetts or Bob Marleys to give this place instant name recognition. This joint stands or falls on its own merits.

It succeeds remarkably well by providing a place where a mostly young crowd (you must be at least 21 to enter) can come and boogie the night away in a cacophonous atmosphere that duplicates big city sophistication. The main difference is that here you will be let in even if you don't meet some snotty doorman's idea of what is currently cool and hip. Intimate it's not, with a maximum capacity of 1,277 on multiple levels, but with crowds comes excitement.

The design conceit is that you are in a century-old theater that is in various stages of renovation, but the dim lighting and pulsing light effects negate much of the intended effect. The various areas of the club provide ample space for those who want to thrash and writhe under pulsating lights to ear-splitting music while offering some refuge to those who just want to watch.

The main dance floor is dominated by a soaring wall of video monitors that operate separately and then coalesce to form a single image. Patterns of light swirl across the floor to disorienting effect. There is a small stage for visiting groups but we've never seen any here. Most nights the nonstop sound assault is provided by a D.J. The music is eclectic; typically the evening starts off with the more widely popular forms of dance music, with the mix changing gradually as the night wears on. Late at night, the music is predominantly "progressive house." If you don't know what that means you probably won't like it. But those who know it love it.

On Thursdays, the groove is successfully pursuing the time-warped clubgoers left homeless by the closure of Disney's "8-Trax" with its own "**80's Nights**." Admission is free before 10:00 p.m., and drink specials are available to get you in the new wave mood.

Wednesdays are often "**Teen Nights**" ($10 to $15), alcohol-free dance parties for 15- to 19-year-olds, lasting from 8:00 p.m. to midnight. The first soft drink is **free**. On these nights, the groove reverts to adult form at the witching hour. Teen Nights are more frequent during the summer months and are listed on the CityWalk Times & Info brochure.

Fortunately, there are some relatively quiet corners (50- to 80-seat bars actually) where you can get better acquainted with that special someone you just met on the dance floor. These are the Red, Blue, and Green Rooms, respectively, and each is decorated differently. The Red and Green Rooms are dim and deliciously decadent but the Blue Room is lit with a ghastly pallor that will flatter only Goths and vampires and seems designed to convince you you've had too much to drink. When it all becomes too much, you can repair to a balcony over the Promenade and look down on the latecomers standing in line.

Rising Star

What:	Karaoke club
Where:	On the Promenade
Hours:	Sunday through Thursday 8:00 p.m. to 1:00 a.m.;
	Friday and Saturday 7:00 p.m. to 2:00 a.m.

Located in an octagonal building almost at the geographical center of CityWalk, Rising Star is your neighborhood karaoke bar given an extreme makeover. The canned "tiny orchestra" on a portable CD player is gone, replaced by a live backing band with concert-quality lighting and sound systems. The only thing they can't upgrade are the vocal talents of the eager volunteers who line up for their shot at small-scale stardom.

The club's two-story design combines the intimate ambiance of a jazz club (its former incarnation) with the great sightlines of a conventional theater. A scattering of memorabilia from *Downbeat* magazine's Jazz Hall of Fame remains on the walls, with the rest covered by velvet curtains. The color scheme of soothing browns and rich reds, along with the plush banquettes, creates an aura of ultra-cool sophistication. The overall effect is at once festive and laid-back.

The format should be familiar: chose a song from their slender list of about 100 selections (classic rock standards and a smattering of Top 40), write it on a slip of paper, and wait your turn. You (and one friend) can join the band on stage, belting away with teleprompter lyrical assistance, while overhead video screens broadcast your performance to the back row. The musicians do a professional job of staying in time no matter how inebriated the intonations, though it's a wonder they don't go mad repeatedly recycling their short set list.

The food and beverage service is also fairly standard. You can have the bartender pour the usual well drinks for about $5, but there are also martinis ($8.50), wines by the glass ($4 to $8) and a variety of specialty drinks ($7 to $10). Food ($5 to $12) is something of an afterthought and includes potato skins, buffalo wings, and chicken fingers.

Rising Star opens at 8:00 p.m., and the band begins performing at 9:00. If you want to sing, get your request in early, as the club can fill up quickly, especially on weekends. On Sundays and Mondays the live band takes a break, so you and your and backup choir will be singing to prerecorded instruments.

SHOPPING IN CITYWALK

The designers of CityWalk had a difficult challenge when it came to creating retail spaces that would both complement and enhance their entertainment district. How do you create an upscale shopping experience that has the strength and credibility of major "brands" without offering "the same old thing," familiar big-name shops just like the ones holiday-goers have back home? And to hold its own against the entertainment venues, the shopping has to be pretty entertaining in its own right, without overwhelming CityWalk's prime reason for being. By and large, management has met the challenge.

The shopping here is fun without being overbearing, and the range of goods for sale fits in very well with the customers who come here — people on vacation, bent on having fun rather than purchasing necessities. There's probably nothing here that you can't live without, but there's also plenty of stuff you'd love to have, either as a special treat for yourself or as a gift for friends and family who couldn't make the trip with you. Prices, on the whole, are surprisingly moderate. Oh sure, you can drop a bundle if you want, but there's plenty here to appeal to a wide range of budgets.

■ Need another souvenir?

As you've probably noticed by now, nearly every entertainment venue has its gift shop selling branded souvenirs. So it comes as a relief that the major retail spaces do not simply repeat the merchandise themes you found in the theme parks.

The one exception is the **Universal Studios Store** that, with its towering and colorful exterior signage, dominates the CityWalk Plaza. Here you will find a tasteful selection of touristy trinkets, with an accent on nicely designed (and, hence, moderately expensive) clothing. The merchandise mix changes frequently to take advantage of seasonal fads or the latest Universal film venture in need of targeted promotion. It's not as large as its sister store in Universal Studios Florida but if you are in desperate need of something to remind you of your visit to either of the theme parks, you should be able to find something suitable, including selected Wizarding World of Harry Potter merchandise.

■ Clothe thyself

Clothing, the kind that doesn't advertise anything, can be found at several locations here. **Fresh Produce**, a large airy shop on the Plaza, features women's, girls', and infants' casual clothing in a limited palette of vibrant pastels. Many dresses and blouses are imprinted with bold and simple floral or animal motifs, for a sort of summery backyard feel. The designers, twin sisters from Colorado, describe their products as "make you feel good clothing." What will also make you feel good are the prices, which are surprisingly modest for the obvious stylishness of the clothes. Many ensembles can be put together for well under $100. Mothers and young daughters should have great fun picking out coordinating outfits here.

More casual clothing, this time with the emphasis on men's wear, can be found at **Quiet Flight Surf Shop**. It is easy to spot on your right, near the Cineplex, as you enter CityWalk; the display window framed by the huge curling wave is the tipoff. In this window, you will see from time to time a craftsman shaping a high-end surfboard. Although you can actually buy a surfboard here, the selection is small and most of the space is devoted to casual clothing designed to make you look like a well-heeled surf bum. There are wildly colorful print shirts for men and equally colorful "baggies," the capacious swim trunks favored by surfers. Women get almost equal time with a goodly selection of swimwear and casual poolside attire. Here you will also find the kind of accessories no well-dressed surfer should be without, from ultra-hip sunglasses to waterproof watches.

Photo Op: Before you move on, check out that curling fiberglass breaker one more time. There's a riderless surfboard perfectly positioned in the curl. Step aboard for a nifty souvenir photo.

Continue through the store and it turns into a **Tommy Bahamas** shop, with another entrance facing the waterway. This is a great place to pick up those high-end "tropical" shirts for men. Not only that, but these back-to-back shops make for a great air-conditioned shortcut when walking to or from the Universal Studios theme park.

Still more casual clothing can be found at the **Endangered Species Store**, which is to your left as you enter CityWalk. The shop's exterior has the look of some long-lost Southeast Asian temple complex, with the doorway flanked by twin elephants and guarded by a huge stuffed toy gorilla. The merchandise isn't quite that exotic, however. There are animal-themed T-shirts here as well as more dressy (and gaudy) examples of the genre. For the rest, it's a mixed bag of animal-themed gifts, figurines (some of them quite handsome), and bric-a-brac along with some stuff that was obviously chosen just because it's fun.

For accessories to go with your new wardrobe, head to the **Fossil** shop, which carries a selection of handbags, belts, and other leather goods, along with men's and women's watches in their signature retro-styled tins. You'll also find a rack of sunglasses at prices that won't blind you.

▌ What on earth was I thinking?

Another recurring theme of holiday shopping is the irresistible pull of the "novelty item." Otherwise sensible people, when far from home and in an expansive mood, will buy the darnedest things, and CityWalk has some wonderfully offbeat shops along Lombard Street that cater to this urge.

Katie's Candy Co., in the middle of Lombard Street, serves up by-the-pound candy that you certainly don't need at prices that are higher than in the theme parks. Of course nothing fits this theme like a tattoo and, if you're game, **Hart and Huntington** is there to oblige. They also sell T-shirts and other gear of the sort that might freak your mom out.

Element, at the bottom of the street, is an offshoot of the professional skateboarding team of the same name. This shop sells customized skateboards, "Von Zipper" sunglasses, stylish sneakers, and any other apparel you need to accessorize your extreme sports lifestyle.

Finally, back up at the top of Lombard Street, opposite the Whopper Bar, is **Cigarz at CityWalk**, which doesn't quite fit into any category. Most obviously it is a cigar store wonderfully decorated to evoke an old Cuban cigar factory, complete with sheaves of tobacco leaves hanging from the corrugated tin roof. A walk-in humidor holds the good stuff, while the rest of the shop offers exotic cigarettes and a variety of paraphernalia for the serious cigar buff. Best of all, at the back is a compact and cozy bar where smokers, preferably cigar smokers, can repair for quiet conversation, a warming scotch, and a fine cigar. Yes, you can actually smoke here, thanks to a loophole in Florida's anti-smoking law. It seems Cigarz doesn't sell enough food to be covered by the law. This is one of CityWalk's few hidden corners where you can actually get away from the noise and the crowds. It's not surprising that it has become a favorite hangout for Universal employees.

CHAPTER FIVE:

THE RESORT HOTELS

In the hospitality industry, the word "resort" refers to a hotel that offers not just a high standard of luxury and extra amenities, but special recreational opportunities, either natural or man-made. Well, two world-class theme parks surely qualify as a recreational opportunity.

Of course, if the visionaries at Universal had done nothing more than add Islands of Adventure and CityWalk to the existing Universal Studios Florida they would have had a vacation destination that could challenge Disney World in appeal and popularity. Fortunately for us they set their sights much higher than that, seeking to turn Universal Orlando into a true resort destination with five distinctively themed hotels surrounding the theme parks. To accomplish that they have partnered with Loews Hotels to provide the hotel part of the equation.

If you've never heard of Loews Hotels, you're forgiven. Loews has forgone the current craze of hotel consolidation, with big chains devouring small chains to create ever larger chains, to concentrate on operating a small portfolio of one-of-a-kind hotels of the four-diamond variety that seek to become the dominant hotels in their marketplace.

The Loews Portofino Bay Hotel, the Hard Rock Hotel (a separate brand managed here by Loews), and the Loews Royal Pacific Resort, described in this chapter, are the first of the five planned hotels but the fourth and fifth hotels have been in "development" forever. From now on, the hotels will be referred to by their shorter, "unofficial" names and nicknames.

Honored Guests

Staying at one of the Universal Orlando hotels has some obvious advantages. For one thing, you will be staying almost literally at the gates to the theme parks. None of the first three hotels is more than a ten-minute complimentary boat ride from CityWalk (just a short walk from the park gates) and some are much closer. For another, these are very nice hotels, far superior to the usual run of tourist hotels that ring Universal Orlando and continue down the tacky environs of International Drive. But there are other advantages to being a Universal hotel guest. Staying at an on-property hotel confers certain VIP privileges unavailable to the average run-of-the-mill tourist.

- **Early Entry to the Wizarding World.** At press time, all on-site hotel guests get into Islands of Adventure an hour before the general public, allowing them to explore the Harry Potter attractions in relative privacy. The *Forbidden Journey* ride currently offers limited Universal Express access for hotel guests (see below), but this privilege nearly makes up for it.

- **Universal Express Priority Access.** Perhaps the most talked-about perk of all is that resort guests get priority access at most of the rides and attractions in the theme parks. Simply use your room key to get immediate access to the Universal Express Plus entrance to the ride. You can use this privilege as many times as you like. Of course, this may change in the future, so it's not guaranteed. Check with the concierge when you arrive.

   You should get a separate room key for everyone in your party when you check in, which will allow your family to split up and still get Express access. If you tour together, a single key will sometimes gain access for more than one person, but attendants are supposed to check the eligibility of everyone in the group.

   This perk is sometimes referred to as "Front-of-the-Line" or FOTL and some people think it means they are supposed to quite literally be the very first person in line. Not so. What it does mean is that your wait to ride will usually be cut to 15 minutes or less, although at extremely busy periods the wait can be somewhat longer.

   It is like the Universal Express Plus system, with the difference that those who have paid for Express access can only use their passes once per ride and cannot use them at all during the first hour the park is open, giving hotel guests first crack at the most popular rides. (For more on Universal Express Plus, see *Chapter One: Planning Your Escape*.)

During very busy periods or at popular attractions like *Forbidden Journey*, this perk may be restricted somewhat during part of the day, preventing you from riding the same ride many times in succession. However, enforcing such restrictions is left largely to the ride attendants, who may not always enforce it vigorously. Guests have reported that they experienced few if any restrictions, even when they were supposed to be in effect.

- *Priority seating.* This perk gets you the best seats for some shows and priority seating Sunday through Thursday nights at some restaurants in CityWalk and the theme parks. Check with the hotel concierge to see which shows and restaurants are offering this perk at the time of your visit.

- *Package delivery.* Any park visitor can get some shops to deliver their purchases to the front gate for later pick-up, but Universal hotel guests can have their purchases sent directly to their rooms, provided they are staying over till at least the next day. Packages are delivered the day after your purchase.

- *Charge privileges.* You can use your room key (which looks much like a credit card) to charge purchases in park shops and restaurants that accept credit cards. You pay just one bill when you check out.

- *Length-of-stay tickets.* Resort guests can purchase park passes valid for however long they are staying at the hotel. These tickets are usually booked as part of a package. They don't represent any great savings on park admission but they have the beneficial effect of giving you a better room rate. They can also come in handy if the length of your stay doesn't match one of the standard pass options. If you wish to purchase length-of-stay tickets once you have checked in, see the concierge.

- *Character Dining reservations.* All resort hotel restaurants play host to characters from the Universal stable of stars. Typically, these events happen a few times a week during the evening meal. As a hotel guest, you will have priority when making reservations for these popular events. Check with the concierge for the nights and restaurants involved in the Character Dining experience during your stay.

Additional perks may be added. It's also possible that some may be changed or discontinued. So make sure to ask the concierge for the latest information when you check in. You are paying a premium to stay in such style so close to the parks, so you should take advantage of the privileges conferred by your status as an honored guest.

Perhaps the best perk is the excellent treatment you're sure to enjoy from Loews famously guest-oriented staff. While you may not receive the personal tour of the grounds and complimentary chocolate rowboat we got on our last visit, you'll find the staff remarkably responsive to any requests.

Room Rates At A Glance

The hotels follow similar patterns when it comes to rooms and rates. Two hotels have "standard" rooms and larger, pricier "deluxe" rooms. In all hotels, the view from the room also affects the rate, with "pool" or "harbor" views costing more. All hotels have a Club floor offering special amenities and perks for a price. Next come the suites. All hotels have "Kids' Suites," specially designed for families. For high rollers, there are larger, more elaborate suites with suitably larger, more elaborate price tags.

If we could give you an exact figure you'll have to pay, we would. But hotel rates are notoriously volatile, rising and falling with the seasons, leisure travel patterns, and a variety of market conditions that are impossible to forecast. The hope here is to provide some general guidelines about the "going rate" that will prove useful in considering your Universal Orlando Resort hotel choices. Then you can use the tips offered in *Getting A Good Deal* (below) to zero in on the best rate for the room you want.

The resort hotels recognize five distinct "seasons." The exact dates for each season change slightly from year to year depending on when certain holidays occur. Here, in ascending order of room cost, is a general overview of those seasons.

Value season. Roughly from early January to mid-February; from mid-August (when Florida kids head back to school) to early October; and from just after Thanksgiving to the Christmas/New Year's holiday.

Regular season. From Spring Break (see below) to early June and from early October to just before Thanksgiving.

Summer season. Early June to mid-August.

Peak season. The Presidents' Day period (mid-February to mid-March); Spring Break (late-March to mid-April); and Thanksgiving weekend.

Holiday season. The two weeks around Easter and the Christmas/ New Year's holiday period, which typically begins a week before Christmas and ends a day or so after New Year's Day.

▮ Standard Room Rates

The hotels play it close to the vest when it comes to room rates. Short of actually booking a room, it's hard to tell what a given room category will cost when. However, the following standard room rates, which were in effect during 2010 provide a basis for making some educated guesses. These are "starting from" prices, which means that the actual price quoted could be as much as $50 higher.

	Value	Regular	Summer	Peak	Holiday
Portofino Bay	$274+	$304+	$304+	$339+	$399+
Hard Rock	$234+	$269+	$289+	$299+	$354+
Royal Pacific	$219+	$249+	$249+	$274+	$334+

To these rates, add $30 per night for a room with a view, $40 to $50 for a "deluxe" room, and $90 to $100 for a club level room. The more expensive hotels add correspondingly more for each step up. Kids' Suites start at about $500 and go up to over $700; nonetheless, they sell out quickly. If you need to ask the price of the so-called "super luxury" suites, you probably can't afford them.

Getting A Good Deal

While the resort hotels offer excellent value for the money, they are not precisely cheap. But the advantages of staying on site are so attractive that figuring out a way to make a stay at one of these great hotels fit into your budget will be worth the effort. Here, then, are a few suggestions on how to get the best possible deal on your resort hotel room rate.

Book a package. Ask your travel agent about purchasing a package that includes an on-site hotel, theme park tickets, and perhaps airfare and car rental. You will probably wind up paying less than if you had booked all the elements separately.

AAA. Members receive a 20% discount.

Purchase an Annual Pass. Annual passholders to the theme parks receive a discount of about 30% off regular rates and are eligible for periodic special offers on a space available basis.

You First. Membership in Loews *You First,* the hotel chain's frequent lodger program, does not get you any discounts, but it qualifies you for some nice perks like a newspaper delivered to your door; free use of the fitness centers; food, spa, and golf credits; and room upgrades at check-in based on availability. You can enroll online at www.loewshotels.com or call (800) 23-LOEWS to have an application mailed to you. Hard Rock has it own, separate *All Access* frequent stay program with similar perks.

Go on the Internet. As a supplement to some or all of the above ploys, you should check out a site called The DISboards.com. The "DIS" in the name stands for Disney Information Station but the site has a discussion group devoted just to Universal Orlando. You will have to register to post messages, but it's free and there are no strings attached. On the DISBoards home page, scroll down until you see the link to "Universal Resorts & Hotels" and click there. When you get to the Resorts board look for permanent threads near the top devoted to each of the hotels. This is where members post information on when they are going to the various resort hotels, the rate they got, and how they got it. This is invaluable intelligence for the budget-conscious traveler.

Go on the Internet, Part II. Once you have done your research on the DISboards, then you might want to try those hotel "discount" sites on the Internet. Among the more prominent are sidestep.com, hotels.com, and hotwire.com.

Making Reservations

If you are not using a travel agent to book a package vacation, you can do so yourself by calling (800) 711-0080 or (888) 837-2273. For the hearing impaired, there is a TDD line at (407) 224-4414. If you are calling from overseas or are already in Orlando, call (407) 363-8000 and ask to be transferred.

If you are interested in booking a room only, you can call Loews central reservations number toll free at (800) 23-LOEWS. Those calling from Orlando or overseas can dial (407) 503-1000 for Portofino Bay, (407) 503-ROCK for the Hard Rock, and (407) 503-3000 for Royal Pacific Resort.

Good Things To Know About...

■ Access for Non-Guests

The resort hotels are tucked away in corners of Universal Orlando, carefully masked from the nearby streets, with grand entrance gates that have an air of exclusivity about them. That may be why many people mistakenly assume the resorts are closed to all but hotel guests. In fact, anyone can drop in for a visit and, if your vacation schedule affords the time, you should by all means come for a meal at one of the restaurants and a stroll through the very special grounds and public areas of the hotels. You can come by boat or on foot from the parks or you can drive in. If you drive, you can choose between valet and self parking. Non-guests must use the main entrances to the hotels since other entrances (like the pool areas) require a room key for access.

■ Business Centers

All resort hotels have a "business center" for those who need to photocopy or fax something or use a computer. You can even find a notary should you need one. Most are conveniently located, although at the Royal Pacific Resort, the business center is a good hike away in the adjoining conference facility. The fees charged won't surprise the average business traveler but might make others gasp.

■ Character Dining

All of the hotels offer "character dining" experiences at their main restaurants — Trattoria del Porto at Portofino, The Kitchen at Hard Rock, and Islands Dining Room at Royal Pacific. During these events, costumed characters such as Scooby Doo, Woody Woodpecker, Spider-Man, Shrek and Fiona stroll the dining room, visiting with kids and posing for photos. Unlike character dining events at some theme parks, there is no separate charge for these events; if you are eating in the restaurant, you will be able to interact with the characters. Character dining takes place once or twice a week, typically between 6:30 and 9:00 p.m. If there is no character dining at your hotel during your stay, there most likely will be at another. You don't even need to be staying at any of the hotels to have dinner during these fun events.

Since schedules and participating characters change from time to time, the best strategy is to call the hotel before your arrival and ask about the character dining schedule during your visit.

■ Concierge Service

All of the hotels offer concierge service. The concierge desk staff is extremely knowledgeable, not just about all things Universal, but about Orlando in general. They can offer tips on what else to see in the area, give you the latest weather report, where to shop, and where to find a baby sitter or get the perfect birthday cake for your kid. You can even stop by the concierge desk for information about and tickets to most local attractions. Although they stock plenty of brochures about Walt Disney World and can arrange transportation to get you there, Disney does not allow them to sell Disney tickets.

■ Checking In and Out

Standard check-in time at all hotels is 4:00 p.m.; if you arrive early, the front desk will happily give you your hotel keycard and hold your baggage so you can go play in the parks. Check-out is at 11:00 a.m., and can be performed in person, "express," or via interactive television.

■ Did You Forget?

All hotels offer a service aimed at the forgetful among us, so if you forgot your toothbrush or razor you can call Star Service (see below) for a complimentary replacement.

■ Drugs

No, not that kind. We mean medicine, the kind your doctor prescribes. The Loews resort hotels have partnered with a nearby pharmacy to provide 24-hour prescription service. For more information, call (407) 248-0437. The fax is (407) 248-2297.

■ Game Rooms

All the hotels have small, unattended video arcades that seem to attract the under-15 crowd. Typically the games, none of them terribly elaborate, run on tokens with a token vending machine that accepts $1, $5, and $10 bills.

■ Golf

None of the resort hotels offers a golf course, but golfers needn't despair. The "Golf Universal Orlando" program has partnered with three nearby courses (MetroWest, Mystic Dunes, and Orange County National) to make golfing easy for hotel guests. Perks include complimentary transportation and "special privileges." Rates and availability vary with the season. To make a reservation for a tee time, the best strategy is to call the golf concierge, headquartered at Royal Pacific Resort, prior to your arrival and let them do it. The direct line is (407) 503-3097, or 3-1097 inside the hotel. Or reserve online at www.universalorlando.com/golf.

▊ Green Lodging

All hotels are "Green Lodging Certified," having passed eco-muster with the Florida Department of Environmental Protection inspectors. You'll find recycling bags in the rooms, and energy-saving compact fluorescent bulbs in the light sockets. Your bed will always have clean sheets upon check-in, but they'll only be changed every three days (unless you request otherwise). You can reuse towels by putting them back on the rack; only towels left on the floor are washed during your visit.

▊ Hotel Hopping

Guests in the hotels are encouraged to visit the other on-site properties and take advantage of their restaurants, amenities, and special events like Dive-In Movies (see below). Your concierge will make dining reservations. Your hotel key will not work in the gated areas of other hotels, so show your key to an attendant, who will grant you access. You can, however, use your hotel key to charge purchases at any other hotel.

▊ Internet Access

High-speed Internet access is available in all rooms of all hotels for a fee of $10 per day. Those staying on the Club level get their wireless access free, as do those who schlep their laptops to the lobby or other public spaces in the hotel.

▊ Kids

Loews has a soft spot for kids. Kids under 18 stay free in a room with their parents and the hotels frequently run special promotions. Check when you make reservations to see if there are any special deals going on during your visit. When you check in, be sure to ask the desk clerk about Character Dining (described above) and Character Wake-Up Calls, tape-recorded telephone messages for your kids. All of the hotels have special children's playrooms with supervised activities (see below) as well as special "Kids' Suites" designed to give families a little extra room.

▊ Kids' Activities

All the resort hotels have special supervised activities programs for children aged 4 to 14. These center around large, colorful playrooms filled with fun things to do, from computers with educational CD-ROMs, to computer games, to arts and crafts, to movies shown on large screen TVs. The programs also take advantage of the hotel grounds for outdoor fun and games when appropriate.

These are typically evening programs, designed to let Mom and Dad go off to enjoy more adult nighttime entertainment knowing that their little darlings are being looked after and well entertained. So expect the programs to run from about 5:00 to 11:30 p.m. or so, a little later on weekends. During busier periods and school holidays, hours can expand. During slow periods, the program at one hotel might close altogether, but since a guest at one hotel can use the program at any other hotel, this should not pose a problem.

Pricing varies from hotel to hotel and is subject to change without notice. $15 per hour per child and $15 for a meal is fairly common. If you think you might be interested in these programs, you will have to check with the hotel at check-in or shortly before arrival to ask about the current schedule and pricing arrangements. The concierge will be able to provide you with a flyer containing complete information on activities offered, hours, and pricing. In the sections on the individual hotels, we will provide information about locations and how to contact that hotel's kids' program. Private child care services provided by reputable outside agencies with licensed and bonded sitters can also be arranged. Ask your hotel concierge for assistance.

▌Mail

If you will need to receive mail or courier shipments while you are visiting the resort hotels, an increasingly likely scenario in our overworked world, have your mail sent to the address given below for each of the hotels. As long as your first and last name is on the letter or parcel, no special markings or additional notations are needed.

▌Parking

Each resort hotel has its own parking lot. Self-parking is $15 per day for hotel guests, unless you take advantage of the valet parking service, in which case there is an $22 per day fee (plus tips, of course). If you fly into Orlando and plan to spend most of your time at the major attractions, you might want to consider foregoing a rental car during your stay and using shuttles and other options to get around Orlando. (See *Good Things To Know About... Transportation Elsewhere* below.)

For non-guests, there is a flat rate of $20 for self parking and $25 for valet service. If you come for a meal, ask to have your parking ticket validated at the restaurant and three hours of parking will be free.

Pets

Loews is a pet-friendly hotel chain and your furry friends are not only welcomed but pampered; they even get their own welcome gifts! If you'd like to bring a pet, be sure to let the hotel know when you make your reservation. A number of rooms in each hotel have been designated as pet rooms and a separate room service menu offers first-class pet dining for about $11.

You will be given a special sign to hang on your room latch to alert staff that a pet is in the room and you will have to make special arrangements with housekeeping since hotel policy is that no staff member will enter a room with a pet without the owner present.

A $25 fee for "extra thorough cleaning" will be charged once per stay. Maps provided by the hotels point out areas in which you can walk your pets. People with allergies should alert the hotel when making reservations to avoid being inadvertently placed in a pet room.

Room Service

There is 24-hour room service in all the hotels offering an abbreviated menu drawn from the main hotel restaurant. As you probably know, you pay a premium for room service, whether it is for a pet or a human. At the Universal resorts there is a $3 per order charge plus a 22% gratuity added to the bill.

Star Service

All the hotels offer "Star Service," a one-stop, one-phone-call solution for just about any need that might arise during your stay. It even has a special button on your in-room phone. The folks at Star Service seem to pride themselves on providing speedy answers to all your questions.

Transportation to the Parks

Once you arrive at the resort, it's possible to spend an entire vacation at Universal without riding any motorized vehicles (other than the ones inside the attractions), since all the hotels are at most a brisk fifteen-minute stroll from the action. The hotels are also linked to CityWalk and the theme parks by complimentary water taxi and shuttle bus. Each hotel has its own water taxi that runs between the hotel and a dock just below the NASCAR Sports Grille; from there, it's a short walk to either park. If you want to go from hotel to hotel by water, you will have to change boats at CityWalk.

Shuttle buses run about every half-hour from each hotel to a bus stop area near the entrance to Universal Studios Florida, but walking or taking the water taxi is a far quicker and more scenic way to get to the parks. If you prefer the bus, check with the concierge for details. Another option is the cadre of pedal-powered two-person rickshaws that play the walkways. There is no set fee; the drivers work for tips.

Transportation Elsewhere

Complimentary bus shuttle service is also provided from all hotels to Wet 'n Wild and SeaWorld. Typically, there is one departure in the morning and, in the evening, one return from SeaWorld and one from Wet 'n Wild, although the schedule varies with park operating hours. Check with the concierge for more precise schedule information.

Mears Transportation operates on-demand shuttle services to and from Orlando Airport to the resort hotels, as well as scheduled shuttle service to and from each of the Universal Orlando Resort hotels and the Disney World parks. Limousine and town car services are also available. Check with the concierge for details.

If you prefer to do the driving yourself, all hotels have Hertz rental cars available. They can be reserved ahead but, if you decide you need a car at the last minute, chances are they will be able to accommodate you. Cars can be returned to the hotel or, for an additional fee, the Orlando Airport.

LOEWS PORTOFINO BAY HOTEL

5601 Universal Boulevard
Orlando, FL 32819
(407) 503-1000; fax: (407) 503-1010

A leisurely eight-minute cruise aboard a gracious nineteenth century motor launch takes you from CityWalk to one of the favorite getaways of Europe's fabled jet set — Portofino, Italy.

Well, okay, it's not really Portofino, Italy, but a near-photographic replica of the picturesque Ligurian fishing village that has long been a retreat for the rich and famous. And while you don't have to be famous to stay at this Portofino, it might help to be rich because the room rates place this property in the super-luxury range. If it's any consolation, staying at the Hotel Splendido (yes, that's its name) in the real Portofino will set you back $800 to $1,200 a night, while a room can be had at this Portofino Bay for under $300, at least at some times of the year.

If you're familiar with the real Portofino, you'll be amazed at how closely the architects and designers have come to re-creating the ambiance. If you're not, you might think the designers have cut corners by painting architectural details on the facades. Not so. This is exactly the way it's done in Portofino, Italy. It's called "trompe l'oeil," French for "trick the eye," and it's considered quite posh. Indeed, Loews brought in Italian artists and local scenic design wizards to cover the hotel's public spaces with a wide variety of trompe l'oeil effects and colorful murals at a reported cost of $70 a square yard. The real trompe l'oeil accomplishment, however, is that what looks for all the world like a quaint fishing village made up of scores of separate homes, shops, courtyards, churches, palazzos, and alleyways is, in fact, a state-of-the-art luxury hotel whose 750 rooms have been artfully hidden behind those picturesque facades.

If you arrive by boat, you will walk from the dock to the large central piazza with all of Portofino arrayed before you. If you arrive by car, you will drive around the Bay to arrive at a portico entrance (dressed with vintage Fiats and Vespas for authentic flavor) where you can turn your vehicle over to a valet and step into a sumptuously appointed marble lobby. Either way, it's a spectacular introduction to a very special experience.

Orientation

Portofino Bay Hotel is located at the corner of Kirkman and Vineland Roads, but it turns its back to those streets and looks out on its own artificial harbor and across to Universal's Hard Rock Hotel and the theme parks beyond. The sole vehicular entrance is on Universal Boulevard near the Vineland Road entrance. You can also arrive by boat from CityWalk or walk onto the hotel property either from CityWalk and the Hard Rock Hotel or from Universal Boulevard.

The hotel wraps around "Portofino Bay," a small man-made harbor dotted with fishing boats and dinghies. A large open piazza faces the Bay and forms the focal point for the entire establishment. Most of the eateries and many of the shops face the piazza and the Bay.

The hotel's East Wing runs down one side of the Bay and the West Wing occupies the other, forming a rough "U." The section at the bottom of the "U" houses the hotel's main lobby area. Behind this, away from the Bay, are the extensive meeting rooms and banquet halls; they are located in such a way that vacationers and convention-goers need seldom cross paths or rub shoulders, except perhaps in the restaurants. Jutting out from the West Wing is the Villa Wing, offering larger rooms and easy access to the hotel's nicest pools and its spa facilities.

There is a downside to the layout, which is that your room can be quite a distance from the lobby and some of the hotel amenities.

Rooms and Suites

One nice thing about staying in a super-luxury hotel like Portofino Bay is that even the most modest room is going to be pretty special. And even the "average" guest is going to feel pampered by a level of service that the typical Orlando tourist never experiences.

All rooms have tall beds covered with Egyptian cotton linens and inviting plush comforters. All rooms include clock/radios with MP3-player connections and sleek flat-screen televisions with DVD players upon request.

The bathrooms feature hand-painted stone-like terra cotta tiles and a few are even tiled in marble. Especially convenient are the his-and-hers dual sinks. Also common to all rooms are such thoughtful touches as lavishly stocked mini-bars, plush bathrobes, an iron and ironing board, a hair dryer, and a safe. Every room benefits from a keen attention to aesthetics, down to matching patterns on the luggage rack and faux ceiling molding. About nine percent of the rooms have balconies; most of them are quite small but a few are large enough to allow al fresco dining.

Standard rooms are a comfortable 400 square feet, while deluxe rooms are 600 square feet. Fax machines are available on request. Deluxe room bathrooms feature a separate shower stall, as well as the dual sinks, and have windows with louvered shutters over the tub that open onto the room. You may find the added perks well worth the added cost.

Beach Pool view rooms offer great views of the often dramatic Florida sunsets. Bay view rooms are ideal for those who want to feel as if they've been transported to the real Portofino. However, rooms in the Villa Wing that look out onto the Villa Pool offer a serenity that's hard to match.

Families with young children might want to consider one of the 18 Kids' Suites, six of which feature Dr. Seuss-inspired decor. All include a separate, themed kids' bedroom that is accessible only through the parent's room. Other multi-room options include a one-bedroom suite with parlor and a two-bedroom suite. If you really want to treat yourself, consider the Presidential Suite, with its spacious outdoor terrace.

See *Room Rates At A Glance*, above, to get an idea of the price range at Portofino Bay and how it compares to the other on-site hotels.

Amenities

The amenities here are as lavish in execution as the hotel itself and may encourage you to put off visiting the theme parks as you linger in the lap of luxury with a masseuse and a poolside waiter at your beck and call. The lobby alone, featuring leather armchairs and today's international newspapers on old-fashioned reading sticks, is an oasis of sophisticated repose.

■ Club Level

Ninety-seven rooms in the Villa Wing have been set aside to give select guests that extra level of service and exclusivity. It's essentially the same concept as that found on the "Concierge Level" at upscale business hotels. However, because the layout of the hotel makes it impossible to restrict access to the Club Level rooms and lounge area with elevators, the system here is slightly different.

The Club lounge is on the lobby level, just paces away from the Bar American. The entrance to the lounge shares space with the hotel's ticket sales and auto rental counter. To gain admission to the private lounge, Club Level guests must use their room keys. Once inside, they are treated to the largest Club lounge of all the resort hotels. This one features free Internet access and a pool table along with more usual amenities. Those include out of town newspapers like the *Wall Street Journal* and DVDs (to watch there or take back to the DVD player in the room). There are also personal concierges on duty from 7:00 a.m. to 10:00 p.m. to attend to guest needs.

There is a complimentary continental breakfast in the morning, beverages and snacks available throughout the day, light appetizers in the afternoon, free drinks from 5:00 to 7:00 p.m., and dessert before bedtime (8:30 to 9:30 p.m.).

▌Pools

There are three pools, ranging from the intimate to the lavish. The **Beach Pool** is the most extensive and, to my mind, the most fun. You find it nestled behind the West Wing. At one end it simulates a beach, with the ankle deep water surrounded by soft white sand; at the other end the pool is deeper, although never more than five feet. It surrounds a replica of the old lighthouse that stands along the Ligurian coast near Portofino. This crumbling ruin hides a short but speedy water slide that is a favorite with kids.

Nearby, against walls that mimic ancient aqueducts, are two small secluded spa pools with hot bubbling water and warm waterfalls that provide a very nice shoulder massage. Also close at hand is a large, separate children's play area, with a pirate ship to climb in and over and a wading pool that is constantly spritzed by a trio of fountains. Campo Portofino, the children's program (described below), is close by.

There are a few "cabanas," gaily striped canvas tents with overhead fans, electricity, and small refrigerators. These can be rented for $125 per day (and up) and provide a modicum of privacy and a touch of class for your poolside lounging. All cabana rentals come with bottled water and include a small selection of soft drinks and fruit. For $25 extra, you can have a TV. Club Level guests receive a $20 discount. Make your reservations at the Beach Pool hut, dial 41745 from your room, or speak with the concierge.

The Beach Pool is near the Splendido Pizzeria and has its own poolside bar, so it's a great place to have a relaxed al fresco meal. Because of its popularity with kids, however, it can get noisy; so adults in search of peace and quiet might want to head elsewhere.

The **Villa Pool**, just a few steps from the Beach Pool and separated from it by a wing of the hotel, is much more elegant. The atmosphere is one of regal gentility. It's easy to imagine that you have your own palazzo or that you are a movie mogul cutting deals along the Italian Riviera. The layout of the pool is crisply formal with stately palm trees lining its borders and, at one end, an elaborate fountain backed by a raised balustrade.

There are more cabanas here, and nicer ones to our taste. These start at a mere $100 per day ($20 less for Club Level guests) and come with the same amenities. Reserve them just as you would a Beach Pool cabana.

There is a heated jacuzzi-like pool too, of course, and attendants are on hand to take food and drink orders at poolside. Just for fun, try out the immaculately groomed bocce ball courts; they make for a perfect no-cost date night. The official rules are posted nearby.

On peak-season Saturday nights there is a "Dive-In Movie" at the Beach Pool. A huge screen is set up at poolside so guests can watch while floating on rented rafts. The films are family fare of fairly recent vintage, often with a tie-in to the theme parks, and never more racy than PG-13.

A good place to go for some real privacy is the **Hillside Pool** tucked away at the end of the East Wing. Much smaller than the Beach Pool, it has the virtue of seclusion and quiet along with a view across the Bay.

Hours at the pools vary by season and occupancy. In summer, you will generally find the Beach Pool open 8:00 a.m. to 10:00 p.m. daily; the Villa Pool, 6:00 a.m. to 11:00 p.m.; and the Hillside Pool, 8:00 a.m. to 8:00 p.m.

■ Mandara Spa

Near the Beach Pool is a state-of-the-art spa. Never mind the serene but somewhat incoherent Malaysian theme: this is your perfect chance to feel like an Italian movie star. Looking like an Italian movie star may be asking too much, but who knows. You can get the full treatment of massages, mud wraps, and facials, all with the latest "all-natural" and "therapeutic" ointments, oils, and unguents, of course. The heated masseuse tables are a particularly nice touch. Or you can simply have your hair and nails done in an elegant European salon setting. If you stroll in here and say, "Give me the works," be prepared to spend a bundle. The six-hour "Day of Perfect Bliss" package, which includes lunch in addition to a dizzying regimen of facial, massages, makeup, manicure, pedicure, hair styling, and aromatherapy, costs $600. Less lavish packages of pampering start at $320 for men and $340 for women. Use of all spa and fitness center facilities are included with any service (see below).

▌Campo Portofino

Located near the Beach Pool, this indoor play area houses Portofino's children's activities program. For more information about the services offered here, see *Good Things To Know About...Kids' Activities* in the introductory section of this chapter. Make your reservations 24 hours in advance by calling 31200 on a hotel phone or (407) 503-1230 from outside.

▌Fitness Center

Adjacent to the Mandara Spa is a sleek health club offering the very latest in pec-pumping paraphernalia. Here you can exhaust yourself on treadmills, recumbent and standing bicycle machines, or stair climbers. For the die-hard traditionalist, there are also free weights. Access to the fitness center costs $10 per day, which entitles you to use all the facilities of the Spa, including showers, roman bath hot tubs, saunas, and steam rooms. You can also relax in the "quiet room" lounge, sipping herbal tea and snacking on dried fruit while you peruse periodicals in a comfy chair. If you are a customer of the Spa, staying on the Club level, or a member of You First, your access to the fitness center is free. Fitness-minded guests also use the paved walkway that surrounds the Bay or the path to Universal Studios Florida and back as a handy jogging trail.

Good Things To Know About...

▌Guest Laundry

Portofino Bay is apparently too posh for anything as down market as a coin laundry. You can either use the hotel's laundry service or carry your dirty duds to the Hard Rock Hotel and use the facilities there.

▌Meetings and Banquets

The hotel has over 42,000 square feet of meeting space, renovated in 2009, ranging from the magnificent 15,000-square-foot Tuscan Ballroom, which can accommodate 1,280 for a sit-down dinner, to a sumptuous boardroom suite for 25. In addition to being beautifully appointed, with lavish hand-painted Italian murals, these facilities offer some of the most advanced telecommunications equipment available anywhere. That's made the Portofino Bay Hotel one of the most sought-after meeting venues in Orlando. If you'd like more information, simply call Conference Management at (407) 503-1130.

■ Musica della Notte

Every night, weather permitting of course, the piazza at Portofino comes alive with the "music of the night." Strolling musicians and classically trained singers appear on balconies and fill the night air with Italian favorites from opera, movies, and a cross-over style known as "popera," which blends classic opera and pop. There is no charge for this spectacle and guests from other hotels and even non-guests are welcome to take a motor launch over to Portofino Bay to enjoy the show.

On Sunday nights, following Musica della Notte, an Italian movie is screened on Mama Della's patio; on Wednesdays, a video concert of Italian opera is shown. Ask the concierge for a schedule.

■ Parking

The parking here is well-hidden and covered, making self-parking a more attractive option than at the other hotels, which have open lots.

■ Weddings

Looking for a very special place to tie the knot? Portofino Bay has quickly become a favorite spot for Orlando's discerning brides. There are two outdoor gazebos that, when adorned with flowers, make lovely wedding chapels. One is above the Villa Pool in a palazzo-like setting; the other is in a courtyard near the main ballrooms and just steps away from a majestic curving staircase that was seemingly custom-designed for bridal portraits. And Universal Orlando, with its panoply of diversions, makes a terrific honeymoon destination. Call (407) 503-1120 for more information.

Dining at Loews Portofino Bay Hotel

Portofino Bay offers some superb gourmet dining, but reflecting the casual ambiance of its namesake, there are also casual, moderately priced eateries dotted around the property. Of course it's all Italian, in keeping with the hotel's theme. Unless you can be satisfied with a burger or a club sandwich, you'll have to travel to CityWalk or the parks for more varied fare.

Most of the hotel's eateries are positioned to take advantage of the piazza and the Bay. This survey begins on the western side of the Bay and heads around the piazza to the east, before describing two venues located elsewhere in the hotel. Guests who just can't get it together to drag themselves to one of these restaurants can take advantage of the hotel's 24-hour room service.

▍ Bice

What:	Fine gourmet dining Northern Italian style
Where:	On the third level overlooking the Bay
Price Range:	$$$$+
Hours:	Daily, 5:30 p.m. to 10:30 p.m.
Reservations:	Not required, but strongly suggested
	(407) 503-1415 or online
Web:	http://orlando.bicegroup.com/

If the name Bice rings a bell, then there's a good chance you are an international jet setter with a generous expense account. The Portofino Bay Bice is just the latest addition to a chain that spans the globe, with outposts in some forty cities, most of them financial or mercantile capitals (like Amsterdam, Tokyo, New York, and Dubai) or resorts of the rich and famous (like Monte Carlo, Palm Beach, and Tahiti). Bice has a proud history and a reputation for superb Italian cuisine.

Bice was founded in Milan, Italy, in 1926 by Beatrice Ruggeri (Bice is an Italian diminutive for Beatrice). It was a family affair and still is, with the Ruggeri family still in control and still zealously maintaining its high standards. The atmosphere is one of hip, casual elegance. The main dining room is open and airy, with tall ceilings and large windows looking out onto the bay; black and white predominate, with elaborate flower arrangements adding a touch of color. Starched tablecloths on widely spaced tables add a certain formality to the trendy feel of the room, which can get extremely noisy when it's busy.

The menu leans strongly to Northern Italian specialties. Antipasti and Insalate ($12 to $21) include Bice's signature tri-color salad with arugula, endive, and radicchio in a Parmesan lemon dressing. Other starters include such standards as mozzarella with tomatoes and basil, prosciutto and melon, superbly sweet fried calamari, and tuna tartare. Primi Piatti (pastas and risottos) ($18 to $32) range from penne in a simple, but spicy, tomato sauce to risotto with lobster and asparagus. The Bice signature here is Pappardelle al Telefono, broad pasta ribbons in a mozzarella and tomato cream sauce, a simple dish that is here done to perfection.

Secondi Piatti ($29 to $45) include fish dishes such as tuna, salmon and the like in simple sauces with vegetable accompaniments. Meat lovers will want to try the Ossobuco alla Milanese, another Bice specialty, a rich veal shank on a bed of saffron risotto. Other entrees include hearty steaks and chops and homey poultry dishes like grilled chicken breast. Side orders of vegetables ($9) are also available. Desserts ($10 to $13) cover the usual Italian bases with the Cioccolatissimo alla Bice the standout.

As you can see, the food here is not cheap, so you may want to take out a second mortgage if you plan on having wine with dinner. The extensive wine list ranges from $40 to $500. Expect to pay around $60 for a decent bottle. As you might expect, the list leans heavily to Italian wines, with a great selection of "Super Tuscan" wines listed from $60 to $495. Montalcinos range from $55 to $80 and the superior Brunello di Montalcino can be had for $95 to $190. Many wines can be ordered by the glass ($8 to $20).

At these prices, perfection seems a reasonable expectation. Based on our experience and reports from other diners, however, both food quality and service have been hit or miss. Or as a wise Italian grandmother once said, "such big prices, and such tiny portions."

Tip: Bice will validate complimentary self-parking for non-hotel guests; valet parking will cost you $5, plus tax, with Bice validation.

■ The Thirsty Fish Bar

What:	Casual bar with snacks and cigars
Where:	Facing Portofino Bay, below Bice
Price Range:	$ - $$
Hours:	6:00 p.m. to 2:00 a.m.; Saturday noon to 2:00 a.m.; Sunday noon to midnight
Reservations:	None

One of the few spots in the hotel that doesn't have an immediate echo in Italy, this casual bar is just a bit too tidy to be called funky. It caters to bayside strollers in need of liquid refreshment. This is primarily a drinking establishment; Italian appetizers ($8 to $10) are served here and you can get a decent cigar.

Outdoor tables that spill into the piazza make The Thirsty Fish a great place to relax and survey the passing scene in the Italian fashion. On sultry summer nights (Thursday through Sunday) there may even be live music.

■ Trattoria del Porto

What:	Casual all-day dining
Where:	Facing the Harbor Piazza
Price Range:	$$ - $$$
Hours:	Breakfast 7:30 a.m. to 11:00 a.m.; Lunch 11:00 a.m. to 2:30 p.m.; Dinner 5:30 p.m. to 11:00 p.m. (closed for dinner Tuesday and Wednesday)
Reservations:	Not required but recommended during busier periods

This spacious 300-seat restaurant is the only eatery serving breakfast, lunch, and dinner. That doesn't mean that you have to settle for so-so food, however. The cuisine here is first-rate, inventive, and well executed.

Large windows look out onto the piazza, where there is plenty of al fresco seating. Should you care to eat outdoors, you'll be happily accommodated. The columns indoors are painted with fanciful scenes of commedia dell'arte figures cavorting under the sea with dolphins and seals. With its high ceilings, tile and mosaic accents in blue and gold, and polished wood trim, the Trattoria projects an air of laid-back elegance.

At breakfast, the Trattoria lays on a sumptuous buffet ($17.50 for adults, $8.50 for kids) that features made-to-order eggs and omelets. You can also order from a more traditional breakfast menu that features such favorites as Eggs Benedict and waffles adorned with fresh fruit.

The same menu is served at lunch and dinner. One half of the menu is given over to a variety of soups, salads, and other starters. For the rest, there are sandwiches, pizza-like flatbreads, and pasta dishes. Starters run from about $6 to $14, sandwiches are about $12, flatbreads are $14, and entrees are $15 to $30. Entrees range from yellow tail snapper to a hearty New York steak with an inventive demi-glace. At certain times an all-you-can-eat "family dinner" or "interactive cooking experience" may be offered ($15 to 19). A special kids' menu features simple dishes for $10. The mini-desserts ($4) include a vanilla panna cotta and tangerine cheesecake.

If the weather's fine, the tables in the large al fresco dining area on the piazza offer the best seats in the house.

Note: Kids are specially welcome. At the back of the restaurant there is a small dining area for little ones, featuring brightly colored toddler-sized tables, a large-screen TV showing appropriate kiddie fare, and big pillows for comfy after-meal sprawling. Some nights a magician will perform or a clown will drop by to create balloon animals. Other nights there is Character Dining with various Universal stars; ask the concierge for the schedule.

▌Mama Della's Ristorante

What:	Home-style Italian dinners
Where:	Facing the Harbor Piazza, next to the Trattoria
Price Range:	$$$ - $$$$
Hours:	5:30 p.m. to 10:00 p.m.
Reservations:	Not required but recommended

A lot of people will tell you this is their favorite Portofino Bay restaurant, and it has attracted a dedicated local following. It isn't as fancy as Bice and the cuisine is more comforting than intriguing, but perhaps that is the attraction. Then, too, Mama Della's comes complete with Mama, a perfectly cast woman of a certain age who greets you warmly at the door and makes you feel as if you never left the Old Neighborhood even if you were never there to begin with.

The decor evokes a large and comfortable country home with its beamed ceilings and colorful wallpaper. Vintage family photographs and gaudy gold-framed floral paintings line the walls of the various rooms. Colorful pitchers, bowls, and other folk ceramics are displayed in niches. Adding to the casual air is an open galley kitchen in the back room where you can see chefs in baseball caps dishing up their homey specialties. And a festive note is contributed by a strolling singer offering popular Italian songs to an accordion accompaniment.

Among the appetizers ($7 to $14), you'll find the tender fried calamari with both marinara and pesto dipping sauces and the Vongole e Cozze, clams and mussels in a garlic-infused sauce especially noteworthy. The mixed antipasto of cured meats, cheeses, and marinated vegetables is also worth sampling.

The entrees ($17 to $34) can best be described as Italian comfort food: chicken a la carbonara, chicken parmigiana, lasagna, and the like. The veal dishes, prepared in various styles, are reliably spectacular: the veal chop in shiitake stew is the best of its kind we've ever had, and big enough for two to share. Another winner is the frutti di mare — grilled shrimp, scallops, and grouper with roasted tomatoes in a garlic sauce. A generous mixed salad comes with your meal, as does fresh bread and dipping oil. Many of the dishes here can be served "family style" on large platters for a group. Family style service typically means a modest discount off the individual price for each additional person.

Vegetable side dishes are not listed on the menu but can be ordered for about $7. Desserts ($6 to $9) range from simple sorbets and tiramisu to a fancy chocolate extravaganza.

■ Sal's Market Deli

What:	Casual sandwiches and pizza
Where:	Facing the Harbor Piazza
Hours:	Varies with the seasons and occupancy level, generally 11:00 a.m. to 11:00 p.m.
Price Range:	$$
Reservations:	None

Sal's offers a casual atmosphere patterned on the famed Peck emporium of Milan but reminiscent of New York's Little Italy, with its marble-topped cafe tables and arched ceiling. It's a nice place to stop for a quick bite.

Panini (grilled Italian sandwiches, $12) are served at the deli-like counter along with cold antipasto-style salads ($8 to $12).

At the back is a sort of pizza bar where you can order one of five styles of pizzas (small $11 to $12, large $13 to $14) and sit on a stool along a marble counter and watch it baking in the open-doored oven. A small pie can feed two people generously. This ain't Domino's, either. The pizza chefs here make their own dough, using a mixture of high-gluten flour for toughness and durum semolina for taste and a rich yellow color. The oven is a true pizza oven, with the base kept at a steady 600 degrees. The result is a crisper and firmer crust than you'll find over at the Trattoria or the Splendido Pizzeria. Sal's version of Pizza Americana, with a generous topping of mushrooms, sausage, and pepperoni, is especially good.

Tip: You can have your pizza made to go, a good thing to know if you are not staying in the hotel.

If you like wine with your pizza, you can get it by the glass for $5 to $7. Sal's is also a good place to grab a cup of coffee. Espresso and cappuccino are available, as is regular coffee. For a stronger cup ask for a Caffe Americano, a shot of espresso with steaming hot water added. Carrying the Italian deli theme to its logical conclusion, Sal's sells Italian specialties such as extra virgin olive oil and dry pasta, but oddly only California wine.

■ Gelateria Caffe Espresso

What:	Ice cream and coffee
Where:	Facing the Piazza, connected to Sal's
Hours:	Open daily, but hours may vary
Price Range:	$
Reservations:	None

The Gelateria serves gelato, the creamy Italian ice cream, handmade daily on the premises. You can have it straight, in a sundae, or in a cream-topped milk shake. Sorbets and Italian ices are also served.

You can also pick up a coffee, espresso, cappuccino, or latte in any of their increasingly elaborate variations. A small selection of cookies, muffins, pastries, and cakes is also served here. In the mornings, croissants, muffins, and fresh fruit are laid out, making this a good serve-yourself alternative to a room service breakfast. There is both indoor and outdoor seating. In the Italian tradition, these establishments take a leisurely midday break.

■ Bar American

What:	Posh formal bar
Where:	Off the main lobby

Hours:	4:00 p.m. to midnight, to 2:00 a.m. on Friday and Saturday
Price Range:	$$ - $$$
Reservations:	None

There are vague echoes of Harry's Bar in Venice here, but Portofino's Bar American is very much its own room and in the fine tradition of upscale hotel bars where patrons signal their status by swirling $150 snifters of fine brandy.

Luckily you can enjoy a drink and the refined atmosphere for less than that. Specialty cocktails are in the $11 range, with appetizers such as smoked salmon, shrimp cocktails, and flatbread pizzas available for under $16. Desserts are also served here. Other specialties here include single malt Scotch ($12 to $20), grappa, an Italian fortified wine ($25), and the aforementioned cognacs ($16 to $150).

▍Splendido Pizzeria

What:	Pizzeria
Where:	Near the Beach Pool
Hours:	11:00 a.m. to 5:00 p.m., but hours vary seasonally
Price Range:	$$
Reservations:	None

The name is a nod to the exclusive hotel in the real Portofino, but the atmosphere is far from deluxe. This is a laid back and ultra-casual eatery whose small indoor and outdoor seating areas are supplemented by poolside service at both the Beach and Villa Pools, which seem to be where most of its food is served.

Salads ($9 to $13) include mesclun, chicken Caesar, and a fruit plate. Wraps (about $11) are served with slaw, onion rings, or French fries and include ham and cheese, as well as turkey. Burgers, a grouper sandwich, and hot dogs are also available ($9 to $13).

The pizza you get here ($12 to $14) is much the same as that served up in the Trattoria del Porto. But here you can eat it poolside, which, of course, makes it taste better. Italian ices and fruit smoothies round out the short menu. A kids' meal, including an entree, fries, and a beverage, is under $10.

The Splendido also serves up some fancy cocktails (about $9) designed to produce that perfect poolside buzz. The Riviera, to cite just one example, is a creative blend of Captain Morgan's Parrot Bay rum, mango, and coconut topped with a "strawberry meltdown."

As with all the poolside eateries at Universal Orlando, an 18% gratuity is automatically added to all bills.

Shopping at Loews Portofino Bay

Shopping is not the main focus at Portofino Bay Hotel. In fact, unlike many posh hotels around the world, this one has remarkably few shops. The ones it has can be roughly divided between the practical and the posh.

On the practical side is **Le Memorie di Portofino**, or Memories of Portofino, where you can pick up a variety of sundries and magazines along with pricey polo shirts bearing the hotel's handsome logo. If you don't like the paper dropped outside your door, you can come here for *The New York Times, Wall Street Journal,* and London's *Daily Mail.* Other reading matter includes glossy magazines and the latest thriller to take to the pool. There is also some posh Italian ceramic ware, and resort wear emblazoned with the Portofino Bay logo.

Another place to stop into to pick up the necessities of resort life is **L'Ancora** (The Anchor) located near the boat dock. It thoughtfully purveys sunscreen and other items you might need as you head for the parks. This shop also stocks chips, nuts, and soft drinks to wash it all down with. In addition, about 50 percent of their business is in ultra-casual clothing.

As you might have guessed, there is an outpost of the **Universal Studios Store** in Portofino Bay. It stocks plenty of T-shirts and polo shirts, some of them quite nice. You'll also find a small selection of toys and plush dolls for the kids.

The remaining shops are for pampering yourself or that special someone. Once you've taken in the luxurious atmosphere of the hotel, you might want to rush to **Alta Moda** (High Fashion) for something you'll feel comfortable being seen in. They have thoughtfully provided the best in contemporary resort wear, with everything from Tommy Bahama clothes and fashion accessories, to swimwear, to lingerie, to evening wear for that special meal at Bice.

Another place to spend the money you didn't spend on a ticket to Italy is **Galleria Portofino**. It features the work of contemporary artists. In addition to paintings, there is some lovely decorative statuary, blown glass from Murano, and jewelry from a variety of artisans. Much of it is not to our taste, but your mileage may vary.

HARD ROCK HOTEL

5800 Universal Boulevard
Orlando, FL 32819
(407) 503-ROCK (7625); fax: (407) 503-ROLL (7655)

Imagine for a moment you are an aging rock star. Changing tastes and slumping record sales have reduced your income to pitiful new lows. Years of hard living and fiscal mismanagement have depleted your assets to the vanishing point. Your groupies have left you to your own devices in the palatial Beverly Hills mansion that you have filled with the memories and memorabilia of your high-flying years of hits and worldwide mega tours. Soon you will have to sell this last remnant of your once lavish lifestyle and move into a shabby condo. Then, inspiration strikes: you'll turn your mansion into a hotel! Paying guests will leap at the chance to experience, however vicariously, however briefly, what it must be like to live like a real live rock star.

That is the "backstory" of the Hard Rock Hotel. It's a story that will never be told in so many words to the guests who stay here, but it is the fanciful tale from which the architects and designers drew inspiration as they fashioned this flamboyant, flashy, and surprisingly elegant hostelry.

The 650-room Hard Rock Hotel draws on the architectural traditions of California's Spanish Mission style, with stucco arches and adobe-like touches, rising to seven stories at its highest point. With its gracious terraces and the towering palm trees that dot the 19 acres of manicured grounds, it looks more like the rambling mountaintop palaces of Hollywood's superstars than the well-appointed hotel it is.

Orientation

The Hard Rock Hotel is located on Universal Boulevard, just south of Vineland Road. Its huge front gates face toward the Portofino Bay Hotel, which lies, unseen, across the boulevard. For guests with hotel keys, there is also a side entrance near the dock where water taxis arrive from CityWalk.

The elegant main approach, an oval lawn flanked by stately palms, suggests pure luxury. The fountain out front, with its sculpture of spiraling guitars, adds a touch of whimsy. The pulsing rock music that subtly envelops guests as they walk over the marble-mosaic Hard Rock logo into the expansive lobby signals that a stay here is literally going to be an upbeat experience. The marble lobby gives way to a spacious sunken carpeted lounge overlooking the palm-dotted pool area out back.

The lobby lounge is decorated with the furniture and souvenirs that the unnamed rock star of our backstory has collected during his world tours. They range from the lavish to the funky, the tasteful to the bizarre, with coffee tables doubling as showcases for rare guitars once owned by rock masters. The effect is at once edgy and elegant and even the oddest looking furniture proves to be quite comfortable. Elaborate floral arrangements that are abstract art in their own right add the perfect finishing touch.

The public areas of the lobby level are dominated by large-scale art paying homage to some of rock's greatest stars. Our favorite is the massive blowup of the cover photo from the Stones' *Beggars' Banquet* album. This is a Hard Rock property, of course, so as you might expect, the ample collection of rock memorabilia spills out into the public areas and down the hallways. In fact, more than $1 million worth of rock memorabilia is scattered throughout the hotel, but judiciously so.

The lobby level, on the hotel's third floor, features the Palm Restaurant, the Velvet Bar, the Rock Shop, and the hotel's small meetings areas. Two floors below, at ground level, is The Kitchen, the hotel's main restaurant, and the extensive pool area. Also on this level are the fitness center and Camp L'il Rock for kids. A single bank of elevators gives access to all the hotel's floors.

The hotel wraps itself around the pool area out back, so the hallways of the upper floors, beautifully carpeted in blue and tan, curve gracefully. Where wings meet, the halls are punctuated by circular mini-lobbies with carpet medallions on the floor and rock memorabilia or rock portraits on the wall. The overall effect is quite classy; the rocker who owned this place obviously had exquisite taste — or hired a decorator who did.

For most people, the Hard Rock Hotel's best feature is likely to be its "ground-zero" location, next to Universal Studios Florida. As noted above, the actual front entrance to the hotel faces Universal Boulevard, looking across to the Portofino Bay Hotel, but the hotel grounds nestle up against the theme park. A side entrance on the ground level leads to a boat dock where you can pick up a motor launch for the short ride to CityWalk. If you prefer to walk, out back, past the pool, is a path that will take you directly to the front gates of Universal Studios Florida. You can leave the hotel on foot and, walking at a leisurely pace, be inside Universal Studios Florida in less than six minutes. It's the next best thing to actually staying inside the park.

Rooms and Suites

In general, the rooms are smaller than those at Portofino but just as nicely appointed. What you will find are beautifully designed and furnished rooms that would make the reputation of any big city "boutique" hotel. Most rooms, which avoid that boxy hotel room look with curved or angled walls, are "standard" rooms, 375 square feet, while the deluxe rooms are 400 square feet and feature a larger sitting area. Pool view rooms, especially those on floors five through seven, are highly recommended. You can reserve either a pool view or garden view room, but if you choose a deluxe room, the hotel will not be able to guarantee the view.

There is no rock memorabilia in the rooms, but the walls are decorated with black and white photos of rock history, in artful black frames with plenty of white matting. Each room has a different selection of photos from the hotel's collection. There are no labels, so your rock knowledge will be tested. If you get stuck, the management has thoughtfully provided each room with a guide to the photographs.

Every room boasts a flat-screen television and a compact but powerful CD-radio player. All rooms also feature iHome clock/radios with built-in iPod docks. When you check in you will get a code allowing you to download three distinct playlists. Eat your heart out, Napster! Otherwise, you can tune the player to the local classic rock station, 96.5 FM. Don't be surprised if you hear the dull throb of bass notes from other rooms lulling you to sleep and waking you up in the morning.

In what may be a subtle reference to a Beatles song, you'll even find a copy of Gideon's Bible. Gideon checked out and left it, no doubt, to help with some rocker's revival.

Hard Rock features a Club Level, with restricted access, on the seventh floor. For more on the Club Level, see *Amenities*, below. Kids' Suites, similar to those offered at Portofino, are also available, as are 685-square-foot "King" Suites.

There is even a Graceland Suite, also named in honor of The King. But don't expect gaudy over the top furniture and pink Caddy fins on the bed. This is a beautifully appointed suite of rooms with antiques, abstract paintings, and beautiful furnishings. The master bedroom features a flat plasma screen TV hanging on the wall and a glass-fronted fireplace that also opens onto a lavish shower area with a jacuzzi that can hold several people. (Groupies not included, presumably.)

Amenities

As a relatively small hotel on a smallish plot of land, the Hard Rock Hotel boasts fewer amenities than the nearby Portofino Bay, but what's here is choice.

▌ The Pool

The Hard Rock's only pool, all 12,000 square feet of it, is like a jewel in a fine setting. The hotel itself almost completely encloses it. The open end looks out past a rocky hill topped by a 30-foot guitar and a forest of palm trees toward Universal Studios Florida. The far side of the pool is an extensive sandy beach, dotted with lounge chairs and cabanas. The near side is dotted with more palm trees and still more lounge chairs. Two heated jacuzzi spas offer soothing massages. As a screenwriter might put it in a pitch meeting, "It's Bel Air meets Palm Springs."

Like the Beach Pool at Portofino, the Hard Rock pool features a water slide, this one a bit longer and a bit zippier. But the feature that will have everyone talking is the underwater sound system, which plays the same toe-tapping rock music you hear at poolside and throughout the hotel. It is possible to float lazily on your back, your ears below the water line, and groove to some of the greatest rock 'n roll ever recorded. And, yes, the sound quality is very good indeed. If you prefer, you can sit on underwater benches along the side where heated jets of water caress your back.

Near the pool is a concrete shuffleboard court, which struck us as a bit incongruous. Yes, of course even rockers grow old, but it's still just a little difficult to picture Twisted Sister hanging out here.

A lot more "happening" is the Beach Club bar (reviewed below). Attractive young servers roam the pool area taking orders for exotic drinks with names like Blue Suede Shoes and Hard Rockin' Lemonade.

Hollywood deal makers can spread out in one of the private tent-like cabanas that can be rented by the day. "Standard" cabanas start at $160, with a premium based on time of year and "Beach Side" locations. Club Level guests get $45 off. There are no half-day rentals. All cabanas have a television, refrigerator, fresh water, fruit basket, towels, and a small selection of soft drinks.

On some nights the pool hosts a "Dive-In Movie." A huge screen is set up on the poolside beach so guests can watch while floating on rented rafts. The films are of fairly recent vintage, often with a tie-in to the theme parks, and never rated higher than PG-13. On other nights there may be a "Dive in Concert" or blacklight volleyball. Some nights a D.J. appears to keep the joint jumpin'.

If there's a downside to all this, it's probably that the pool is just too popular. So expect it to be crowded. The pool is open daily from 8:00 a.m. to 11:00 p.m. or midnight during warmer months. Access is through a gate that can be opened with your room key.

■ Club Level

The rooms and suites on the seventh floor have been set aside for those who insist on a little extra from their hotel stay. The concept is much like the Concierge Levels you may have encountered at those high-priced hotels that cater to business travelers, except this one has the hip, rock star name "Club 7."

For starters, access to the seventh floor is strictly limited. Just to make sure you are not bothered by the riffraff, you have to insert your room key into a slot in the elevator before it will take you to seven. Once there, you can step into a spacious lounge staffed with friendly hosts and hostesses, who serve as your personal concierges from 7:30 a.m. to 11:00 p.m. This is where you come in the morning for a complimentary continental breakfast and to glance through the tony out-of-town papers high rollers insist upon. The lounge serves refreshments throughout the day; hors d'oeuvres, beer and wine in the evening; and cookies and milk before bedtime.

Club Level guests can borrow from the Club's collection of 500 rock CDs for private listening in their rooms. If they're feeling more sociable, the Club lounge offers two large screen TVs with DVD players in an area with very comfy seating. Club level guests also receive free access to the hotel's fitness center and a discount on those pricey poolside cabanas (see above).

■ Camp L'il Rock

Hard Rock's kiddie club is located on the ground floor not far from the pool. For more information about the services offered here, see *Good Things To Know About...Kids' Activities* in the introductory section of this chapter. Make your reservations 24 hours in advance by calling 32230 on a hotel phone or (407) 503-2230 from outside.

■ Workout Room

The compact fitness center on the ground floor has a small selection of treadmills and weight machines and even some free weights for purists. After your workout, you can relax in a steam room or sauna and then change in the locker room. Separate facilities are provided for men and women. There is an $10 per day fee; multiday passes are available. Club Level guests and All Access members get in free. Hours are 6:00 a.m. to 9:00 p.m. Kids 12 through 15 are allowed, but only if they have adult supervision. Joggers can take off for a loop around either the Bay at Portofino Bay in one direction or CityWalk in the other.

Good Things To Know About...

■ Guest Laundry

The Hard Rock Hotel has small guest laundry rooms on the second and fourth floors near the elevators, each with two washers and two dryers. The cost is $2.50 to wash, $2.50 to dry.

■ Meetings, Weddings and Banquets

There is very little meeting space at the Hard Rock. The largest space is the Avalon Ballroom, 3,000 square feet divisible into three separate sections, with a total capacity of 300 people. Two smaller rooms, the Apollo Boardroom and the Fillmore Meeting Room, are suitable for receptions or small meetings. For more information, call (407) 503-2100.

■ Parking

Parking is outdoors in two lots that flank the impressive main entrance. Because the Palm Restaurant draws so many locals, however, finding a good spot (or any spot!) can sometimes be a challenge. Valet parking is another option.

■ Velvet Sessions

On the last Thursday of each month, the Velvet Bar (see below) spills out into the lobby for Velvet Sessions, "a rock and roll cocktail party," and a guest rock band pumps up the volume from 6:30 to 9:00 p.m. or later. Past acts have included Cheap Trick, Joan Jett, Eddie Money, and Flock of Seagulls. Various liquor companies use the events to tout new brands and concoctions, and presumably a good time is had by all. Tickets range from

$25 to $50, depending on the band.

Visit www.velvetsessions.com to find out who's playing when and to purchase tickets.

Dining at the Hard Rock Hotel

There are just two full-service restaurants at Hard Rock, one offering gut- and wallet-busting steaks for the expense account crowd in the evenings, the other serving up moderately priced casual fare all day long. An ice cream parlor doubles as a casual, take-out breakfast spot in the morning. Guests who are too pooped to pop or too old to stroll can call on the hotel's 24-hour room service.

■ Palm Restaurant

What:	Steak house
Where:	On the lobby level, near Velvet; also has an outside entrance
Price Range:	$$$$+
Hours:	Monday to Thursday 5:00 p.m. to 10:30 p.m.; Friday and Saturday 5:00 p.m. to 11:00 p.m.; Sunday 5:00 p.m. to 9:30 p.m.
Reservations:	Not required but highly recommended, especially on weekends. Call (407) 503-7256.

The original Palm opened in New York in 1926 and over the years developed a reputation as a place where movers and shakers gathered to devour mammoth steaks and cut big deals. In the intervening years, the Palm has branched out to many other cities and has now established itself in Orlando. Those who know the original will find the Hard Rock incarnation familiar, if larger. Like the other branches, the walls of this one are filled with colorful caricatures of regular patrons and local celebrities from the business world and the media. The dark wooden wainscoting and room dividers evoke an earlier, male-dominated era when the steak house was something of a boy's club. The waiters in long white meat cutters' aprons complete the vintage picture.

This is a noisy, boisterous steak house that fits in well with the spirit of Hard Rock and is proving equally popular with tourists and high-rolling locals, which is probably the whole point. It's a great place to come in a celebratory mood with a bunch of friends who don't mind shouting to make themselves heard as they tuck into huge slabs of prime aged meat or crack open a five-pound lobster, all washed down with some pricey wines. Figure a bare minimum of $60 per person for the standard Palm blowout meal, much more with cocktails and wine. Those looking for a quiet table in the corner or a moderately priced meal should look elsewhere.

Steaks are the center of attention here and they are quite good. They range in price from $42 to $47, with a mammoth 32-ounce double steak for two going for $92. Three-pound lobsters start at $65; at times you can get a four-pounder for two with salad and side for $90. If you don't know exactly what you want, our advice would be to rely on the server's recommendation. Steak and lobsters at the Palm are traditionally accompanied by a number of side dishes served "family style for two or more" ($9 to $11). The creamed spinach is justly famous and the others are good, too.

For those not into thick slabs of steak or gargantuan crustaceans, the Palm offers a selection of fairly standard Italian veal dishes (about $30) as well as some pasta dishes. For lighter appetites, two of the Palm's signature salads are worth recommending. The Gigi ($13) is a blend of tomatoes, bacon, onions, chopped shrimp, and green beans in a light vinaigrette and the Monday Night Salad ($12) is mixed greens, pimentos, onions, tomatoes, anchovies, and radishes.

Desserts ($6 to $12) are fairly pedestrian versions of old standbys and strike some as a tad overpriced. They include New York cheesecake, tiramisu, key lime pie, and creme brulee.

The Palm has two entrances. One leads from the hotel lobby down a stately corridor lined with psychedelic day-glo posters from the heyday of San Francisco acid rock; the other offers access from the hotel's front drive for those arriving by car.

▌Velvet Bar

What:	Trendy watering hole
Where:	Off the main lobby lounge
Price Range:	$ - $$
Hours:	4:00 p.m. to 2:00 a.m. daily
Reservations:	None

Plasma TV screens on the wall provide a never-ending flow of music videos for the crowds that gather in this intimate, postmodern lounge. It has quickly proved to be the place for groups of friends to meet before an evening at the hotel or CityWalk.

The decor relies on the same artfully mismatched furniture that fills the lobby. To this is added some wonderfully tacky faux zebra chairs, abstract art, and portraits of rock stars in a color-filled mish-mash that makes you feel like you've had a bit too much to drink before you take your first sip. A well-placed divider splits the room into a bar area and a more secluded lounge area, and servers in chic black prowl the bar and the adjacent lobby lounge taking orders. For serious drinkers there is cognac ($10 to $175) and single malt Scotch ($11 to $55). There are about two dozen specialty drinks ($10.50 and up) on offer as well as an abbreviated menu ($10 to $16) of things to nibble on, including shrimp cocktail, burgers, and salads. Hookah water pipes ($20) and cigars ($6 to $20) are also available.

■ The Kitchen

What:	Casual all-day dining
Where:	On the ground floor with an entrance facing the pool
Price Range:	$$ - $$$
Hours:	7:00 a.m. to 11:00 p.m. daily
Reservations:	Not required but accepted at (407) 503-DINE (3463)

This artfully casual eatery features "New American" cuisine in a glamorous open setting that seems to run the length of the hotel. The long main dining area features an open kitchen and a brick pizza oven. There is a separate, more intimate dining room at the far end for private parties, a small bar area, and a "Kids' Crib," a separate area where kids can dine apart from their hectoring parents. The furnishings and table settings follow the pattern of eclectic mismatching found throughout the hotel and the overall effect is delightful. The entire restaurant looks out through generous glass walls to the pool area and there is an outdoor seating area where the tables are shaded by snazzy square canvas umbrellas.

In keeping with the kitchen theme, many dishes are served in what appear to be cooking utensils like colanders and frying pans. The open kitchen sometimes serves as a venue for cooking demonstrations by stars and "Kids Can Cook, Too" events.

Breakfast is the most traditional meal, as the counters by the open kitchen are transformed into a sumptuous buffet. You can choose the full Breakfast Buffet (about $18, $9 for kids), or you can order a la carte from a menu of standards, from bacon and eggs to waffles with fruit, all of them well executed.

Lunch and dinner share most of the same menu items. Pizzas are $14, with the most interesting choice topped with ancho grilled chicken and roasted corn. Main dishes ($13 to $31) range from a simple Mac and Cheese to Seared Ahi Tuna and vegetable chow-chow, and include straightforward interpretations of salmon, chicken pot pie, and roasted chicken. Otherwise, there are salads and sandwiches ($10 to $14).

It's rather like what you'd expect to find over at the Hard Rock Cafe, and perhaps that's the point. The food is good without making an attempt to be exceptional. Salads are in the $9 to $16 range, pizzas $14, burgers $12 and up. Heartier entrees range from the $11 Mac and Cheese to a $31 filet mignon and a $30 New York Strip steak.

In the center of the restaurant is a "chef's table" where you can sit at a curving counter and watch a sous chef prepare the evening's specials. A tilted overhead mirror gives you a good view of the techniques being employed.

■ Emack & Bolio's

What:	Ice cream parlor
Where:	On the ground floor on the way to the pool
Price Range:	$
Hours:	6:30 a.m. to 11:00 p.m. daily
Reservations:	None

In the morning, Emack & Bolio's serves up quick, easy-to-carry breakfast items like yogurt, fruit cups, Starbucks coffee, and pastries. There are also take-to-your-room snacks and drinks. Its main line of business, however, is upscale, high-fat, premium ice cream and fruit smoothies, which have made it one of the hotel's most popular "dining" spots.

The ice cream flavors have cutesy Ben & Jerry's-style names, often with a rock and roll twist. A single scoop costs $3.75 and a pint goes for $7.50. Sundaes start at $5.50, but why not round up seven friends and splurge on a $24 Emack Attack?

■ Beach Club

What:	Bar and snacks al fresco
Where:	By the pool
Price Range:	$ - $$
Hours:	11:00 a.m. to 10:00 p.m., later when it's busy
Reservations:	None

The pool enjoys its own casual bar serving light fare, with optional poolside service. The circular bar is open to the pool and raffishly decorated with rusted metal sculptures of musicians. Tables spill out from under the conical roof, but roaming servers will take your order and fetch you food and drink anywhere in the pool area. You can order up a daiquiri, margarita, or other fancy drink ($9 to $12) or opt for a non-alcoholic smoothie ($6).

The abbreviated menu ranges from the sort of salty snacks that will encourage you to order another beer, to salads and sandwiches, to simple desserts. The sandwiches ($10 to $13) range from wraps and burgers (including veggie burgers) to more refined fare. Or you can build your own pizza ($10 and up). Salads ($10 to $15) range from a simple dish of mixed greens to Caesar salad with shrimp. The desserts ($3 to $5) include ice cream treats from Emack & Bolio's. As with all the poolside eateries at Universal Orlando, an 18% gratuity is automatically added to all bills.

Shopping at Hard Rock Hotel

"Love all. Serve all. Sell all a tchotchke." That's not really the Hard Rock motto, of course, but it's hard to escape noticing that the Hard Rock empire must make as much money selling branded clothing, souvenirs, and memorabilia as it does selling burgers, shakes, and booze. So it's fitting that the only shop is the coyly named **Rock Shop** just off the main lobby.

Most of the room in this spacious emporium is given over to souvenir clothing, from T-shirts to snazzy leather jackets with equally snazzy price tags. If you have arrived only to discover that your wardrobe isn't what it should be, you can remedy that here. There are some suitably slinky dresses and beachwear for women. Somehow, the men's clothing, while very nice, is rather staid, the kind of thing that would look great on the PGA tour.

There are some nice things for kids here, too, including black leather jackets. Almost as an afterthought, a corner of the shop is given over to a small selection of the sort of sundries you usually find in a hotel gift shop. You will have to head to Le Memorie di Portofino shop in Portofino Bay's lobby for a larger selection.

LOEWS ROYAL PACIFIC RESORT

6300 Hollywood Way
Orlando, FL 32819
(407) 503-3000; fax: (407) 503-3010

Like the Hard Rock, the Royal Pacific Resort has a "backstory" that subtly informed the design of the hotel and the themes of its restaurants. This one involves the Royal Pacific family of companies, a made-up travel and transportation conglomerate that flourished in the 1930s, the "Golden Age of Travel." Its holdings included Royal Pacific Airways, a fleet of dashing sea planes that linked the sprawling island chains of the South Pacific, and Royal Pacific Steamship Lines, a fleet of luxury ocean liners that plied the tropical seas. The Royal Pacific Resort, it would seem, is the latest jewel in the Royal Pacific crown, a luxury getaway located somewhere in Bali. Of course, none of this is terribly overt. It's a muted story, told with subtlety — a welcome message in the in-room hotel directory, the 30s-style jazz that plays throughout the property, the retro art on the travel posters in your room, and the occasional display case of memorabilia dotted around the property, not to mention the Royal Pacific Airways Grumman Albatross sea plane floating near the water taxi dock. Everything here has been inspired by, rather than copied from, Indonesia and Fiji, so the hotel reminds you of the South Seas while remaining very much its own place.

If the fictional Royal Pacific was a company of the 30s, the present seven-story hotel is very much of the twenty-first century. Its public spaces are open, airy, and luxurious, tastefully decorated with genuine Indonesian woodcarvings and other art works. Its lobby is gorgeous, our favorite of the three resort hotels. Its amenities are state of the art and the dining venues, including a snazzy restaurant by Emeril Lagasse, are a cut or three above standard hotel fare.

The hotel's facade, which reflects its Balinese inspiration, is rather featureless, a mustard-colored slab concealed by lush greenery. The exterior looks better at night, when artfully placed spotlights and the shadows cast by palm trees add texture and depth to the building's flat surfaces.

While the other hotels have meeting space — Hard Rock a little, Portofino Bay somewhat more — the Royal Pacific was designed as a full-fledged convention hotel. The attached convention center is vast. In fact, all of Portofino Bay's meeting space could fit into Royal Pacific's Grand Ballroom with enough space left over to swing quite a few cats. Of course, with its fabulous and fun pool and its proximity to two great theme parks, the Royal Pacific has drawn a large leisure and family business as well.

Orientation

Your Royal Pacific Resort experience begins when you cross a broad, thatched-roofed, bamboo-accented bridge over an artificial river. Step into the massive rectangular lobby and you enter a Balinese demi-paradise. Pause to admire the intricately carved Indonesian wood panels hanging on the walls on either side of the entrance. The lobby completely surrounds a glassed-in, orchid-accented courtyard pool. Statuary elephants cavort in its shallow depths while fountains in the form of Southeast Asian temple statuary constantly replenish its waters. At night, with a crescent moon high overhead, this courtyard is ravishingly romantic.

To the left of the courtyard pool is the reception area, to the right an elegant staircase that descends two stories to the hotel's main restaurant and the swimming pool area. Also to the right, just around the corner and past the staircase, is a spacious seating area complete with expansive views and the elegant Orchid Court Lounge bar with an adjoining sushi bar. The floor to ceiling windows overlooking the pool area evoke the open-air pavilion architecture that represents the finest in Balinese living.

The hotel's 1,000 rooms are arrayed off the lobby in three Y-shaped, seven-story wings, called Towers. Tower 1, The Windward, is to your right as you enter, Tower 2, The Leeward, is to your left, and Tower 3, The Royal, which houses the hotel's Club Level rooms on its seventh floor, is directly opposite the main entrance. (In your four-digit room number, the first digit indicates which tower you're in and the second digit denotes the floor.)

The swimming pool is located between the Windward and Royal Towers, and beyond the pool the rides and attractions of Islands of Adventure form an antic skyline. The space between the Leeward and Royal Towers, in contrast, is given over to a quiet croquet lawn and open spaces, such as the Wantilan Pavilion, designed for outdoor events. The Leeward and Windward Towers frame the main entrance.

The lobby is on the third level. Most of the dining and other amenities will be found two floors below. From the Islands Dining Room, the hotel's main restaurant, a covered walkway hugs the building as it makes its way

257

past the pool to Tchoup Chop, another creation of Emeril Lagasse, and the vast convention center beyond that is attached to the hotel.

The water taxi dock is near Tchoup Chop, most convenient to rooms in the Royal Tower and a longish walk past the pool from the lobby area. From the water taxi stop, the "Garden Walkway" runs along the shore of the Bali Sea, past the pool and on to CityWalk. It takes less than ten minutes to stroll there at a leisurely pace. The main entrance can be reached by foot from the Garden Walkway, but is most conveniently reached by car.

Rooms and Suites

Compared to the wide-open public spaces, the rooms seem small. They are decorated in pale pastels like lime and mango, with sisal-style carpeting and rattan touches in the furniture evoking the tropics and making the space seem airier. Flat-screen TVs add a sleek modern touch, while the bamboo patterned screens and vintage posters from Bali remind us that we are a world away. A number of other small touches in the rooms echo the hotel's backstory and are fun to look for.

Since the Royal Pacific was designed as a convention hotel, there is one distinct difference from the other hotels: all rooms are standard rooms. There are no slightly larger rooms designated as "deluxe rooms" as there are at Portofino and the Hard Rock. Most rooms have a compact vanity area with a sink just outside the bathroom (which has no sink), while others have full bathrooms. All rooms have 32" (or larger) flat-screen televisions, coffee makers for that morning jolt of java, iHome clock/radios with iPod docks, as well as the usual blow dryer for damp hair and an iron and ironing board.

The next step up from a standard room is a suite. Like the standard rooms, the suites were designed with the convention trade in mind. They are the nicely appointed two-room suites you would expect in any business hotel; aside from the extra space, they feature the same amenities as in the standard rooms. The Royal Pacific has eight Jurassic Park-themed "Kids' Suites," complete with dinosaur murals and raptor-cage headboards, as well as a Club Level with restricted access in the Royal Tower. For more on the Club Level, see *Amenities*, below.

For high rollers, the best option is The Captain's Suite, located on the seventh floor Club Level of the Royal Tower. It is exquisitely decorated with Indonesian art and fabrics and features a full kitchen and a guest bathroom off the entry foyer. All the super luxury suites at the resort hotels are grand and splashy, but this one is the most quietly elegant, the kind of place you could imagine yourself having as a permanent residence. It also has the best view in the hotel, a sweeping vista of the pool area and Islands of Adventure. Compared to the rates for other luxury suites at Universal, the Captain's Suite here is a positive bargain.

Pool view rooms are obviously much sought after. Unfortunately, the hotel has just 173 such rooms, so your odds of getting one are approximately one in six. The hotel will try to honor requests for a specific view but they cannot guarantee them.

See *Room Rates at a Glance,* at the beginning of this chapter, to get an idea of the price range at Royal Pacific and how it compares to the other on-site hotels.

Amenities

One thing you might expect of a hotel with "resort" in its name is a spa, but Royal Pacific lacks this amenity, directing its guests to the Mandara Spa at the Portofino Bay Hotel. For the rest, the choices are limited but well executed.

■ Club Level

The rooms and suites on the seventh floor of the Royal Tower have been set aside for those who enjoy that extra little bit of pampering. The concept is much like that used at the Hard Rock, and if you've enjoyed Club Level service there, you'll no doubt want to see how the Royal Pacific compares.

As at the Hard Rock, access is strictly limited; a slot in the elevator reads your room key before it will take you to seven. At the end of the corridor, you will find a spacious V-shaped lounge. Picture windows looking out across Interstate 4 to the International Drive area give this room an edge over similar rooms at the other hotels. It is staffed with friendly hosts and hostesses, who serve as your personal concierges from 7:30 a.m. to 11:00 p.m. Head here in the morning for a complimentary continental breakfast (7:00 a.m. to 10:30 a.m.) and to glance through the tony out-of-town newspapers so imporatant to high rollers. The lounge serves refreshments throughout the day; hors d'oeuvres, beer, and wine in the evening; and "Something Sweet" before bedtime.

Club Level guests can borrow from the Club's collection of DVDs for viewing on the large screen TVs at either end of the lounge. Club Level guests also receive free access to the hotel's fitness center and discounts on poolside cabanas.

■ Lagoon Pool

The Royal Pacific may have only one pool, but it's the largest in the city of Orlando (although not, it should be noted, in the greater Orlando area). It sprawls languorously between the Windward and Royal Towers beside the Bali Sea end of the winding waterway that links all the resort hotels with CityWalk. The heated pool is like a small tropical sea itself, with an irregular, sinuous shape and even a tiny palm-dotted island. It's shallow, too, designed more for playing than serious swimming, with no spot deeper than about four feet seven inches.

One side is dominated by the superstructure of the Royal Bali Sea, a ship of the Royal Pacific line that seems to have run aground and buried itself in the sand. Actually it's an elaborate water play area (think *Curious George* over at Universal Studios) that gushes cold, bracing water from every conceivable orifice, while kids man a battery of water cannons, never seeming to tire of squirting each other and unsuspecting swimmers who venture too close to shore. This is Royal Pacific's answer to the water slides at the other resorts and kids love it.

On this side, the pool bottom slopes gently up to water's edge, affording little ones easy entry. Nearby is a white sandy beach area and a fenced children's play area complete with wading pool and sandbox (pails included). Close by is an ice cream parlor. It's just a walk-up kiosk, but it dispenses a surprising variety of fast-melting treats.

Near the middle, the pool narrows to accommodate a volleyball net strung from shore to shore and an impromptu game between former strangers always seems to be in progress. The opposite side is more adult-oriented. Here you will find the **Bula Bar and Grille** (reviewed below), three cabanas, a red-topped pool table, and two hot tubs — one somewhat larger than the other. Between the pool and the hotel is a concrete shuffleboard court; you will often see a ping-pong table in this area when the weather cooperates.

Cabanas are small (two lounge chairs fill them up) canvas-sided shelters with a TV, ceiling fan, and a small, modestly stocked fridge. Full day rentals (8:00 a.m. to pool closing) start at $75, with half-day rentals (8:00 a.m. to 3:00 p.m. or 3:00 p.m. to pool closing) at $45. Club Level guests get full day rentals starting at just $45. Rentals are handled by the staff at The Gymnasium (see below) and cabanas can be reserved weeks or months in advance, just like rooms.

On most summer nights at sunset, near the Bula Bar end of the pool, the wail of conch shells and the sonorous singing of a Samoan chieftain signal the start of a brief "torch lighting ceremony." Many people drift over to watch from the shallow water. The ceremony is staged only on Friday and Saturday during the rest of the year.

Just outside the fenced-in pool area is the "Garden Walkway" that takes you to CityWalk. The gates are usually open during the day, but in the evening you will need your room key to gain entry.

▌ Volleyball Court

Also just outside the pool, on the very edge of the Bali Sea, is a splendidly inviting white sand regulation volleyball court. It's first come, first served and **free**. Grab a ball at the pool towel hut.

▌ The Mariners' Club

Just past the Game Room is Royal Pacific's children's playroom. For more information about the services offered here, see *Good Things To Know About... Kids' Activities* in the introductory section of this chapter. Make your reservations 24 hours in advance by calling 33230 on a hotel phone or (407) 503-3230 from outside.

▌ The Gymnasium

This sleek, modern, but rather spartan fitness room is close by the Lagoon Pool, just past the Treasures of Bali shop as you head to the convention center. The equipment is state-of-the-art but free weights are also available for the old-fashioned pumping iron crowd. The fee is $10 per day; it includes use of the sauna, steam bath, and a unisex whirlpool room, which is a particularly lovely place to hang out and relax. Club Level guests and You First members receive complimentary use of the fitness facilities. Kids 12 through 15 are allowed, but only if they have adult supervision. The Gymnasium is open from 6:00 a.m. to 9:00 p.m.

▌ Croquet Lawn

Far from the frenzied activity of the pool area, on the other side of the Royal Tower wing, is a meticulously groomed croquet lawn, where the harried executive can come to unwind and practice those tricky cannon shots. You can pick up **free** mallets and balls at The Gymnasium.

Good Things To Know About...

◼ Guest Laundry

Each Tower has a guest laundry room. In the Royal Tower, it is on the second level. In the other two towers, it is on the bottom floor with an outside entrance. There are three washers and three dryers in each room. The cost is $2.50 per load to wash and the same to dry.

◼ Meetings and Banquets

Loews Royal Pacific was designed as a convention hotel, with some 75,000 square feet of meeting space. The Grand Ballroom alone is 41,500 square feet. The convention area, which is adjacent to but quite separate from the hotel itself, is spacious and airy and decorated with a South Seas nostalgia theme. The walls are dotted with fanciful 1930s-style travel posters and memorabilia. If you'd like more information about how your company might take advantage of all this, call (407) 503-3100.

◼ Parking

There is less guest parking available at the Royal Pacific than at the other resort hotels, which means that if you are self-parking, finding an empty space can sometimes be a challenge. One choice is to park at the rear of the hotel in the convention center parking area. Or you might want to consider paying the extra money for valet parking to avoid the hassle.

Dining at Loews Royal Pacific Resort

The food at Royal Pacific tends to be of the sit-down variety and on the pricey side. The good news is that the food served here is worth the premium prices charged. Those looking for a quick bite or more moderately priced fare will have to travel to CityWalk.

◼ Orchid Court Lounge and Sushi Bar

What:	Lounge bar with continental breakfast, hors d'oeuvres, and sushi at night
Where:	In the main lobby
Price Range:	$ - $$$
Hours:	6:00 a.m. to midnight
Reservations:	None

This elegant lobby bar and lounge area is awash in the gorgeous orchids from which it takes its name. It serves up exotic drinks ($9). The potables range from martinis, to frozen drinks, to elaborate "South Seas" concoctions like Mai Tais and the signature Pacific Paradise. They arrive garnished with colorful little umbrellas or enormous tropical palm leaves. Wine is available by the glass.

In the morning, from 6:00 a.m. to 11:00 a.m., the bar at the Orchid Court turns into a cafeteria line serving an a la carte continental breakfast featuring cereal, fruit, and a variety of breakfast breads and pastries. It has proven to be a popular option and the lines are frequently quite long. Careful! If you have a hearty appetite the cost can quickly approach that of the buffet breakfast downstairs at the Islands Dining Room. One saving grace is that coffee refills are free and unlimited until 11:00 a.m.

From 5:00 to 11:00 p.m., the **Orchid Court Sushi Bar** operates at the opposite end of the lobby from the bar. Here you can get your favorite rolls or sashimi specialties prepared to order by a team of experienced sushi chefs. This section of the lobby has been partitioned off, creating a de facto restaurant, which makes the sushi bar a perfectly good choice for dinner if you're in the mood for sushi.

Prices are moderate ($4 to $7 for two pieces of *nigiri*, $6 to $14 for rolls) although some of the sushi and sashimi platters can be quite pricey ($30 to $90). Some of the rolls are quite creative, like the Tropical (salmon and tuna with mango and kiwi) and Pacific (four fishes with cucumber wrapping and ponzu sauce). But pass on the *uni* (sea urchin); it's frozen and overpriced. Hot "nybbles" are also offered ($9 to $17), but the quesadillas, paninis, and other snacks don't quite fit the theme.

▎ Islands Dining Room

What:	Full-service all-day dining
Where:	Directly below the lobby overlooking the pool
Price Range:	$$$ - $$$$+
Hours:	7:00 a.m. to 10:00 p.m. daily.
Reservations:	Not required but highly recommended. Call (407) 503-3463.

The hotel's large main dining room (the restaurant seats 380) is styled in the Indonesian fashion with louvered walls and ceiling fans hand-fashioned from silken hand fans. Indonesian carved wooden panels divide the room into separate seating areas. Floor to ceiling windows seem to bring the pool area indoors and huge carved frogs from Indonesia stand sentinel-like, adding a whimsical touch. Alcoves along one side of the room serve as added dining space, or buffet lines, one of them set aside for the special evening kids' buffet ($6), complete with kiddie-sized tables and chairs, a great way to give the grown-ups a mealtime break.

Most breakfast tastes can be accommodated — there's even a Japanese breakfast option — with the typical a la carte breakfast running just over $15. Unless, of course, you order one of the fancier Eggs Benedict offerings, in which case your bill could easily exceed $17.50, the price of the sumptuous, all-you-can-eat breakfast buffet that includes made-to-order eggs and omelettes. The children's version of the breakfast buffet is $8.50.

Dinner is where the kitchen at Islands Dining Room comes into its own. Islands turns out some of the best dinner entrees at any of the resort hotels, with prices to match. It is easy to spend $30 to $35 or more per person on food alone, without drinks, tax, or tip. For many people that will put dinner here in the "special occasion" category, although the aforementioned $6 kids' buffet may lessen the impact on the old wallet. The menu also calls out some less expensive (and less adventuresome) choices. That being said, you will probably not leave the table disappointed.

The appetizers ($9 to $15) feature potstickers and a "surf and turf" summer roll. Salads ($9 to $18) include a wonderfully simple "Seven Leaf" with lemon-soy vinaigrette.

Entrees ($13 to $29) range from upscale versions of homey dishes like Korean-style crispy pork cutlets to a grilled beef tenderloin. The seafood choices ($17 to $23) change seasonally so it's hard to predict what you'll encounter. A Teriyaki Beef Stir Fry is $19. Sandwiches ($13 to $17) are also available and include South Seas versions of the standard burger and the traditional club sandwich. Mini-desserts ($3.50) include guava flan and tropical fruit trifle.

The Islands Dining Room features Character Dining (Curious George and Woody Woodpecker are common sightings) and strolling entertainers. Several nights a week a Southwestern or Italian buffet is offered for $25, with entertainment to match. You may also see a witch-doctor magician moving from table to table or hear strolling Pacific islands musicians.

▌ Jake's American Bar

What:	Bar and light meals
Where:	Downstairs, near Islands Dining Room
Price Range:	$$
Hours:	4:00 p.m. to 2:00 a.m.; "late nite" menu from 11:00 p.m.
Reservations:	None

Jake McNally was quite a guy, a sea plane pilot for Royal Pacific Airways who won the "World Series of sea plane racing" in 1927. Jake's exploits in love were as dismal as his airborne feats were glorious. Dumped by the love of his life, Jake disappeared and is rumored to be flying from one backwater dive to another trying to forget. This bar is a tribute to his memory by his friends, who have donated memorabilia to help decorate the joint. It's all made up, of course, but this fanciful story forms the basis for one of the most successful themed restaurants in all of Universal Orlando Resort.

The decor is colonial men's club and casual, echoing the open architecture of the South Seas, where any breeze is welcome. In fact, it's worth peeking into Jake's just to marvel at the ceiling fans. Also a great deal of fun is the Jake McNally memorabilia and the framed love letters that grace the walls.

The food is as jaunty as the decor with the accent on casual bar fare that won't overly tax the wallet, another reason Jake's has become so popular with guests. The "To Start" section of the menu ($8 to $15) consists of appetizer-like nibbles such as volcano shrimp and chicken quesadillas. For veggie lovers there are salads like Caesar and Cobb, with the mixed garden greens a light-bite winner, especially with the ginger soy dressing.

Slightly more substantial are the sandwiches and burgers. The most expensive item on the menu is Slow Roasted BBQ Ribs ($20), melt in your mouth guava-glazed ribs served with potato salad and baked beans.

Of course, Jake's is a bar and dining is not mandatory. Jake's would make an excellent choice for drinks before (or after) dining at Islands. Happy hour is 4:00 p.m. to 6:00 p.m. daily. Along with the usual, the bartenders here whip up a variety of lethal "South Seas" concoctions with don't-tell-me-I-didn't-warn-you names like Tsunami. Setting new heights for exotic concoctions is the flaming Mt. Kumuneyewanadrinkya, a 32-ounce behemoth with at least eight ounces of rum and other booze lurking in its depths.

If you stop by for a nightcap, you should check out the small outside seating area under the bridge that forms the entrance to the hotel. Here you can enjoy the lingering warmth of a summer night with a waterfall providing a romantic soundtrack. A limited "late nite" menu ($8 to $13) will take care of those midnight munchies.

■ Bula Bar and Grille

What:	Casual poolside dining
Where:	By the pool, near the Royal Tower
Hours:	11:00 a.m. to 11:00 p.m., kitchen closes at 9:00 p.m. (10:00 p.m. on weekends)
Price Range:	$ - $$

Reservations: None

An inviting palapa-like bar beckons thirsty swimmers with exotic drink concoctions (about $9) ranging from Mai Tais to less well-known potions with names like "Witch Doctor," whose lengthy list of ingredients might give even the heartiest boozer pause. Other drinks are available as well, of course, with beers going for $5 to $6. Non-alcoholic Tropical Smoothies (about $6) in strawberry, mango, and passion fruit flavors are also on tap for those who want to get into the South Seas swing of things and still walk.

Snacks and light meals are available from the Grille part of the establishment, cooked up in a small kitchen a few paces away. They range in price from $8 to $14 and include nachos with a roasted pepper cheese sauce, fish tacos, and (at about $12) the Big Bula Burger. More adult choices include grilled mahi mahi, chimichuri steak wrap, and Pacifica ceviche. The food here is surprisingly substantial and quite good, making the Bula Bar an option for your main meal of the day.

As with all the poolside eateries at Universal Orlando, an 18% gratuity is automatically added to all bills.

▌Tchoup Chop

What:	Another Emeril's extravaganza
Where:	Near the convention center
Price Range:	$$$ - $$$$+
Hours:	5:30 p.m. to 10:00 p.m.; to 11:00 p.m. on Friday and Saturday.
Reservations:	Highly recommended. (407) 503-2467

Located at the point where the Royal Pacific Resort meets the massive convention center attached to the hotel, Tchoup Chop (pronounced "chop chop") is to Royal Pacific what Bice is to Portofino Bay, the signature restaurant for the hotel and a destination in its own right. And being an Emeril Lagasse restaurant, the cooking is as bold as the decor.

Guests arriving by boat from CityWalk pass through a carved wooden moon gate and cross an open patio to reach the restaurant. The dining area, carefully designed according to feng shui principles, is a riot of blue tile, orange glass chandeliers, pale beige bamboo and rattan and dark teak furniture. A long, narrow pool bedecked with lily pads runs down the middle with a chic and well-stocked bar at one end. The overall effect is at once vibrant and soothing. Unfortunately, the design has been spoiled somewhat by an ungainly curtain that's been installed as a partition for private parties.

Facing the entrance is an open kitchen and food bar that allows "interactive" experiences between chefs and diners. Tchoup Chop was destined to become instantly popular and the Lagasse touch has kept the place booked up well after the initial curiosity was satisfied. So if you plan to dine here, be on the safe side and book your dining reservation when you book your hotel room.

Fortunately, the food lives up to the hype. Chef de Cuisine Gregory Richie has received raves from local food critics. The cuisine is inspired both by the Polynesian islands of the South Pacific and Asian cooking techniques, with the fresh seafood of the Gulf of Mexico and the nearby Atlantic playing a strong supporting role. But don't expect a re-run of Trader Vic's, which is the stereotype of a Polynesian restaurant, or even Emeril's over at CityWalk for that matter. Here the emphasis is on relatively straightforward preparation of superb ingredients. Get a burger for your kid and it will be made from the finest beef. The menu changes with admirable regularity as the chefs take advantage of the seasonal availability of fish and produce, so it's difficult to predict what will be available when you visit. However, a survey of past dishes will give you some idea and help whet your appetite. Rest assured that everything we've tried here has ranged from excellent to life-altering.

Your meal begins with complimentary prawn chips (like a potato chip with the texture of packing styrofoam, but redeemed by a tangy citrus dipping sauce). Appetizers ($6 to $12) might include Emeril's take on Shanghai dumplings, "kicked up" crab cake, or wasabi-cured lomi lomi salmon, all very good. Dinner soups and salads ($5 to $8) range from simple miso soups to elaborate salads with exotic dressings, and a limited menu of sushi rolls, nigiri, and sashimi ($8 to $12) is offered.

Entrees ($19 to $35) include innovative takes on filet mignon, short ribs, and salmon, which might be crusted with macadamia nuts and served with coconut purple sticky rice. The roasted duck breast with pastrami confit is exquisite, as are jumbo scallops on risotto with Thai-curry lobster sauce. Meats are often served over mashed potatoes laced with roasted garlic or wasabi paste. Desserts ($6 and up) also change too often to keep up with. Suffice it to say, they're all terrific.

Sake ($60 to $99 the bottle) features in the culinary concept here, much as wine would in a fine French restaurant, with a small but choice selection of premium brands available. A tasting flight of sake samples is about $12. A more traditional wine list is also available.

Tip: Tchoup Chop owns a small outdoor "tiki bar," which serves all the elaborate cocktails ($9 to $19) served inside. What is less well known is that you can order anything else on the menu here to be served outside. It makes for a fun blending of the elegant and the casual.

▌ Wantilan Luau

What:	Hawaiian-themed dinner show
Where:	On the Wantilan Terrace
Price Range:	Adults, $58 plus tax; children under 13, $32
Hours:	Saturday at 6:00 p.m. year round; Tuesday and Saturday at 6:00 p.m. seasonally
Reservations:	Required. (407) 503-3463 or see the concierge.

Wantilan is Indonesian for "gathering place," and at the outdoor Wantilan Terrace, on Saturday nights, the hotel gathers its guests together with that tried-and-true staple of warm weather tourism, a Hawaiian luau complete with roast suckling pig on your plate and Hawaiian hams on stage, but thankfully no poi.

The generous buffet meal starts with fruits and salads, continues with Lomi Lomi Chicken Salad, the "Catch of the Day," Teriyaki Chicken, Flank Steak, and the aforementioned Pit-Roasted Suckling Pig, before wrapping up with a dessert station with goodies like White Chocolate Macadamia Nut Pie and Chocolate Banana Cake. Wine, beer, Mai Tais, and soft drinks are included in the price and a cash bar is available. The entertainment is as rich and filling as the meal, featuring a medley of Polynesian song stylings and hula dancing.

There is a cancellation fee of $20 per person unless you cancel prior to noon on the day of the performance.

Shopping at Loews Royal Pacific Resort

Shopping here is muted and low key, which after the mercantile madness of the theme parks is a refreshing change of pace. Off the lobby, you will find **Toko Gifts**, a small shop that at first glance seems entirely devoted to casual clothing and souvenirs, all with Royal Pacific and Universal logos. Peek around the corner at the back and you will find magazines and sundries of the sort you'd expect at any hotel lobby store.

More elaborate is **Treasures of Bali**, located near the pool on the way to the convention wing. This is the place to come if you forgot to pack your swim gear. Swimsuits for men and women are stocked here, along with a variety of balls and toys suitable for pool play. You will find some very nice resort wear for after-pool occasions, much of it with a South Seas flavor. A small selection of Indonesian crafts can be found here and, if you poke around in the back of the shop, you'll discover some magazines and popular novels for poolside reading.

CHAPTER SIX:

STAYING NEAR THE PARKS

I f you aren't staying at one of Universal Orlando's on-property hotels, you may want to consider staying close by. The following hotels are located along Major Boulevard, just opposite the Kirkman Road entrance to the Universal Orlando property. They are listed in order of their distance to CityWalk, with the nearest listed first. Major Boulevard is also served by the Super Star Shuttle (see *Chapter One*).The price range refers to the cost of a standard double room, from low season to high, as follows:

$	Under $60
$$	$60 - $100
$$$	$100 - $150
$$$$	Over $150

Be aware that at particularly busy times the cost of a room can soar to astronomical levels, regardless of what it says here.

■ DoubleTree Hotel

5780 Major Boulevard
Orlando, FL 32819
(800) 222-8733; (407) 351-1000; fax (407) 352-8556
www.doubletree.com

A sleek corporate-style hotel (there's a convention center attached) that is a favorite with upscale overseas visitors.

Price Range: $$ - $$$$

Amenities: Large pool, five restaurants, playground, exercise room, business center, shops, hi-speed Internet

Holiday Inn

5905 South Kirkman Road
Orlando, FL 32819
(800) 327-1364; (407) 351-3333; fax (407) 351-3577
www.holiday-inn.com

Standard mid-range hotel with ten-story all-suite tower.

Price Range: $$ - $$$$

Amenities: Pool, volleyball, restaurant ("kids eat free"), fitness center, business center

Hyatt Place

5895 Caravan Court
Orlando, FL 32819
(888) 492-8847; (407) 351-0627; fax (407) 351-3317
www.hyattplace.com

Upscale hotel chain.

Price Range: $$ - $$$

Amenities: Outdoor pool, fitness center, 42" flat-screen TVs, free continental breakfast or hot breakfast for purchase, wine and coffee bar, free hi-speed Internet

Days Inn

5827 Caravan Court
Orlando, FL 32819
(800) 329-7466; (407) 351-3800; fax (407) 363-0907
www.daysinn.com

Typical budget-class motel.

Price Range: $ - $$

Amenities: Pool with tiki bar, in-room movies, game rooms, 24-hour restaurant

Baymont Inns and Suites

5652 Major Boulevard
Orlando, FL 32819
(407) 354-3996; fax (407) 354-3299
www.baymontinns.com

Spartan budget motel.

Price Range: $ - $$
Amenities: Pool, continental breakfast

▎Comfort Suites

5617 Major Boulevard
Orlando, FL 32819
(800) 424-6423; (407) 363-1967; fax (407) 363-6873
www.choicehotels.com
All-suite hotel.
Price Range: $$ - $$$
Amenities: Pool, continental breakfast, shuttle to Universal

▎La Quinta Inn

5621 Major Boulevard
Orlando, FL 32819
(866) 725-1661; (407) 313-3100; fax (407) 313-3131
www.lq.com
Standard budget motel.
Price Range: $$ - $$$
Amenities: Pool, HBO, continental breakfast, some rooms with
refrigerator/microwave, hi-speed Internet

▎InTown Suites

5615 Major Boulevard
Orlando, FL 32819
(800) 553-9338; (407) 370-3734
www.intownsuites.com
Budget all-suite property with kitchenettes; weekly rentals only, limited
office hours, and no Sunday check-ins.
Price Range: $$ - $$$
Amenities: Pool, HBO, free Internet

▎Extended Stay America

5620 Major Boulevard
Orlando, FL 32819
(800) 398-7829; (407) 351-1788; fax (407) 351-7899
www.extstay.com
Budget-priced all-suite property with well-equipped kitchenettes, including pots, pans, dishes, a microwave, and a coffee maker.
Price Range: $ - $$

Amenities: Laundry room, Showtime, hi-speed Internet

▌ Extended Stay Deluxe

5610 Vineland Road
Orlando, FL 32819
(888) 788-3467; (407) 370-4428; fax (407) 370-9456
www.extstay.com
    Mid-range all-suite property, a more upscale variant of the Extended Stay America formula.
    Price Range: $ - $$
    Amenities: Laundry room, Showtime, pool, hi-speed Internet

▌ Holiday Inn Express

5605 Major Boulevard
Orlando, FL 32819
(877) 863-4780; (407) 363-1333; fax (407) 363-4510
www.hiexpress.com
    Eleven-story hotel with both standard rooms and suites.
    Price Range: $$ - $$$
    Amenities: Outdoor pool, exercise room, continental breakfast, free shuttle to Universal, Wendy's next door

▌ Fairfield Inn & Suites

5614 Vineland Road
Orlando, FL 32819
(800) 936-9417; (407) 581-5600; fax (407) 581-5601
www.marriott.com
    Standard budget hotel with some suites.
    Price Range: $$ - $$$
    Amenities: Outdoor whirlpool, exercise room, continental breakfast

▌ Best Western Universal Inn

5618 Vineland Road
Orlando, FL 32819
(800) 313-4616; (407) 226-9119; fax (407) 370-2448
www.bestwestern.com
    Standard mid-range motel chain.
    Price Range: $$ - $$$$
    Amenities: Pool, continental breakfast

CHAPTER SEVEN:

DINING AT A GLANCE

A s Napoleon once said, "A family visiting a theme park travels on its stomach." With that in mind, here is a quick look at Universal Orlando's many dining options — all 84 of them! The table that follows, lists the restaurant name, its location, its type, the cuisine featured, and the estimated price range. Locations are abbreviated as follows:

Universal Studios Florida (USF):

FL	Front Lot
Hwd	Hollywood
KZ	KidZone
WE	World Expo
SF	San Francisco-Amity
NY	New York
PC	Production Central

Islands of Adventure (IOA):

PoE	Port of Entry
SL	Seuss Landing
LC	Lost Continent
HP	Wizarding World of Harry Potter
JP	Jurassic Park
TL	Toon Lagoon
MS	Marvel Super Hero Island

The hotels are Portofino Bay (PBH), Hard Rock (HRH), and Royal Pacific Resort (RPR). We estimate the cost of an "average" meal at each restaurant based on its type. Prices are as follows:

273

$	Under $15
$$	$15 - $25
$$$	$25 - $40
$$$$	Over $40

Restaurant	Location	Type	Cuisine	Price
Alchemy Bar	IOA/LC	Bar	n/a	$
Amity Fried Chicken	USF/SF	Walk-up	American	$
Arctic Express	IOA/PoE	Walk-up	Ice cream	$
Backwater Bar	IOA/PoE	Bar	n/a	$
Bar American	PBH	Bar	Italian	$$ - $$$$
Beach Club	HRH	Poolside	American	$ - $$
Beverly Hills Boulangerie	USF/FL	Cafeteria	American	$
Bice	PBH	Full-service	Italian	$$$$+
Big Kahuna Pizza	CityWalk	Walk-up	Pizza	$ - $$
Blondie's	IOA/TL	Cafeteria	American	$
Boardwalk Snacks	USF/SF	Walk-up	Funnel cakes	$
Bob Marley	CityWalk	Nightclub	Caribbean	$ - $$
Bone Chillin' Beverages	USF/PC	Bar	n/a	$
Bubba Gump	CityWalk	Full-serve, Bar	Seafood	$$ - $$$
Bula Bar and Grille	RPR	Full-serve, Bar	American	$ - $$
Burger Digs	IOA/JP	Cafeteria	Burgers	$
Cafe 4	IOA/MS	Cafeteria	Italian	$
Cafe La Bamba	USF/Hwd	Cafeteria, Bar	Barbecue	$
Captain America Diner	IOA/MS	Cafeteria	Burgers	$
Cathy's Ice Cream	IOA/TL	Walk-up	Ice cream	$
Chez Alcatraz	USF/SF	Bar, Walk-up	Seafood	$
Chill Ice Cream	IOA/MS	Walk-up	Ice cream	$
Cigarz	CityWalk	Bar	n/a	$
Cinnabon	CityWalk	Walk-up	American	$
Cinnabon	IOA/PoE	Walk-up	American	$
Circus McGurkus	IOA/SL	Cafeteria	American	$
Classic Monsters Cafe	USF/PC	Cafeteria	American	$
Comic Strip Cafe	IOA/TL	Cafeteria	Various	$
Confisco Grille	IOA/PoE	Full-service	Eclectic	$$ - $$$
Croissant Moon	IOA/PoE	Cafeteria	American	$

Restaurant	Location	Type	Cuisine	Price
Emack & Bolio's	HRH	Walk-up	Ice cream	$
Emeril's	CityWalk	Full-service, Bar	Eclectic	$$$$+
Fat Tuesday	CityWalk	Walk-up bar	n/a	$
Finnegan's	USF/NY	Full-service, Bar	Irish/British	$$ - $$$
Fire Eaters Grill	IOA/LC	Walk-up	Mid. Eastern	$
Frozen Desert	IOA/LC	Walk-up	Ice cream	$
Fusion Sushi	CityWalk	Walk-up	Japanese	$$
Galaxy	CityWalk	Walk-up bar	n/a	$
Gelateria Caffe Espresso	PBH	Cafeteria	Italian	$
Hard Rock Cafe	CityWalk	Full-service, Bar	American	$$ - $$$
Hop on Pop	IOA/SL	Walk-up	Ice cream	$
Hog's Head Pub	IOA/HP	Bar	n/a	$
Int'l Food & Film Festival	USF/WE	Cafeteria	American, Asian, Italian	$
Islands Dining Rm	RPR	Full-service	Asian	$$ - $$$$+
Jake's American Bar	RPR	Full-service, Bar	American	$$ - $$$
Jimmy Buffett's Margaritaville	CityWalk	Full-service, Bar, Nightclub	Caribbean	$$ - $$$
KidZone Pizza	USF/KZ	Walk-up	Fast food	$
Latin Express	CityWalk	Walk-up	Latin Amer.	$
Latin Quarter	CityWalk	Full-service	Latin Amer.	$$$
Lombard's Seafood	USF/SF	Full-service	American	$$ - $$$
Lone Palm Airport	CityWalk	Walk up, Bar	American	$
Louie's Italian Restaurant	USF/NY	Cafeteria	Italian	$
Mama Della's Ristorante	PBH	Full-service	Italian	$$$- $$$$
Mel's Drive-In	USF/Hwd	Cafeteria	Burgers	$
Midway Grill	USF/SF	Walk-up	Hot dogs	$
Moe's SW Grill	CityWalk	Walk-up	S'western	$
Moose Juice...	IOA/SL	Walk-up	Soft drinks	$
Mythos	IOA/LC	Full-service	Eclectic	$$ - $$$

Restaurant	Location	Type	Cuisine	Price
NASCAR Sports Grille	CityWalk	Full-service, Bar	American	$$ - $$$
Nathan's Famous	CityWalk	Walk-up	American	$
NBA City	CityWalk	Full-serve, Bar	American	$$ - $$$
Orchid Court	RPR	Bar	n/a	$ - $$
Orchid Court Sushi Bar	RPR	Full-service	Japanese	$ - $$$
Palm Restaurant	HRH	Full-service	Steaks & Seafood	$$$$+
Panda Express	CityWalk	Walk-up	Chinese	$
Pastamoré	CityWalk	Full-service	Italian	$$ - $$$
Pastamoré Market-place Cafe	CityWalk	Walk-up	Italian	$
Pat O'Brien's	CityWalk	Full-service, Nightclub	New Orleans	$$ - $$$
Pizza Predattoria	IOA/JP	Walk-up	Pizza	$
Red Coconut Club	CityWalk	Nightclub	Eclectic	$ - $$
Richter's Burger Co.	USF/SF	Cafeteria	Burgers	$
Rising Star	CityWalk	Nightclub	American	$ - $$
Sal's Market Deli	PBH	Cafeteria	Italian	$$
San Francisco Pastry Company	USF/SF	Cafeteria	American	$
Schwab's Pharmacy	USF/Hwd	Cafeteria	Ice cream	$
Splendido Pizzeria	PBH	Cafeteria	Italian	$$
Starbucks	CityWalk	Coffee house	Coffee	$
TCBY	CityWalk	Walk-up	Ice cream	$
Tchoup Chop	RPR	Full-service	Asian	$$$-$$$$
The Kitchen	HRH	Full-service	American	$$ - $$$
Thirsty Fish Bar	PBH	Bar	Italian	$
Three Broomsticks	IOA/HP	Full-service	British	$$
Thunder Falls Terrace	IOA/JP	Cafeteria	Barbecue	$$
Trattoria del Porto	PBH	Full-service	Italian	$$ - $$$
Universal Cineplex Concessions	CityWalk	Walk-up	Snacks	$
Velvet	HRH	Bar	American	$ - $$
Wantilan Luau	RPR	Dinner show	Polynesian	$$$$
Watering Hole	IOA/JP	Bar	n/a	$
Whopper Bar	CityWalk	Walk-up	Burgers	$
Wimpy's	IOA/TL	Walk-up	Burgers	$

Index

This Index lists rides, attractions, and restaurants mentioned in the text, along with other topics of interest. Where appropriate, the location of each entry is indicated by the following abbreviations: (CW) - CityWalk; (HR) - Hard Rock Hotel; (IOA) - Islands of Adventure; (PB) - Portofino Bay Hotel; (RP) - Royal Pacific Resort; (USF) - Universal Studios Florida; (WDW) - Walt Disney World Resort.

W

Other Books from The Intrepid Traveler

The Intrepid Traveler publishes money-saving, horizon expanding travel how-to and guidebooks dedicated to helping its readers make world travel an integral part of their everyday lives.

For more information, visit our web site, where you will find a complete catalog, the latest news about our books, travel articles from around the world, Internet travel resources, and more:

■ **http://www.IntrepidTraveler.com/store**

If you love theme parks, you'll love zoos. *America's Best Zoos: A Travel Guide for Fans and Families* provides in-depth reviews of the country's 60 best zoos, plus information on scores more. Arranged geographically to inspire road trips, this is a must-have reference for your next family vacation.

■ **http://www.AmericasBestZoos.com**

If you are interested in becoming a home-based travel agent, visit the Home-Based Travel Agent Resource Center at:

■ **http://www.HomeTravelAgency.com**

For this book's companion volumes, *SeaWorld, Discovery Cove & Aquatica: Orlando's Salute To The Seas, The Hassle-Free Walt Disney World Vacation, Hidden Mickeys: A Field Guide To Walt Disney World's Best Kept Secrets,* and *The Walt Disney World Trivia Book* (Vols. 1 and 2), plus updates to all our Orlando guidebooks, visit:

■ **http://www.TheOtherOrlando.com**

Come Back Next Year!